ONE
CHEESE
TO RULE
THEM ALL

PATRICK MCGUIGAN AND CARLOS YESCAS

ONE CHEESE TO RULE THEM ALL

IN SEARCH OF THE WORLD'S 100 BEST CHEESES

murdoch books
London | Sydney

Contents

Foreword

Cheese can make you cry. It was October 2021 and we had convened the World Cheese Awards in Oviedo, northern Spain, having had an enforced sabbatical due to the Covid pandemic the previous year. It was the first time the awards hadn't taken place since they started more than 30 years earlier, and we were determined to bounce back with a bang after those long months of separation and isolation.

As I led our expert cheese judges from their briefing in the vast auditorium of the Palacio de Exposiciones y Congresos, I was joined by local cheesemakers and political dignitaries. The procession snaked down a long, curved, white-washed stairway into the judging arena, and I shed a tear. More than a tear; I blubbed.

It may have been the sight of our dedicated team standing to attention at the end of 100 tables of cheese. It could well have been pent-up emotion from the preceding 18 months. But I'm pretty sure it was the landscape of 4,000-plus cheeses, coupled with a parade of 50 local drummers and bagpipers following me, bellowing out Asturian anthems with genuine pride and a heap of emotion.

Cheese has been made by humans for thousands of years. It is, in its simplest form, the way in which we preserved the goodness in milk, before we could throw it, casually, into the door of a refrigerator. By ageing a cheese (essentially removing moisture from it in the right conditions), milk could be enjoyed and would nourish for months and possibly years after being harvested from whatever animal could be persuaded to co-operate.

And it is that simplicity that makes cheese the most enigmatic of foodstuffs. Cheese is an unromantic word for the planet's most romantic by-product, yet personality and romance are as much in the recipe as the science that combines its ingredients: milk, starter culture, rennet and salt.

My father, Bob, consistently aided by my stepmother, Linda, is the personality that launched the World Cheese Awards in 1988, in part out of sheer panic at the decline in traditional cheesemaking. I was cheap labour at that inaugural event, aged 16. During his career, my father had published magazines, written books and trained counter staff, centred around a genuine interest in – possibly an obsession with – cheese. That obsession crosses over into his paternal calling, so much so that our children call him Papa Cheese.

Bob wasn't unique in seeing the startling demise of traditional cheesemaking at the time, but only a few were willing to do something about it. His solution was a forum, where cheese experts could celebrate the very best in cheesemaking through measured assessment. The community was small back then; everyone knew each other, business was done, and excellence was celebrated. The World Cheese Awards is still that forum today, except it has become a global network with those same values – and there's now an enormous following. The community remains tight, invested and concerned in equal measure.

The subject of cheese normally elicits quiet amusement or a smile, and I am acutely aware that the very act of organising the awards may seem flippant. It is far from flippant. Its simple objective is to shine a light on cheesemakers who excel, accrediting them, which in turn provides a fillip and can help increase sales. But dig deeper and it can provide a mechanism to discuss, address and highlight the issues affecting our beloved trade. It can also enable cheesemakers to improve and even shore up family farms.

In 2018, Norwegian cheesemaker Jørn Hafslund of Ostegården was crowned World Champion for Fanaost, an aged Gouda-style cheese. At the time, his son, Magnus, was hell-bent on leaving the farm to chase the Norwegian Krone in Oslo, but the success, publicity and sheer feel-good factor of that prize persuaded the formerly reluctant son to stay, saving the cheese from extinction.

The relentless drive towards sanitised mass production in food and drink can be seen clearly in cheese. And this removes the romance. Cheese factories take milk from herds and flocks of animals from different terroirs, regions and even countries to manufacture consistent products. And in this case 'consistent' is a bad thing, removing distinctiveness, character and often taste.

This shift away from the artisan to mass production removes skills throughout the cheese chain. There is a shortage of those willing to understand, care for and breed the animals that provide milk of the required quality for cheesemaking. And while there has certainly been a global renaissance in artisan or small-scale production, the teachers, or those with the skills to formally educate the makers, are vanishing from our agri-food establishments worldwide.

And that is why the premise for this book is so important. It might be fun to hunt out and debate which is the One Cheese to Rule Them All, but ultimately this book is a celebration of the community that defines our awards scheme and gives it colour to this day.

Tortie, my wife, who has worked on the awards for over 20 years, will maintain that the event is as much about the people as the cheese: the cheesemakers that enter, the logistics people that deliver, the workers that stage the cheeses in the judging room, the judges who travel from all corners to carefully assess every entry, the journalists that write about it and the food lovers who await the verdict.

If you can seek out and try these 100 cheeses, you'll understand the alchemy of personality, romance and science, and how they combine to make the perfect food. Some will inspire you, some delight you, but when you find your favourite, it will make you cry.

John Farrand
Managing director, Guild of Fine Food, organisers of the World Cheese Awards

With my thanks to the Guild of Fine Food team who ensure the continued success of this unique event.

Introduction

Like elite athletes limbering up before an Olympic final, there's a nervous energy when the judges assemble at the World Cheese Awards.

Clad in pristine white coats, they come from all corners of the planet and comprise highly skilled cheesemongers, makers, maturers and food writers, who hug and high five ahead of what is the biggest day in the cheese calendar. 'Judge' pin badges are proudly fastened to lapels, apples are crunched to keep palates fresh, and there's a final check of specialist knives that can carve a wheel into a wedge in seconds. The buzz of anticipation is palpable.

These are the cream of the cheese world (excuse the pun), gathered together to put their taste buds to the test to help you find your next favourite cheese. To see hundreds of international cheese experts in one room is a humbling sight – but it's eclipsed by the scene that greets them when they finally walk out into the main judging arena.

A room the size of an athletics field filled with over 4,500 cheeses is guaranteed to quicken the pulse of any self-respecting lover of cheese. Each one carries the hopes of cheesemakers around the world. Neatly laid out on tables covered in white cloths, the cheeses come in all shapes and sizes, from tiny goat's cheeses that could be eaten in one mouthful, to hulking wheels of Emmentaler that weigh as much as a person. And everything else in between, from giant blocks of plastic-wrapped Cheddar and shiny drums of Parmigiano Reggiano, to blues that are so gooey they can be scooped with a spoon, and a rainbow of cheeses soaked in red wine, infused with truffles or decorated with herbs, flowers and chocolate.

Each one will be carefully poked, squeezed, sniffed and tasted by over 250 experts in a series of blind judging rounds, with medals given to the very best, through Bronze, Silver, Gold and Super Gold. Most get nothing at all (see page 12 for more details on how the judging and awards work).

As the epic festival of tasting continues, the cheeses that reach Super Gold are reassessed in further rounds until a live televised final in which a 'Super Jury' of experts vote to decide which cheese will be named World Champion for that year. In other words, the best cheese in the world.

From Cheshire to Quebec

This remarkable spectacle takes place every year in different towns and cities across Europe, from London, England and San Sebastián, Spain to Bergamo, Italy and Trondheim, Norway. Organised by a British organisation called the Guild of Fine Food (you've met the MD, John Farrand, in the Foreword), the awards started in London in 1988.

It was John's dad, Bob Farrand, who came up with the idea, building on a formative period in his youth in the 1960s when he worked in what he describes as a 'high class provisioners' in Dorset (a kind of fancy grocer's shop), where he would portion cheese for discerning locals. A career in food magazine publishing followed, leading to the acquisition of a trade magazine called *Good Food Retailing* (now *Fine Food Digest*) in 1985.

By all accounts, the first event, in March 1988, was a modest affair. Part of the London Food Exhibition at the Wembley Conference Centre, it was initially called the London

International Cheese Show (it was rebranded as the World Cheese Awards in 2000). Only 250 cheeses were entered, 100 of which were British, while all but one of the 19 judges that took part were from the UK. After the judging, visitors were allowed to help themselves to whatever was left in what turned into something of a bun fight (or should that be cheese fight?), according to Farrand Senior.

An article in a dusty copy of *Good Food Retailing* contains a great photo of a few of the judges, peering with great concentration at tiny pieces of cheese held aloft for the cameras. But the best snap is of the very first World Champion cheese – a Blue Cheshire – along with its beaming makers, Mr and Mrs Hutchinson-Smith, flanked by Bob Farrand and food broadcaster Glynn Christian.

From these humble beginnings, the awards began to gain traction, slowly growing in terms of both the number and variety of cheeses that were entered. The first non-British World Champion was Fourme d'Ambert from France, in 1991. And the first non-European cheese to take the title was Le Cendrillon in 2009 – a triangular, log-shaped goat's cheese from Quebec, Canada. The awards that year were held in Las Palmas, Gran Canaria, the first time judging had taken place outside of the UK or Ireland. Since then, the event has moved between European locations pretty much every year.

At the same time, the origins of the cheeses that are entered have become more diverse, with countries including Australia, Brazil, India, Japan, Turkey, South Africa and the USA joining the party alongside those from Europe. Cheeses from nearly 50 countries were judged at the most recent awards by experts representing 40 nations.

What makes a winner?

We've both been lucky enough to don the white coats and cast our verdict as judges ourselves for more than 10 years each [Carlos started judging in 2009 and Patrick in 2010].

We even sat next to each other on the Super Jury panel, which was where the first seeds for this book were sown. Being chosen to judge in the final is a great professional honour, although nibbling cheese in front of an audience of hundreds with a camera relaying every chew to a big screen is one of the more surreal parts of the job.

After all those years of handing out medals, you'd think we'd know a fair bit about cheese, but there's always more to learn. The more we have tasted our way across the field of cheese, the more questions have been raised about what makes a good cheese into a great one. And a great cheese into a World Champion.

There's a lot to consider, not least the animals and their milk. Species, breed, age, diet, season, climate and geography make a huge difference. Make cheese with milk from Jersey cows chewing silage in a barn during an English winter and you will end up with very different flavours and textures to a cheese made from milk from a French Manech sheep grazing summer herbs and flowers in the Pyrenees.

Then there's what you do with the milk, from the thorny issue of pasteurisation, to whether cheese is made in an automated factory or by hand in a chalet at the top of a mountain. The impact of moulds, yeasts, bacteria and time in the maturing room also comes into play. Even the packaging it's wrapped in and the temperature it's served at make a difference.

How these factors influence cheese are explored in this book, and by their nature can be technical. If you're not sure of the difference between raw, thermised or pasteurised milk, or want to know what Protected Designation of Origin (PDO) and starter cultures refer to, then it's worth having a skim through the glossary at the back of the book.

But we also wanted to get to the bottom of other vexing questions that are often the subject of heated conversation among cheese judges once they've retired to the nearest pub or restaurant to unwind (an important part of the judging day). Questions such as, why are Cheddar, Gouda and Brie so universally popular, while other cheeses are on the brink of extinction? Why do some styles of cheese win the World Cheese Awards more than others? And, most heated of all, is it ever okay to eat Wensleydale and Cranberries?

Most of all, we really wanted to explore what makes a winner at the World Cheese Awards, and whether there really is such a thing as 'the best cheese in the world'. Of all the cheeses that have been named World Champion down the years, is there one that trumps all the others? Is there really One Cheese to Rule Them All? And if so, why?

The final 100

With these questions in our minds, we set about choosing 100 cheeses that we thought were worthy of the title. The starting point for this was to analyse decades of data from the Guild of Fine Food, which was easier said than done. Apart from the fact that there are literally thousands of cheeses that have won awards over the years, records from before 2010 hadn't been digitised, which meant many (not unpleasurable) hours poring over old magazines in the Guild's archives. The format of the awards has also changed over the years. The idea of awarding medals to cheeses didn't start until 1995. Before then there were various classes, such as 'hard pressed' or 'soft ewe's milk', and changing categories from Best Cheddar to Best Irish Cheese.

There has always been a World Champion cheese at the awards, but not all of them are in this book. That might be because they are not being made any more, or because the same style of cheese has won on multiple occasions (Gruyère being the prime example). Picking our 100 contenders for the One Cheese to Rule Them All was not a scientific process. We used the awards as a base – most of the cheeses we picked have been successful and won medals – but there was also quite a large amount of personal opinion that went into the mix. To be clear, those opinions were ours [Patrick's and Carlos's] and not those of the Guild of Fine Food, who generously gave us access to all the winners from over the years.

It was important to us to explore cheeses with a wide spread of milk types, styles and geographies. We also wanted the majority to be fairly accessible to all – available to buy in supermarkets, specialist cheese shops or online – but with a decent sprinkling of rare and unusual cheeses that hardcore cheese geeks could hunt down on their travels. To this end we cover most of the European big-hitters (Comté, Manchego, Gorgonzola) and well-known brands (Rogue River, Cornish Yarg, OG Kristal), as well as lesser-known cheeses from overlooked cheesemaking nations such as Japan, Brazil and Ukraine (Mount Fuji Chèvre, Passionata, Syrna Torbynka).

Our final 100 cheeses are spread over five chronological sections, charting the four decades of the awards, with entries listed alphabetically in each section. We've also listed their main awards in their respective eras, as well as others we think are relevant, but the list is not exhaustive. In each section we've also highlighted one hero cheese, which we think is a heavyweight contender to the title of 'best cheese in the world'.

It's been fascinating to see how cheese fashions have changed from the 1980s to the 2020s. There's a lot less block Cheddar and Brie, and a lot more cheese from Latin America, Japan and India, reflecting our increasingly globalised world.

The final section, 'The Future', covers 10 cheeses that have not yet won major honours at the World Cheese Awards (they may not even have been entered), but we think they offer a glimpse of where and how good cheese can prosper in the years to come. Think of them as authors' picks.

The book can be read cover to cover or used as a reference to look up individual cheeses. Each profile is a self-contained story that delves into subjects from climate, geography and history to economics, politics and science. We also introduce you to the cheesemakers, as well as to some of the judges who have made an impact on the awards. The author of each profile is indicated with their initials at the end. Read them together and they build into a broad overview of the traditions, ideas and struggles that make cheese so special.

So, let's put on our white coats, sharpen our cheese knives and start our quest to find the One Cheese to Rule Them All.

World Cheese Awards: the judging process

Before we strike out on our journey of cheese discovery, let us give an overview of what it takes to be a winner at the World Cheese Awards, and what judges are looking for when it comes to bestowing medals. Welcome to the world of professional cheese-tasting!

The 250 or so judges who are picked each year to taste their way through thousands of cheeses come from all walks of life, including cheesemongers, buyers, sales and distribution professionals, cheesemakers, chefs and food journalists. There's an emphasis on having a balance of ages, genders and nationalities.

On competition day, teams of two to four judges are formed, with a mix of experience and expertise. Judges are put together based on a common language when possible, though with over 40 nationalities represented, many communicate using English, French, and the shared language of cheese.

Each team is assigned a table with around 50 cheeses that must be tasted and scored in three hours. Rather than judging just one type of cheese, judges have a range of different styles to taste, such as fresh, bloomy-rind, washed-rind, goat's cheeses, Cheddars, Alpines and blues, with five to ten cheeses in each category. It's easier to judge smaller batches of different cheeses than tasting just Cheddar or just Brie, which would soon become monotonous. All the cheeses are judged blind: the name of the cheese, who makes it and where is never revealed. Team captains record the scores but all decisions are made by consensus.

Cheeses are evaluated in four key areas: visual appeal (5 points), body and texture (5 points), aroma (5 points), and most important of all, flavour and mouthfeel (20 points), for a total of 35 points. Judges can award multiple Gold (31–35 points), Silver (27–30 points) and Bronze (23–26 points) medals, since cheeses are judged individually rather than against each other. So if they had five blue cheeses to taste and they were all fantastic, they could all get Gold medals. Once all the cheeses have been assessed, the team selects one cheese for the Super Gold medal, moving it forward to the next rounds of judging.

There are various signs that judges look out for when they're putting a cheese through its paces, from checking for cracks, holes (known as 'eyes') and moulds where they shouldn't be, to assessing the body and texture by literally squeezing pieces of the cheese between their fingers to test moisture and fat levels. For hard cheeses, a special tool known as a cheese iron (or 'trier' in the US) is used to bore a plug of cheese from the centre, which gives a cross section of the whole wheel or block. To do this, cheeses are unwrapped of any cloth, wax or plastic coverings. For soft cheeses, judges check moisture levels, with deductions for excessive wetness or dryness.

Next, judges evaluate the aromas of both the rind and paste. Aromas are assessed upon cutting, and again by smelling small samples held close to the nose. Before tasting, all judges smell the cheese. Off aromas such as ammonia, sulphur (cooked

egg) or manure may indicate contamination or defects. However, not all unusual smells are faults. Some, like butyric acid (baby-sick scent), neral (citrussy-oily notes coming from the presence of cheese mites) or geosmin (earthy or wet stone smells), are natural characteristics of certain cheese styles or maturation techniques.

The final stage is tasting. Judges take a small piece and spread it across their palates to assess mouthfeel. They evaluate the length of finish, as well as the presence and balance of the five essential flavours: salty, sweet, acidic, bitter and umami. They also consider nuanced notes influenced by milk quality, terroir, cheesemaking techniques and maturation. With a value of 20 points, flavour is the most crucial aspect.

Judges often describe flavours as balanced, harmonious or complementary, meaning that milk, salt and other ingredients create a pleasant combination. Assessing this can be challenging, as individual tolerance for saltiness or bitterness varies. To align their sensory perception, judges begin the day by tasting a few samples without scoring, ensuring consistency within the team. The Guild of Fine Food also offers a tasting and judging workshop beforehand to refresh judges' skills.

Most cheeses arrive in the host country just one day before the competition, a major logistical challenge. They travel in refrigerated cargo or with frozen packs to maintain a temperature of around 5°C (41°F). Some samples spend up to two weeks in transit before reaching the host city, making it remarkable that most arrive in good condition. Still, some fresh and surface-ripened cheeses can suffer from prolonged packaging without air circulation. Judges are instructed not to penalise cheeses for damage caused during transport.

In the second round, Super Gold winners are grouped and re-evaluated by members of the Super Jury, with judges focusing on exceptional quality. Each judge selects one cheese, advancing it to the final, where it is tasted once again in front of a live audience of hundreds of people. The final is also live-streamed online, with viewers tuning in around the world. Judges award up to 7 points for each cheese by holding up scoring cards in unison in a scene that is reminiscent of talent shows. The drama was for many years stoked by British food broadcaster Nigel Barden, who hosts the final with a mix of insightful questions, cheese stories and one-liners, all delivered in a deep Yorkshire accent. After each cheese has been voted on, the judge who picked it then makes an impassioned speech as to why they think it should win and what makes it so special.

The scores are tallied and the names of the cheeses (and the countries in which they are made) finally revealed as the entry with the highest total is crowned World Champion. It's an emotional moment, especially if the winning cheesemaker is in the audience and can be welcomed onto the stage to join the hosts and judges. There are frequent tears, cheers and hugs as they claim their golden globe trophy, proving their cheese is the best in the world, for that year at least.

The World Cheese Awards in numbers

1988

First awards held in London, UK

4,700+

cheeses from over 40 countries entered in 2024

250

judges from over 40 countries

14

Super Jury judges in the final

19

cheese distribution hubs worldwide, including 7 in the Americas, 8 in Europe, and additional locations in Australia, India, Japan and South Africa

circa

60

entry categories for cheeses, including buffalo, sheep, goat and cow's milk

18

national trophies and one regional trophy (Latin America), plus various other category awards, such as Best New Cheese, Best Female Cheesemaker and Best Cheddar

1980s –90s

Cheddar, Stilton and big-hitters from Continental Europe hold sway in the early years of the World Cheese Awards. But there is also the emergence of exciting new-wave cheeses as a renaissance in artisan skills in the UK, Ireland and Spain starts to gather pace.

Above: Le Gruyère (see page 31)

Brie de Meaux

It feels appropriate to start our odyssey into the world's greatest cheeses with one that is a true global heavyweight. Ask anyone, anywhere to name a cheese and there's a good chance they will answer 'Brie'. The soft, white French *fromage* is served on cheeseboards from Sydney to Sydenham, thanks to its earthy flavour and oozy centre, so it's no wonder the French proudly call it the 'King of Cheeses'.

It's become such an international phenomenon that liberties have been taken with its name through the decades. All manner of cheeses are described as Brie these days, when they bear only a passing resemblance to the real thing. Virtually every country now makes its own version in a multitude of shapes and sizes, and with various milk types.

So what is real Brie? Well, the easiest answer is that it's a cheese from the place of the same name in northern France. Brie is a historic region close to Paris, which is now part of the Seine-et-Marne *département* in Île-de-France. Its proximity to France's capital has made it a hotbed of cheesemaking for centuries, producing several varieties of Brie named after the villages in which they are made.

Head to a farmers' market in Paris and you might find Brie de Nangis, Brie de Coulommiers and Brie de Melun. But the most famous of all – the classic Brie that defines the genre – is Brie de Meaux. Originating from the village of Meaux, just 25km (16 miles) from Paris, it's protected by a PDO and made with raw cow's milk in impressive 3kg (6.5lb) wheels. The disc-shaped cheeses have an ivory, slightly wrinkly rind with coppery flecks, and a soft interior that combines a wonderfully complex mix of damp earth, wild mushroom and buttered cabbage flavours when ripe.

It's a very different beast to Camembert (though that doesn't stop people mixing the two up all the time). Camembert hails from Normandy and is much smaller (just 250g/9oz) with more powerful flavours (see page 56).

Most Brie de Meaux is made by *laiteries* (dairies) today, which pool milk from local farms. Dongé, Rouzaire and Renard Gillard are good names to look out for. There is also one *fermier* (farm-based) producer still using milk from its own cows to make cheese on the farm, called Le Cellier de la Ferme des 30 Arpents.

Brie has a remarkably long history, taking in monks, emperors and revolutions. Legend has it that it was first invented by monks in the seventh century and became a favourite of the nobility after it was discovered by Emperor Charlemagne in 774. The story goes that he stopped at an abbey and was served the cheese but made the mistake of cutting away the rind. A helpful bishop set him straight, advising the emperor to eat the rind, and he was so impressed he placed an annual order for the royal court.

The cheese was voted *Le Roi des Fromages* (King of Cheeses) in 1815 in a famous taste test that could be seen as a forerunner of the World Cheese Awards. This was at the Congress of Vienna after France's defeat in the Napoleonic wars, where cunning diplomat Tallyrand encouraged his counterparts to bring cheeses from their own countries to take part in a competition to find the best in Europe. Brie promptly triumphed over Stilton, Gouda and Emmentaler, gifting France a morale-boosting cheese victory in the wake of defeat.

Despite this long history, Brie de Meaux would have still seemed rather exotic and sophisticated back in 1994 when it was named World Champion at the World Cheese Awards held in London. It was supplied by a cheese maturation company (affineur) called Hennart, run by two brothers, which is still going strong today, overseen by the second and third generations of the family.

To win the top prize, the Brie Hennart entered must have been perfectly ripe, although what constitutes the perfect state of maturity for these kinds of cheeses is open to argument. The rind of a Brie is a living coat of mould and yeast, most notably a snowy white mould called *Penicillium camemberti*, which breaks down the chalky interior of young cheeses into the most delicious glossy goo.

In other words, Brie literally ripens from the outside in. But how far you want your goo to go is a matter of taste. Many people love their cheese broken down all the way to the middle, but others (including me) like a thin line of chalk in the centre. The contrast between the tangy lactic core and the custardy paste is rather glorious. PM

ORIGIN: Seine-et-Marne, France

PROTECTED STATUS: PDO

MILK: Raw cow's milk

RENNET: Animal

AROMA: Mushroomy, earthy, fruity

FLAVOUR: Cabbage, mushrooms, butter

TEXTURE: Springy when young; gooey as it ages

MATCH: Champagne is often hailed as a good match, but we prefer orange wines. Chilli jam adds pizzazz in a very pleasing way.

WORLD CHEESE AWARDS: Multiple awards, including World Champion 1994 (Hennart), 2007 (Renard Gillard)

Caerphilly

Proud Welsh men and women might want to sit down before hearing the following news about their national cheese. Caerphilly (or 'Caerffili' to give it the Welsh spelling) is named after a small town just north of Cardiff. But today some of the best Caerphilly in the world is not actually made in Wales; it's made in Somerset, England.

Don't just take our words for it. Both Duckett's and Gorwydd (pronounced 'Gor-with') Caerphilly have been serial winners of Gold and Super Gold medals since the early days of the World Cheese Awards. Judges have been smitten by the cheeses' moist textures, mushroomy flavours and grey rinds, very different to the sharp and crumbly Caerphillies found in supermarkets. Those rindless block cheeses are made in large creameries, using a modern recipe developed after the Second World War. But Gorwydd, made by the Trethowan Brothers near Weston-super-Mare, and Duckett's, made at Westcombe Dairy near Shepton Mallet, are cut from a more traditional cloth.

They are made by hand, as they would have been on farms across South Wales 200 years ago, and develop a velvety grey rind during maturation. Each cheese has its own personality – Duckett's is slightly firmer and has a thinner rind, while Gorwydd has a more savoury note. But they also have plenty in common, including a beautiful two-tone appearance, comprising a darker fudgy layer under the rind and a pale crumbly centre that is bright and citrussy.

A tip when you taste: always eat the rind; it's an integral part of the experience, bringing a lovely hit of chestnut mushrooms.

How a Welsh cheese ended up being made in Somerset requires a dash through cheese history. Caerphilly was made on farms across Wales in the nineteenth century and became a favourite among miners. The mineral-rich cheese was a good way to replace salts lost through sweating, and the grey rind made it easy to handle with black fingers.

Caerphilly is only matured for a couple of months, compared to a year or more for

ORIGIN: Caerphilly, Wales

PROTECTED STATUS: Caerphilly is not protected, but there is a PGI for Traditional Welsh Caerphilly

MILK: Raw or pasteurised cow's milk

RENNET: Animal or vegetarian

AROMA: Damp earth, milky, tangy

FLAVOUR: Mushrooms, savoury, lactic

TEXTURE: Crumbly, fudgy, velvety

MATCH: White Burgundy or other oaky whites. Strangely delicious with a piece of dark chocolate.

WORLD CHEESE AWARDS: Multiple awards, including Best British 1991 (Duckett's), 2005 (Gorwydd)

Cheddar, a fact that was not lost on Cheddar-makers in nearby Somerset. They spotted an opportunity for a much quicker return on their milk, so started making Caerphilly as a sideline. Somerset was soon making more of the cheese than Wales, although farmhouse production collapsed both sides of the border in the twentieth century as two world wars and the rise of industrial production took their toll.

By the 1950s there was only one farmhouse Caerphilly-maker left in Britain: Duckett's Farm in Wedmore, Somerset. The late Chris Duckett kept the flame of traditional Caerphilly alight during that dark period, eventually passing his secrets on to Cheddar-maker Westcombe, which continues to make his cheese today. He also trained a fresh-faced cheesemonger called Todd Trethowan in the art of Caerphilly-making, who started making Gorwydd in Wales with his brother Maugan in 1996.

They went on to introduce Caerphilly to new generations using the old-fashioned tactic of getting people to try the cheese for themselves at markets and in good cheese shops, converting people one taste at a time.

The brothers moved production to a farm in Somerset in 2013 when they outgrew their original site, echoing Caerphilly's border-hopping past. They also decided to make a Cheddar at the farm, which is called Pitchfork.

The good news for patriotic Welsh cheese-lovers is that Welsh Caerphilly has also been revived, led by the late Thelma Adams of cheese company Caws Cenarth. She brought back traditional Welsh Caerphilly-making in the 1980s when milk prices collapsed due to new quotas, and once famously dressed as Cleopatra and sat in a bathtub of milk in Carmarthen town centre to protest that milk was cheaper than water.

The Adams family successfully campaigned to get protected status for the name Traditional Welsh Caerphilly under EU law in 2012, which has led to other cheesemakers starting up production. Her son Carwyn continues to make Thelma's Traditional Caerffili today – in fact it was named Best Welsh Cheese in 2022 when the World Cheese Awards were held in Newport, Wales.

If you've only ever tried supermarket Caerphilly, it's definitely a cheese to reconsider, rind and all. PM

HERO CHEESE

Cheddar

There appears to be a human skeleton in the corner as I walk into the damp gloom of Gough's Cave. I'm here in Somerset on a Cheddar pilgrimage to witness Britain's most famous cheese being matured in the limestone caves of Cheddar Gorge, just like it was hundreds of years ago. I wasn't expecting to stumble across a murder scene.

Thankfully, it turns out the bones are not real, but are in fact a recreation of a Mesolithic skeleton, known as the Cheddar Man, who now resides in the Natural History Museum. The exhibit is a bit of macabre fun for the thousands of tourists that visit the show cave each year.

This was all explained to me by affable cheesemaker John Spencer of the Cheddar Gorge Cheese Company – the only Cheddar-maker still in Cheddar – who back in 2019 took me to see his prize cheeses ageing among the stalactites and stalagmites deep underground. The Longleat Estate, which owns Gough's Cave, allows the company to age some of its Cheddars in much the same way local cheesemakers would have done before the invention of refrigerators.

With a cool, constant temperature of 11°C (52°F) all year round, and humidity well above 90 per cent, thanks to a constant drip of water that trickles through the porous rock from the Mendip Hills above, it's the perfect place for ageing cheese. When we finally arrive at the wooden racks of round Cheddars (known as truckles), their cloth-covered rinds are camouflaged against the rock wall with a mottled patina of different moulds, from grey and brown to white and blue. This is proper cave-aged Cheddar, with a snappy texture and deep savoury flavour to match, as I discover when Spencer plunges a cheese iron into the side of one of the cheeses and extracts some of the golden core for us to taste. It's tangy, creamy and beefy, with a pleasant hint of the damp limestone that surrounds us.

It's hard to convey to non-cheese geeks just how exciting it is to taste Cheddar in the place where it was first made and matured. Of all the cheeses in this book, Cheddar is arguably the most successful and well known. It's regularly hailed as the most popular cheese in the world, made and consumed everywhere from Australia and the US to Argentina and South Africa. There's something about the sharp flavour and firm texture, as well as being easy to store, slice and melt, that gives it a universal appeal. If ever there was a cheese to be crowned king of the world, it's Cheddar.

This is confirmed at the World Cheese Awards, where Cheddars have won more awards than we can count over the years, including World Champion on four separate occasions. There were two wins in 1990 and 1998 for traditional cloth-bound Cheddars made by a dairy in Sturminster Newton in Dorset, England, while block Cheddars won in 2000 and 2002. The Cheddar Gorge Cheese Company has had its successes too, most notably Best Cheddar in 2009.

Understanding the difference between cloth-bound and block Cheddar gets to the heart of the story of why and how the cheese has gone from being a little-known regional delicacy to a multibillion-dollar global industry.

The village of Cheddar was known for its

cheese as far back as the sixteenth century, when it was mentioned in the historical reference book *Brittania* as being 'famous for the excellent and prodigious great cheeses made there, some of which require more than one man's strength to set them on the table'.

As this quote suggests, Cheddar cheeses were known for their huge size. Locals would pool their milk to make a single cheese weighing 45kg (99lb) or more, which could then be aged for long periods in the Cheddar Gorge caves. It was the creation of the canal and rail systems in the nineteenth century that brought Cheddar to a wider audience, starting with London.

Most of these earlier cheeses would have been made in a similar way to those at the Cheddar Gorge Cheese Company, as I find out when we head back to the dairy in the village, where Spencer lets me try my hand at Cheddar-making. It's hard work in the warm, steamy make room, bent over the vat, cutting and heating the curd before piling it up to squeeze out moisture in a process known as Cheddaring ('Cheddar' is a place, a cheese and a verb). The curd is then milled, salted and pressed in cylindrical moulds to make truckles that are wrapped in muslin.

It's a very different proposition to the rectangular block Cheddar found in most

ORIGIN: Somerset, England

PROTECTED STATUS: Cheddar is not protected, but there is a PDO for West Country Farmhouse Cheddar

MILK: Raw or pasteurised cow's milk

RENNET: Animal or vegetarian

AROMA: Buttery, earthy, brothy

FLAVOUR: Block: creamy, sharp, sweet; traditional: rich, buttery, savoury

TEXTURE: Block: smooth, malleable; traditional: brittle, flaky

MATCH: Cider is a classic West Country match – the sweetness and sharpness frame the cheese. A few slices of ripe apple work in a similar way on the side.

WORLD CHEESE AWARDS: Multiple awards, including World Champion 1990, 1992 (Dairy Crest), 2000 (Brue Valley), 2002 (Carbery)

supermarkets. This is the modern, industrial version of the cheese, which came to prominence in the second half of the twentieth century and is made at scale on automated lines. It's quicker, cheaper and easier to make than the traditional cheese.

These pasteurised cheeses have no rind because they are pressed in 20kg (44lb) blocks and then vacuum-packed in plastic so that no moisture can escape during the maturing process. It's why block Cheddars still have a putty-like texture, even when they've been matured for over a year. A cloth-bound cheese by contrast can lose up to 10 per cent of its weight through evaporation, resulting in a cheese with a firmer, waxier texture and more concentrated flavour.

The other trick that block Cheddar-makers came up with is to add a starter culture called *Lactobacillus helveticus*, which brings a fruity flavour to the cheese. Modern Cheddar is easy to enjoy because it's sweet, creamy and salty, but it doesn't have the earthy and savoury length of a traditional cloth-bound cheese.

Cheddar's journey to global commodity is a long and complicated story involving characters such as Somerset-native Joseph Harding – the so-called 'father of Cheddar' – who developed a systematic method of Cheddar-making in the 1850s. He was particularly influential in the US, where the world's first cheese factory was set up in New York in 1851, and the industrialisation of the cheese began. The innovations introduced by Harding set in place changes that came back to haunt traditional Cheddar-makers in the early twentieth century, when cheaper cheese imports from the US and Canada seriously undermined British production.

But it was the creation of the Milk Marketing Board in 1933 that really spelled the beginning of the end for farmhouse Cheddar-making as the norm. The government-run board guaranteed stable milk prices, which prompted many farmers to abandon cheesemaking altogether. This was compounded by rationing during the Second World War, which saw cheese production in the UK centralised and scaled up to make what was derisively known as 'Government Cheddar'.

By the time the EU's protected food names scheme came into being in the 1990s, it was too late for the cheesemakers of Somerset. Cheddar was being made all over the UK and further afield, mainly in block format. There is however a PDO for West Country Farmhouse Cheddar, secured in 1996, although the definition is so broad, covering four counties and both block and cloth-bound versions, that small producers have not signed up to the scheme.

Today there are only five cloth-bound Cheddars left in Somerset: Montgomery's, Keen's, Westcombe, Pitchfork and Cheddar Gorge, although there are a handful of others made in different parts of the UK, as well as overseas. Coolattin from Ireland and Cabot Clothbound from the US are particularly fine examples from countries where block Cheddar rules supreme.

What's remarkable about the five still made in Somerset is that although they are made in a similar way, following what you could loosely call the same 'recipe', they each have their own distinct personality. The differences are so marked that it's not unusual for cheese shops in the UK to stock several different Somerset Cheddars next to each other on the counter because customers tend to have a strong personal favourite.

All five have regularly won major trophies and made the final at the World Cheese Awards over the years, but sadly the traditional Cheddars made in Sturminster Newton, which were named World Champion in the 1990s, are no more. The dairy was owned by a much larger company called Dairy Crest, which bought Britain's most popular block Cheddar brand, Cathedral City, in 1995. It closed the Sturminster Newton site five years later, so it could concentrate on cheese wrapped in plastic, not cloth, which sums up the history of Cheddar in a nutshell.

There was a worry that Cheddar Gorge might go the same way as Sturminster Newton when John Spencer and his wife Katherine wanted to retire in 2022, but thankfully the business was taken over by another company. Which means there is still cloth-bound gold slowly ageing in the limestone caves in Cheddar today, just as it has for centuries. PM

Fourme d'Ambert

This is the cheese of pagan rituals, developed before the ninth century and probably enjoyed by Celtic druids and Gauls in central France as part of long-forgotten celebrations. And they must have known a thing or two about making blue cheese back then, because Fourme d'Ambert is still going strong today.

Its long heritage has been codified in a PDO that governs every aspect of its production, from shape and weight to the provenance of the milk, animal husbandry practices and ageing period. The creamy blue takes its name from the commune of Ambert in the Puy-de-Dôme *département* of Auvergne, as well as an old French word from the Latin *forma* (shape). This is in reference to the cheese's unusually tall, cylindrical form, which is higher than it is wide.

It's also a relatively *petit fromage*, weighing no more than 2.5kg (5.5lb). This means it has a large surface area, which develops a crusty rind, bringing interesting flavours to the cheese within. In perfect examples, the rind can appear like a light grey rock with a blue sheen.

The shape also helps the blue mould to grow. Fourme d'Ambert is never pressed, and freshly made cheeses are turned during the first 48 hours, creating an open texture with small air pockets inside. After four days of the cheese being made, it is pierced and the exposure to oxygen sparks *Penicillium roqueforti* spores into life. The blue mould blooms inside, filling the pockets with a delicious grey-blue mould, which slowly softens the cheese, releasing fruity and spicy flavours at the same time. The cheese must be aged for a minimum of 28 days to be called Fourme d'Ambert, according to its PDO.

To make great cheese, you need amazing milk. This is particularly true of Fourme d'Ambert. The milk must come from cows grazing in fields located between 600 and 1,600 metres (1,970–5,250 feet) altitude in the mountainous region of Puy-de-Dôme. At this altitude there is higher biodiversity in the soil and plants. Only pastures in five cantons of the Cantal region and eight communes in the Loire are recognised as meeting the requirements for milk production of this cheese.

Cows should be on pasture for a minimum of 150 days per year. Their diets can be supplemented with grain, but there is a limit

per cow per year. This ensures that cows mostly eat a grass or hay diet and live outside of barns.

The regulated altitude is important as it recognises the historical existence of mountain *jasseries*, from the eighteenth century to the early twentieth century. These were high-altitude dwellings, which also doubled as stables and dairies, used during the summer months when women would move to higher pastures with their cows while men grew hay in the valleys. The hay was used to feed cattle in the colder months. Rent for these mountain chalets is said to have been paid in cheese. The custom has long since died out, but there is a beautifully restored *jasserie* (du Coq Noir) high up in the Puy-de-Dôme, which has been turned into a museum and visitor attraction for hikers.

Like many other cheeses regulated by PDOs, there is a panel of tasters that constantly assess batches to ensure there is consistency and fair play between all producers. In the case of Fourme d'Ambert, there are 17 experts, who mark batches from all producers based on shape, appearance, texture and taste. While most of the production of this cheese is industrialised, there is a new group of makers producing *fermier* (farm-based) varieties.

Fourme d'Ambert won best cheese in the world at the World Cheese Awards in 1991, and its mild, delicate flavour continues to be popular. Close your eyes and it might even transport you to an ancient mystical time when we adored the sun and the elements. CY

ORIGIN: Auvergne, France
PROTECTED STATUS: PDO
MILK: Raw or pasteurised cow's milk
RENNET: Animal
AROMA: Saline and woody from the rind
FLAVOUR: Creamy, mushroomy, mineral
TEXTURE: Firm but moist and easy to crumble
MATCH: Dessert wines such as Sauternes. A drizzle of honey is a happy match.

WORLD CHEESE AWARDS: Multiple awards, including World Champion 1991 (Hennart)

Garrotxa

ORIGIN: Catalonia, Spain
PROTECTED STATUS: PGI
MILK: Pasteurised goat's milk
RENNET: Animal
AROMA: Earthy, milky, yoghurty
FLAVOUR: Citrus, goaty and mushroom notes from the rind
TEXTURE: The paste is firm but creamy when young, and dry as it ages
MATCH: Fino or Amontillado sherry is a great combination, especially with salty roasted nuts and dried fruits.

WORLD CHEESE AWARDS: Multiple awards, including Gold 1995 (Formatgeria del Montseny)

Gastronomists are worried about certain cheeses disappearing. Why? Well, once a food becomes extinct, whether that's because it falls out of fashion or can no longer be produced because of issues such as climate change, a big part of the culture around that food also ceases to exist. The dishes that were made with it need to change, the producers who benefited from its cultivation or production must adapt, and in some cases the rituals, words and expressions associated with it also change. This loss of culture leads to homogenisation and standardisation of food.

Garrotxa – a firm goat's cheese from Catalonia, Spain – was almost one of these stories. During the dictatorship of General Franco from 1939 to 1975, milk quotas almost wiped out small-scale cheesemaking. Fortunately, it was revived by a devoted group of farmers and cheesemakers in the 1980s before it was lost forever.

A group of young, idealistic city dwellers moved to the countryside near Girona and started making Garrotxa once again, using recipes from local women who could remember how it used to be made. The movement gained traction down the decades, until the EU recognised the cheese with a PGI in 2023. There are now around a dozen makers of the cheese, hopefully ensuring this cheese and the culture around it won't be lost.

Garrotxa is made with the milk of hardy goat breeds that can subsist in areas with limited feed. The animals graze in the foothills of the Pyrenees during the summer.

The cheese is often described as *pell florida* (bloomy rind) in Catalan. This is a reference to the texture of the rind, which has a distinctive fleecy grey appearance from the growth of natural moulds. Each wheel weighs either 500g (1.1lb) or 1kg (2.2lb) and is aged for 21 days before it is ready to be sold. It is a very rustic cheese – firm but creamy with a distinct goaty flavour – which is beloved as a table cheese. It is served as a snack with honey and hazelnuts, or with ripe tomatoes and olives as a classic Mediterranean lunch.

We particularly like the one made by Bauma dairy in the town of Borredà. The dairy was originally set up by pioneering cheesemaker Toni Chueca and is today owned by a group of goat farmers, all of whom have been integral to the great Garrotxa revival. CY

Gouda

Where is Gouda from? The obvious answer is the Netherlands. But the name 'Gouda' is not protected in the same way as many other European cheeses so has evolved into a generic cheese style that is made all over the world. It's a situation that must be both a source of great pride for Dutch cheesemakers, as well as being quite frustrating.

The global reach of Gouda helps explain the different ways to say its name. The Dutch say 'how-duh'; the English prefer 'gau-duh'; while in the US, people call it 'goo-duh'.

However you say it, Goudas are generally covered in wax and have a beautiful sheen to their rinds. The most common colour is yellow, but red, white, green and black are not uncommon, and occasionally even pictures and motifs appear. Most wheels are approximately 12kg (26.5lb). But as a cheese that is made globally, there are many variations between producers. There are some made with goat's milk, others with pineapple flavouring, and even bright green ones with a wasabi taste.

In 1999, Kollumer, made by Dutch company Frico and aged for 18 months, won the top prize at the World Cheese Awards. You may have seen this cheese marketed as Old Dutch Master in your local supermarket. In 2004, the cheese again won top honours in another international competition, this time in the US, in the prestigious World Championship Cheese Contest in the state of Wisconsin.

The thing that unites all Goudas is their sweet, butterscotch flavour, which comes from a couple of special steps during production. After cheesemakers have coagulated the milk, they cut the curds into pieces, which are then partially washed in warm water. This process reduces lactose in the curd and limits the

production of lactic acid, which allows the sweetness of the milk to shine through.

Cheesemakers also use specific lactic cultures that help in flavour and texture development. These cultures are widely available and many producers around the world purchase them to use in their own productions.

Finally, the wheels of Gouda are salted in a brine bath, allowing for the slow absorption of salt. The resulting cheeses always have a warm, buttery flavour, and as they age those caramel notes get more intense. The best Goudas are those that balance sweet and savoury. Many industrially made cheeses can be overly sweet, almost cloying.

The reason for the lack of EU protection for Gouda is that during the nineteenth century, following the industrialisation of dairy production in Holland, the cheese was heavily marketed by Dutch traders. This created a market beyond Europe, and copies of the cheese soon started to spring up, principally in North America. When Dutch producers tried to follow other European producers and protect the name of their cheese, it was too late. Gouda had become common property and enforcing such rules would have been impossible. For cheesemakers in the Netherlands this means that there is a lot of competition, while their competitors can sell their cheeses using the iconic name.

There are incredible Gouda-style cheeses made around the world, including some of our favourites: Fanaost, the 2018 World Champion, made in Norway using the milk of a herd of just 12 cows, is a rare treat. There's also Coolea made in Ireland; HolaAndes made in Colombia; and Marieke Gouda made in Wisconsin, USA. These Irish, Colombian and American producers are Dutch migrants, who have used their cheesemaking expertise to set up dairies in their new adoptive countries. However, each one of those cheeses takes on characteristics from the local terroir, making them distinct in their own right.

You could say there's Gouda, and then there's Gouda. CY

ORIGIN: Gouda, Netherlands

PROTECTED STATUS: Gouda is not protected, but there is a PDO for Noord-Hollandse Gouda and a PGI for Gouda Holland

MILK: Raw or pasteurised cow's milk

RENNET: Animal or vegetarian

AROMA: Whey, butter, caramel

FLAVOUR: Sweet, buttery, aromatic

TEXTURE: Pliable to crystalline with age

MATCH: Malty beers like a doppelbock work well. Pair with fresh fruits, such as apples and pears.

WORLD CHEESE AWARDS: Multiple awards, including World Champion 1999 (Kollumer/Frico)

Le Gruyère

In our search for the One Cheese to Rule Them All, Gruyère is a serious contender for the title. This mighty mountain cheese from Switzerland, which comes in hefty wheels weighing up to 40kg (88lb), almost always has at least one representative in the final of the World Cheese Awards, and often goes on to win the whole thing. No other cheese has been named World Champion more often than Gruyère, which has taken the title five times in total.

What's remarkable is that four of these wins belong to one particular company. Von Mühlenen in Fribourg doesn't make cheese. Instead it works as an 'affineur', or cheese maturer, buying young wheels from dairies and maturing them for many months in specially built rooms where temperature, humidity and air flow are carefully controlled.

The skills and techniques used in these cave-like spaces can transform a good cheese into a world-class one. Maturing rooms have their own unique microbiomes, which have a big influence on flavour development in cheeses in ways we don't yet fully understand. Communities of bacteria, moulds and yeasts, which are naturally present in the air, walls and wooden shelves, influence how a cheese will develop and taste.

Affineurs also rub the outside of Gruyère with a microbe-rich brine (called 'morge') to create a pungent rind, and regularly flip and brush the cheeses as they mature from 5 to 24 months. Taste Gruyère near the rind and you'll pick up meaty and farmy notes, while the supple paste towards the centre of the cheese is often creamy and fruity with notes of roasted nuts and even flowers. It's a cheese that melts like a dream in fondue but also takes centre stage on a cheeseboard. There's a lot to get your teeth into.

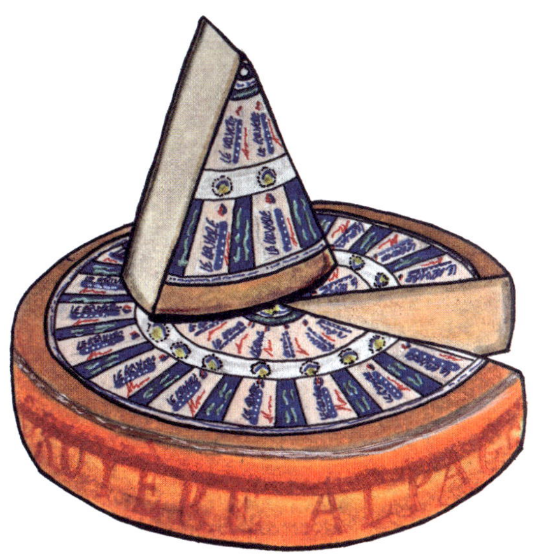

The microbiome of Von Mühlenen's caves must be particularly conducive to good cheese because its Premier Cru Gruyère, aged for 14 months, was named World Champion in 1992, 2002, 2005 and 2015. A Gruyère from affineur Gourmino, matured in a former military bunker deep within a mountain in the Bernese Oberland, also won the top prize in 2022.

There's more to Gruyère than maturation, however. The complex flavour also comes from where it is made, in the Alps of western Switzerland. Under the terms of its AOP, which protects where and how it is produced, the cheese can only be made in Switzerland in the cantons of Fribourg, Vaud, Neuchâtel and Jura, and a few municipalities of Bern. The AOP also

ORIGIN: Fribourg, Vaud, Neuchâtel, Jura, and parts of Bern, Switzerland

PROTECTED STATUS: AOP

MILK: Raw cow's milk

RENNET: Animal

AROMA: Brothy, roasted nuts, farmyard

FLAVOUR: Young: sweet, buttery, hazelnutty; mature: savoury, fruity, spicy

TEXTURE: Pliable and dense when young, firm and crumblier when mature

MATCH: Light whites (Chasselas is popular in Switzerland) with young cheeses. Fruity reds, such as Pinot Noir and Gamay, with mature cheeses. Smoked charcuterie on the side is a fine match.

WORLD CHEESE AWARDS: Multiple awards, including World Champion 1992, 2002, 2005, 2015 (Von Mühlenen), 2022 (Gourmino)

specifies that it should be known as Le Gruyère ('the Gruyère') for reasons I'll explain later.

Western Switzerland is a seriously beautiful place, with sweeping hills and valleys backed by snow-capped mountains. The fairytale town of Gruyères in Fribourg, which the cheese is named after, looks like the inspiration for a Disney movie, complete with cobbled streets and a turreted castle. More importantly for cheese-lovers, the foothills of the Alps are carpeted in lush grass, while higher up there are mountain meadows full of wildflowers and herbs, which keep the cows well fed during the summer.

By law, the milk for Gruyère can only come from cows fed on grass in the summer and hay in the winter. And the milk must not be pasteurised, thereby ensuring that the cows' diverse diet is fully expressed in the complex flavours of the final cheese. It's similar to the idea of terroir in wine – Le Gruyère is made to reflect the soil, grass and landscape of where it is made.

The ultimate expression of this idea is Le Gruyère Alpage, a special category of the cheese made between June and September. Cheesemakers take their cows high up into the Alps to access pristine pastures and flower meadows, making Gruyère in copper cauldrons over fires in wooden chalets. This was how Gruyère used to be made hundreds of years ago, and there are only around 50 of these chalets now left in the cantons of Fribourg, Vaud and Bernese Jura, each with their own unique conditions and flora.

At the end of the summer, the cows are brought down to the valleys with great fanfare in an ancient tradition known as *la désalpe*. Their horns garlanded with flowers, the cows are welcomed back to the villages like returning heroes, with yodelling, Swiss horns and dancing. This joyful celebration of cheese, landscape and tradition has been happening for centuries; Gruyère's history stretches back almost 1,000 years, with medieval chronicles extolling the full-fat cheese, which was durable enough to be packed into barrels and exported to France and Italy.

It became so popular as an export that production spread from its heartland of Fribourg to other Swiss cantons, as well as into neighbouring France. Comté cheese used to be known as Gruyère de Comté, but the Swiss campaigned long and hard to protect the name of their national cheese, eventually securing full AOP status for all of Europe in 2011 for the name Le Gruyère. The 'Le' was included to make it clear that it was the one and only.

Today there are more than 1,800 small farms in Switzerland, 160 Le Gruyère dairies, and around a dozen affineurs involved in the production of Le Gruyère. It's an impressive system of collaboration and co-operation that ensures the livelihoods of thousands of families, while also maintaining ancient craft skills, traditions and the landscape itself. Not to mention creating a seriously delicious cheese that wins a lot of awards. PM

Majorero

Cheese pre-dates modern countries, making it hard to explain how some cheeses are associated with a specific national culture. At the same time, government regulations impact and transform foods. Majorero is a great example of the balance between a local icon and a national product that is protected by European regulations but also accommodates regional nuances.

Majorera goats are found on Fuerteventura in Spain's Canary Islands. The breed is a mix of North African and Iberian Peninsula goats. Over decades the animals have evolved to fit in with the specific climate of this island in the Atlantic Ocean, near the north-west coast of Africa, a semi-arid terrain with plenty of small bushes for goats to graze on.

The climate on the island is temperate most of the year, with some torrential rains in the winter and heavy breezes and sandstorms from the Sahara Desert, known as Sirocco winds. These specific conditions influence the goats' diet and ultimately the flavour of the cheese.

Majorero cheese is made from milk from these goats. Up to 15 per cent Canarian sheep's milk is also allowed to be added, but it's the goat's milk that is the star of the show. The cheese has a distinctive tang to it, partly from the milk itself, but also from special starter cultures used during cheesemaking and ageing. The cheese is a stubby wheel weighing anywhere from 1 to 6kg (2.2 to 13.2lb), with a striking criss-cross pattern on the rind. The pattern on the rind originally came from moulds made of braided palm leaves, which left their imprint on the cheese – an effect now replicated by the plastic moulds used today.

You can find raw and pasteurised milk versions, some aged for a couple of weeks, others for a couple of months or more. The different age profiles are split into separate categories: *tierno* (soft), aged for 8–20 days and often eaten at breakfast; *semi-curado* (semi-cured), aged for 21–60 days and typically served as an aperitif; and *curado* (cured), which can be matured for a year or more and is used on cheeseboards.

The rind can be natural or rubbed with *pimentón* (paprika), *gofio* (milled wheat or corn) or olive oil. The cheese can also be salted by rubbing with salt or submerging in brine.

All of these variations are permitted by the PDO, which was introduced in 1996 to help promote the cheese outside of the Canaries and the Spanish mainland. It was the first goat's cheese in Spain to receive a PDO under the EU's protected food names scheme, giving it a certain cachet and commercial advantage over other *quesos* in the country.

The PDO also established a Comité de Cata – a judging panel formed of local tasters – who work to ensure Majorero meets strict quality standards. The palates of these cheese experts dictate quality for all producers. They are re-trained periodically, and new people are invited to join the judging panel when someone retires. The current 12-strong committee of tasters includes a fascinating mix of people, who reflect island society, from a police officer and social worker to an industrial chemist and a receptionist (who is also a judo instructor!). What they have in common is a deep knowledge and love of their local cheese.

Majorero is therefore remarkably consistent and regularly wins awards in local and international competitions. That's good news for cheesemakers from a remote part of the world, helping them to profit from their land and animals. CY

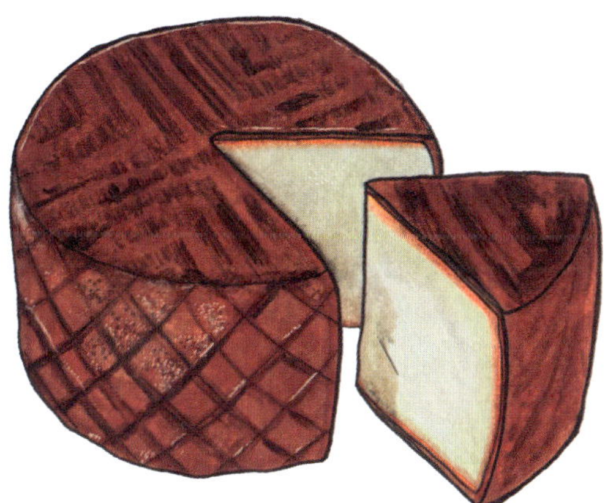

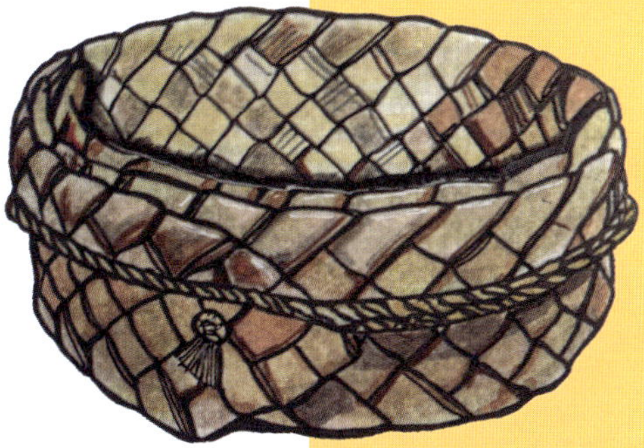

ORIGIN: Fuerteventura, Canary Islands, Spain

PROTECTED STATUS: PDO

MILK: Raw or pasteurised goat's milk; a maximum of 15% Canarian sheep's milk is also permitted

RENNET: Animal

AROMA: Nutty, milky, goaty

FLAVOUR: Nutty, sharp, tangy

TEXTURE: Hard, firm and a bit elastic

MATCH: Fruity red wines, such as Tempranillo. Marmalade is a good match.

WORLD CHEESE AWARDS: Multiple awards, including Best Hard Goat's Cheese 1993 (Co-op Fuerteventura)

Milleens

ORIGIN: County Cork, Ireland
PROTECTED STATUS: N/A
MILK: Pasteurised cow's milk
RENNET: Animal
AROMA: Barnyardy, funky, meaty
FLAVOUR: Smoky, lactic, buttery
TEXTURE: Depends on ripeness, but the best are soft and silky beneath the rind with a line of chalk at the centre
MATCH: A medium dry cider or strong Belgian ale. Cornichons and cured meats on the side.

WORLD CHEESE AWARDS: Multiple awards, including Best Soft Cheese 1997

There's something in the air in West Cork that makes it the perfect spot for smelly cheeses. That something is rain, which sweeps in from the Atlantic and soaks this south-western corner of Ireland so often that rainforests grow there. It's also great for growing grass to feed cows and creates the perfect conditions for maturing washed-rind cheeses – a style notorious for pungent orange rinds.

Durrus and Gubbeen are world-famous examples from the area, as was Ardrahan until the owners decided to call it a day back in 2015. But Milleens, made on the rain-lashed Beara Peninsula, which juts out into the Atlantic, was the first to lead the way.

This soft cow's milk cheese, which comes in different shapes and sizes, including rings and small rounds (called 'dotes'), has a buttery interior that runs from chalk to silk depending on ripeness. But it's the sticky rind that is central to its personality. Ranging from a blushing peach to a fiery orange, it gives the cheese a powerful barnyard aroma and intense flavour that takes in everything from smoked bacon and mushrooms to soil and sea.

The rind is developed by washing the exterior with salt water during maturation to encourage funky bacteria to grow, but the humid, briny environment also plays its part in creating the ideal natural conditions for this style of cheese to thrive.

Veronica Steele started experimenting with cheesemaking in 1976 when she and her husband, Norman, decided to give up their lives in Dublin to move to Milleens Farm in Cork. They only had one cow – a one-horned beast called Brisket – and Steele would use the milk to make cheese in the farm kitchen. Initially she tried to make Cheddar, Gorgonzola and Emmentaler, but the salty air kept turning the rinds orange. So rather than fight the elements, she decided to work with them by actively encouraging the bacteria to grow with regular brine washes.

The resulting cheese, named after the farm, went on to influence others in the area. Jeffa Gill of Durrus, Giana Ferguson of Gubbeen, and Mary Burns of Ardrahan all took inspiration from Steele.

Irish cheese had become so industrialised in the post-war years that there were no farmhouse cheesemakers left until Milleens came along. Steele helped to pioneer a new generation of makers through classes, and by co-founding Cais – the Irish Farmhouse Cheesemakers Association – in 1983. Today the country boasts more than 30 small, farmhouse producers, making everything from goat's logs and blues to Cheddar and, of course, washed-rind cheeses.

Steele sadly passed away in 2017, but her cheeses are in safe hands. They are made by her son Quinlan on the same farm on the Beara Peninsula, where they continue to turn wonderful shades of orange in the salty air. PM

Monte Enebro

Sheep's milk cheeses reign in Spain. From Zamorano and Idiazabal to Roncal and Manchego – these are the traditional hard cheeses that the country is best known for. But there's another more experimental side to Spanish cheese, led by innovative goat's cheese makers.

The soft, hand-moulded goat's cheese Nevat from Catalonia is part of this new wave, as is Olavidia from Andalusia, which has a line of ash through the middle (see page 186). But arguably the most influential of them all is Monte Enebro, made in Castile and León.

This goat's cheese log with a kick was created by visionary cheesemaker Rafael Báez Bravo-Murillo. After retiring from a career as a civil engineer in the 1980s, he started cheesemaking in Ávila as a hobby.

Working with consultant Enric Canut, he developed a cheese that took inspiration from a popular local hard sheep's milk cheese known as Pata de Mulo, which is so-called because its elongated shape resembles a mule's leg. They kept the shape but used goat's milk instead to make a soft cheese with a wonderful blue-mould rind.

Named Monte Enebro, after the *enebro* (juniper) bushes found in the region, it is truly unique because it changed the rules of blue cheese. Made in a 1.4kg (3lb) log with a grey-blue, fuzzy rind, which becomes darker and more piquant with time, it has plenty of the spicy notes you would expect from a blue cheese, but there is no actual blue veining inside. The cheese is not pierced, so the interior remains snowy white.

Depending on age, the cheese goes from a chalky, crumbly texture to gooey and creamy, while very mature cheeses are robust and spicy. It has a noticeable blue cheese flavour, but this is balanced with the creaminess and freshness of the goat's milk. We prefer it when it is young or a bit creamy, and it is glorious slightly heated on a grill and served on top of fresh spring vegetables.

What started as a hobby quickly evolved into a business called Queserías del Tiétar, which continues to make Monte Enebro today under the watchful eye of Báez's daughters María Jesús and Paloma. The cheeses are exported far and wide and have become a familiar site on cheese counters in the US and the UK, proving that there is more to Spanish cheese than Manchego. CY

ORIGIN: Castile and León, Spain
PROTECTED STATUS: N/A
MILK: Pasteurised goat's milk
RENNET: Animal
AROMA: Lactic, herby, piquant
FLAVOUR: Lemony, milky, mineral
TEXTURE: Dense and firm
MATCH: Cava or any other sparkling wine. Match with honey and pears for a perfect dessert.

WORLD CHEESE AWARDS: Multiple awards, including Best Goat's Cheese 1997

Parmigiano Reggiano

It's a magical moment to witness the birth of Parmigiano Reggiano. A delicate mass of ivory curd, submerged under whey at the bottom of a copper vat, is collected in a large rectangle of muslin held at either end by two cheesemakers. They then proceed to gently raise the curd by rhythmically rocking the cloth between them until the baby cheese breaches the surface for the first time.

What happens next is even more surprising. The giant lump of curd is split in half to make two cheeses, which are swiftly swaddled in cloth and hung side by side to drain. In other words, every Parmigiano Reggiano has a twin.

Very little has changed about this scene for hundreds of years. The cheese has a venerable history stretching back 1,000 years, and the way it is made is enshrined in a powerful PDO. This sets out strict rules, from what is fed to the cows to how long the cheese is aged, as well as limiting production to two cheeses per copper vat at a time. It can also only be made in a small part of northern Italy, running along the Po Valley.

The rules are designed to maintain quality and tradition, but they also make it hard to industrialise the cheesemaking process. Put simply, if you want to make more Parmesan (as it's known in the UK), you need more people and more vats. Caseificio Vittoria di Quistello, whose cheese was named World Champion in 1997, is a case in point. The co-operative is relatively large, producing 45,000 drums of cheese a year, each weighing around 40kg (88lb). But this is not an automated, push-button operation. Instead, the company has grown by installing more vats. Its flagship dairy near Quistello is home to row after row of shiny copper cauldrons – 44 in total – which are still tended by cheesemakers, who cut the curd with a giant whisk (called a *spino*) and deliver the twin cheeses into the world by cloth.

Over 3,000 farms and 300 dairies make Parmesan in Parma, Reggio Emilia, Modena and parts of Bologna and Mantua as part of the PDO. It's a relatively small area and cheeses made outside of it, or that don't conform to the rules laid out in EU law, cannot be labelled as Parmigiano Reggiano. Try making Parmesan in other parts of Italy or other countries in Europe and you will soon receive a stern letter from Italian lawyers. It's not so clear cut outside of Europe, however, where EU law is not recognised. Plenty of American and Australian cheesemakers produce cheeses branded as Parmesan, much to the chagrin of Italy.

That said, it's a system that is generally extremely effective. More than 4 million drums of Parmigiano Reggiano were produced in 2023, 40 per cent of which were exported. That represents a very decent return for the farmers and cheesemakers of northern Italy, with sales estimated to be worth €3 billion, making Parmesan the most valuable PDO cheese in Europe. That makes sense when you find out that a single drum of cheese is worth £1,500 or more. There is even a bank in northern Italy, Credito Emiliano, which accepts young cheeses as collateral for loans made to cheesemakers. There's money in cheese.

The value of Parmigiano also explains why cheese heists, involving hijacked lorries full of Parmesan, are more regular than you might expect in Italy. The Parmigiano Reggiano Consortium has also been battling counterfeiters, who make cheeses that look like Parmesan but are produced outside the production zone, and often outside Italy altogether. To this end, cheesemakers and maturers have taken to micro-chipping their cheeses. The edible micro-transponders, which are the size of a grain of sand and fitted into the cheese's food-grade casein label embedded in the rind, can be scanned to give a unique ID number that proves it is the real deal. It's highly unlikely, but if you do accidentally end up eating one of the micro-chips, the Consortium have assured cheese-lovers it is safe.

Price is not the only reason why Parmigiano Reggiano is so sought after. Made only with raw milk and animal rennet, the cheese has a remarkable flavour and texture, which develops over its long maturation period. Cheeses must be matured for at least 12 months, though often up to three years.

ORIGIN: Emilia-Romagna, Italy
PROTECTED STATUS: PDO
MILK: Raw cow's milk
RENNET: Animal
AROMA: Fruit, milk, spice
FLAVOUR: Pineapple, broth, piquant sharpness
TEXTURE: Crystalline and crumbly
MATCH: Lambrusco is a classic match, but also robust reds, such as Barolo. Chunks of pineapple complement the fruit flavour, or drizzle with aged Balsamic vinegar for a sweet, sharp kick.

WORLD CHEESE AWARDS: Multiple awards, including World Champion 1997 (Caseificio Vittoria di Quistello)

Visiting an affineur of Parmigiano Reggiano is another cheese experience not to be missed. Hundreds of wheels of cheese stacked on wooden shelves reach up to the ceiling in cathedral-like maturing rooms. Each one is turned and brushed to maintain its hard, polished exterior, and will be assessed for quality by special inspectors, called *battitores*, who tap the outside with a hammer. They can tell just by the sound it makes whether a cheese is fit to be branded with the Parmigiano Reggiano logo, or if there are holes or cracks that mean it won't make the grade.

The best Parmesans are typically aged for around 24 months and have a beautiful balance of pineapple fruitiness, piquancy and satisfying salty and savoury depths. Then there's the texture, which becomes progressively more granular with time as the proteins in the cheese break down into crystalline amino acids called tyrosine.

If you want to complete the hat-trick of Parmigiano Reggiano experiences, then the other event not to be missed is when a wheel is opened for the first time. It's a wonderful bit of cheese theatre, which involves a cheesemonger scoring the hard rind with a special hooked knife before plunging other stubby blades deep into the cheese. These are levered back and forth until it splits in half with an audible crack, revealing the crystalline cheese in its full glory and a room-filling scent of fruit, nuts and spice. PM

Pecorino Toscano

The name tells you all you need to know about this cheese: honesty in advertising, some might say. *Pecora* means 'sheep' in Italian, so Pecorino Toscano translates as 'Tuscan sheep's milk cheese'.

This cheese dates back to when the Etruscan civilisation ruled central Italy (c.500 BCE), and has become one of Tuscany's most iconic foods. It is one of six Pecorino styles made in Italy, each from a different region, and with distinct characteristics based on the breed of animals and the terroir of each area.

There are three breeds of sheep used to make Pecorino Toscano. Most shepherds have flocks with a mix of different animals, and the PDO does not have a specific amount for each type. These are Massese from Tuscany, Sarda from Sardinia, and Comisana from Sicily. They live outdoors year-round, as the cheese is produced in a region with a temperate Mediterranean climate.

You can find the cheese in two versions: fresh and aged. Younger cheeses, known as *fresco* or *tenero*, must be aged for a minimum of 20 days, though it can be found aged up to 60 days. Past this time, *stagionatori* (cheese maturers) prefer to wait 120 days to sell their cheeses as *stagionato*. We prefer this aged version as the flavours have developed and the cheese has complex umami and savoury notes. It's perfect for pasta.

The Consorzio Tutela del Pecorino Toscano DOP was established in 1985 and then encompassed under European Union rules in 1996. It recognises 17 dairies. Cheese can weigh from 2 to 4kg (4.4 to 8.8lb). As the cheese ages it loses moisture and size, so the older versions will be slightly smaller. CY

ORIGIN: Tuscany, Italy
PROTECTED STATUS: PDO
MILK: Raw or pasteurised sheep's milk
RENNET: Animal or vegetarian
AROMA: Milky, herbaceous, sheepy
FLAVOUR: Young: sweet, creamy, nutty; mature: spicy, animal, umami
TEXTURE: Fresh pecorino is soft and creamy; aged pecorino is harder and easier to shave in flakes
MATCH: Grate into risottos and creamy pasta sauces. Pair with Chianti or Brunello di Montalcino.

WORLD CHEESE AWARDS: Best Ewe's Milk Cheese 1997 (Il Fiorini)

Perroche

Perroche is an unassuming little cheese. The snow-white cylinder of goat's curd, sometimes rolled in herbs, is so fresh it is almost still milk.

But this dainty cheese with a lemony twang is part of a much bigger story of how one cheese shop almost single-handedly saved British cheese from oblivion. More on that later.

Perroche is made in Herefordshire by Charlie Westhead, who owns Neal's Yard Creamery. He makes the kind of goat's cheese you might find at village markets in the Loire Valley in France. Fresh goat's milk is curdled overnight, before the mousse-like curd is hand-ladled into moulds the next morning.

Log-shaped Ragstone and fluffy Dorstone are his most popular cheeses, but we have a soft spot for the bright flavours of Perroche – especially when it's rolled in dill, rosemary or tarragon.

There's none of the billy goat flavour that some people complain about with these styles of cheese. Typically, Perroche is eaten within just a few days of being made, so there's no time for those barnyardy flavours to develop.

Neal's Yard Creamery is an important link in what has been a remarkable revival in artisan cheese in the UK. The company used to be part of London cheese shop Neal's Yard Dairy, which has been banging the drum for British cheese for more than 40 years.

Neal's Yard Dairy was set up as part of a hippy collective in Covent Garden in 1979 by an idealistic cheesemonger called Randolph Hodgson. Initially, he made yoghurt and fresh cheeses like Perroche in the basement, but soon started selling cheeses from the last few farm-based cheesemakers in Britain.

Traditional cheesemaking was in a sorry state at the time. When Neal's Yard Dairy opened, there were just a few dozen small cheesemakers left. Hodgson drove round the country in a clapped-out van, visiting as many as he could (he would find their details in the phone book), filling the boot with traditional Cheddars and Cheshires.

Charlie Westhead joined Neal's Yard Dairy in 1987 and ended up buying the cheesemaking side of the business from Hodgson in 1990. It made sense to split the business in two. Hodgson could focus on selling cheese at the Dairy, while Westhead relocated the Creamery to Herefordshire, close to some excellent goat farms.

These were the early days of the British cheese revolution, but today there are more than 200 artisan cheesemakers in the UK, and many of their cheeses (including Perroche) can be found in Neal's Yard Dairy shops.

No wonder Randolph Hodgson was once described as the 'patron saint of British cheese'. Still, Charlie Westhead and his pretty Perroche also played their part. PM

ORIGIN: Herefordshire, England
PROTECTED STATUS: N/A
MILK: Pasteurised goat's milk
RENNET: Vegetarian (thistle)
AROMA: Milky, citrus, herbaceous
FLAVOUR: Yoghurty, herby, lemony
TEXTURE: Silky and delicate
MATCH: Dry whites, such as Sancerre. Lovely with cherries and raspberries.

WORLD CHEESE AWARDS: Best Goat's Cheese 1992

Stilton

It's the ultimate trivia question. Which British cheese can't be made in the village it is named after? The answer, as all good cheese geeks know, is Stilton. Britain's most famous blue takes its name from the Cambridgeshire village of Stilton, but in a quirk of history it is actually illegal to make the cheese there. That's because where and how the cheese is made is codified by a PDO, which means, by law, Stilton can only be made in the more northerly counties of Derbyshire, Leicestershire and Nottinghamshire.

How we ended up with such a confusing state of affairs is controversial and needs a bit of explaining. For many years cheese historians (there are more of them than you think) believed that Stilton cheese was never actually made in the aforementioned Cambridgeshire village. It was only ever sold there. Stilton was an important staging post on the Great North Road to London, and in the eighteenth century traders from the north would stop over at the Bell Inn coaching house in the village, run by an enterprising landlord called Cooper Thornhill. The inn is still there today, complete with a cheese and coffee shop, which does a roaring trade in Stilton cheeseboards.

Cooper Thornhill had an entrepreneurial streak and quickly spotted an opportunity to sell cheese to the people passing through the village and into London. He teamed up with a cheesemaker in Leicestershire, Frances Pawlett, who made a blue cheese for him to sell, which was promptly named Stilton.

Pawlett encouraged other cheesemakers in Leicestershire to make the cheese and production spread throughout the Midlands. When Britain's Stilton-makers got round to protecting the cheese in the 1990s, they naturally limited it to its traditional heartland of Derbyshire, Leicestershire and Nottinghamshire.

But a few determined Stilton scholars have also unearthed plenty of evidence to show the cheese was in fact made in Stilton as early as the seventeenth century and have got quite hot under the collar about the fact that it is forbidden today. In 2013, amateur historian Richard Landy, and Liam McGivern, then landlord of the Bell Inn, even petitioned the British government to change the PDO and expand the production area to Cambridgeshire. The UK Department for Environment, Food and Rural Affairs and the Stilton Cheesemakers' Association rejected the request out of hand.

What makes it even more confusing is that historical documents describe Stilton in various different ways, from being a hard aged cheese like Parmesan to a spoonable cream cheese. In the eighteenth century, Daniel Defoe said the cheese was 'brought to the table with the mites, or maggots round it, so thick that they bring a spoon with them for you to eat the mites with as you do the cheese', which is enough to put you off Stilton for life.

That would be a terrible shame, however, because Stilton today is one of the great blue cheeses of the world – if not the greatest. Roquefort and Gorgonzola makers would disagree, but when it's on song there is nothing to beat Stilton. The intricate web of blue veins break down the ivory curd inside to create a wonderfully soft and tender texture, while there's also a fudgy layer beneath the knobbly brown rind that is particularly delicious. The best Stiltons have a dark rind, with a peachy blush to the paste just beneath, plus deep blue veins. The flavour ticks every box going: sweet, salty and savoury with a little sharpness and bitterness. Think digestive biscuits, double cream, plus miso and a touch of radicchio.

That's not to say that every Stilton tastes that way. The clamour for Stilton is so monumentally high at Christmas in the UK – somewhere between 40 and 60 per cent of annual sales take place in November and December – that many cheeses are sent out too young, when they are crumbly, acidic and bitter.

The best Stiltons need time in the maturing room to mellow and soften; around 10–12 weeks is about right. It's why Stilton is such a Christmas tradition in Britain in the first place. Cheeses produced in early autumn are made with the best milk – rich in butterfat because the cows are starting to dry off after the summer. These super-creamy cheeses mature just in time for Christmas.

Yet Stilton's pre-eminence at Christmas has come under pressure in recent years, with softer, milder Continental blues eating into sales. There's also a new wave of British blues in various styles that are muscling in on Stilton territory, not least several Stilton-style cheeses. There's Young Buck made in Belfast, and Bath Blue, named World Champion in 2010. Perhaps the most famous of these alternatives is Stichelton, which, like Stilton, is made in Nottinghamshire. However, it cannot carry the name because it is made with raw milk, and under the rules of the PDO Stilton can only be

ORIGIN: Derbyshire, Leicestershire and Nottinghamshire, England
PROTECTED STATUS: PDO
MILK: Pasteurised cow's milk
RENNET: Animal or vegetarian
AROMA: Creamy, earthy, biscuity
FLAVOUR: Savoury, salty, piquant
TEXTURE: Crumbly and fudgy

MATCH: Tawny Port is a classic match. Excellent with a slice of dark, dense Christmas fruit cake.

WORLD CHEESE AWARDS: Multiple awards, including World Champion 1989 (Dairy Crest, Hartington), Best Blue 2001 (Cropwell Bishop), Best British Cheese 2013 (Colston Bassett)

made with pasteurised milk. Stichelton-maker Joe Schneider, an American with a decidedly dry and wicked sense of humour, has long campaigned for the terms of the PDO to be changed to allow raw milk Stilton, but Stilton-makers remain unmoved.

The slow and steady decline of Stilton sales in recent years has been mirrored by a drop in the number of dairies making the iconic cheese. Today there are only four blue Stilton-makers left in the world: Clawson in Leicestershire, Hartington in Derbyshire, and Colston Bassett and Cropwell Bishop in Nottinghamshire. There's also one dairy, Shirevale in Nottinghamshire, that specialises in White Stilton.

Clawson, the largest producer, has been doing its bit to counter the recent slump by developing different packaging, launching a new premium Stilton brand called 1912, and developing recipes to encourage people to cook with the cheese all year round. These efforts are starting to encourage a new generation of cheese-lovers to rediscover the joys of Britain's most famous blue, which can only be a good thing in our book. It's one of the greatest blue cheeses of the world, which should be eaten at all times.

Stilton is for life, not just for Christmas. 

Tomme de Savoie

With its gnarly brown and grey rind, a wheel of Tomme de Savoie looks a little like a rock you might find in the French Alps, where it's made. But pick it up and it is surprisingly sleek, smooth and velvety to the touch. The grey mould that grows on the rind is known as *poil de chat* (cat's fur), and brings a fruity, earthy flavour to the mild cheese beneath.

Tomme de Savoie, made in the mountainous Savoie and Haute-Savoie regions of eastern France, is the most famous of a huge family of Tomme cheeses (known as Toma in Italy). The name is thought to have come from the Latin word *tomus*, meaning a slice or a book. Perhaps people would historically ask for a *tomus* of cheese and it eventually became the name for the whole cheese itself. Nobody knows for sure.

What we do know is that these ancient cheeses were (and still are) a daily staple for cheesemakers and farmers. If there wasn't enough milk to make a large cheese like Beaufort, or perhaps there was a little bit of milk left over at the end of the day, the cheesemaker would skim the cream to churn into butter and use the remaining skimmed milk to make a small pressed cheese for the kitchen table. Typically weighing a few kilos and aged for just a few months, they were eaten as a nutritious, high-protein meal that would be hacked away at by all the family throughout the day. A few slices with a coffee is still a popular snack.

You can find these types of cheese throughout the Alps and the Pyrenees in France, Switzerland and Italy. There's a saying that there are as many Tommes as there are mountains and valleys, but Tomme de Savoie is certainly the most famous. It rose to prominence during the Duchy of Savoy, which comprised lands stretching into modern-day Switzerland and Italy (its capital was Turin at one point), from 1416 to 1860.

There's still an independent streak to the people of the area, who see themselves as Savoyard as much as French, and take great pride in their cheeses. As well as Tomme de Savoie, the region is also home to Reblochon, Beaufort, Abondance and the goat's milk Tomme Chevrotin.

It's a similar story in the vineyards (some of the highest in France) with unique grape varieties, such as Mondeuse and Jacquère, which pair very nicely with the cheeses.

Tomme de Savoie was protected by a PGI in 1996, which ensures that it can only be made in the Savoie region with raw or thermised milk from three French cow breeds: Abondance, Montbéliarde and Tarentaise. These hardy animals are adept at traversing the steep slopes and mountainous terrain of the Savoie, grazing dramatic Alpine pastures under snowy peaks.

There are more than 700 farms and nearly 40 dairies involved in the production of Tomme de Savoie, and the flavour of their cheeses can vary depending on their location, what the cows have been eating and how long they have been aged beyond the minimum 30 days. A big chunk of production is now relatively industrialised, but raw milk *fermier* (farm-based) cheeses are delicious, ranging from sweet and lactic to woody and farmy.

Much also depends on how the cheeses have been matured. Given the right conditions the grey mucor mould grows rampantly, resulting in cheeses that look like giant grey balls of fluff in the maturing room. These are brushed and patted down to more manageable levels by the affineur, which is what gives Tomme de Savoie its distinctive final coat. It's definitely a rind to eat as part of the cheese, although it's almost impossible not to give it a little stroke before you do. PM

ORIGIN: Savoie, France

PROTECTED STATUS: PGI

MILK: Raw or thermised cow's milk

RENNET: Animal

AROMA: Forest floor, damp cellar, milky

FLAVOUR: Lactic, woody, walnuts

TEXTURE: Springy when young; becoming fudgier with time

MATCH: Dry whites, such as Savoie wines made with Jacquère grapes. Fresh grapes or fig chutney is a nice pairing.

WORLD CHEESE AWARDS: Best Hard Cheese 1993 (Conus)

2000s

A decade dominated by the rise of celebrity chefs and Michelin-starred restaurants also marks the opening up of the cheese world. Genre-defying cheeses from the US, Australia and the Netherlands make their mark at the awards, while a Canadian goat's cheese, named after a fairytale princess, becomes the first World Champion from outside Europe.

Opposite: Roquefort (see page 90)

Appenzeller

It's not just Coca-Cola and KFC that have built their businesses on secret recipes. The cheesemakers of Appenzellerland in the north-east of Switzerland have been fiercely guarding the recipe for their cheese for 700 years. Ask an Appenzeller-maker what goes into the secret herbal brine, known as *sulz*, that they use to wash the rind of their semi-hard cow's milk cheese, and you will be greeted by a stern look and pursed lips.

According to the Appenzeller trade association that represents the 800 farms, 40 cheesemakers and five affineurs that make the supple, spicy cheese, only two people know the exact brine recipe, although it does reveal that it is made with 25 different herbs, roots, leaves, petals and seeds. These are mixed in oversized 'tea bags' and steeped in high-proof alcohol for around six to eight weeks. During this cold maceration process, the alcohol extracts a range of aromas and flavours from the secret mixture, resulting in the herbal essence, which is diluted with water and salt.

The mysterious recipe is a marketing boon to the association, which is fond of images of traditional dairymen with their fingers held firmly to their lips. Dressed in traditional festive costumes, including red waistcoat embroidered with flowers, yellow leather trousers, and black hats festooned with flowers (plus a spoon-shaped earring and watch chain), they make an impressive sight.

Historically, cheesemakers would have made their own brine using the herbs and flowers that grew around their dairies, but today the association encourages all cheesemakers to use the same centrally produced *sulz*, which is rubbed on the exterior of the cheeses as they mature, creating a pungent, slightly tacky rind.

Appenzeller is made between Lake Constance and the Säntis mountains in an area that is more hilly than mountainous. The wheels

ORIGIN: Appenzell, St Gallen and Thurgau, Switzerland
PROTECTED STATUS: Collective trademark
MILK: Raw cow's milk, although thermised milk is now also being used
RENNET: Animal
AROMA: Brothy, floral, spicy
FLAVOUR: Creamy, meaty, tangy
TEXTURE: Supple with occasional holes
MATCH: Off-dry Riesling whites cut through the rich cheese. Cured meats and roasted nuts are good partners.

WORLD CHEESE AWARDS: Multiple awards, including Gold 2004 (Arla)

are relatively small for an Alpine cheese, at around 7kg (15.5lb), which means they do not need to be aged for too long. Three to nine months is typical, resulting in a pliable texture, plus a high ratio of washed rind to paste, so it has more impact on the flavour of cheese beneath. Appenzellers are surprisingly powerful, balancing rich, creamy notes with intensely savoury, floral and spicy flavours from the rind. 'Like Gruyère on steroids,' is how a friend once described it to me.

Appenzeller does not have a government-recognised AOP. Instead it is protected by a registered trademark, which is enthusiastically protected by the trade association.

Appenzeller has undergone something of a makeover in recent years to try to boost its appeal, with colour-coded labels indicating age profiles, ranging from Silver (around three months) to Purple (around nine months). There's also White, which is made with added cream, Green for organic, and Brown for a longer-aged version made with skimmed milk.

In 2023 the association unveiled a completely new cheese, called Appenzellerin Elegant, made as a hard cheese with a much milder flavour – more floral and fruity – for shoppers who find the traditional Appenzeller too much.

But back to the secrets of *sulz*. Speculation about what goes into the secret brine is rife. One clue is that it is produced at the Ebneter Distillery in Appenzell, which also makes Alpenbitter brandy, leading some cheese sleuths to speculate that the brine must include the same aromatics as the brandy. Cloves, tarragon, oregano, juniper, rosemary, sage and white wine have all been suggested as key ingredients over the years, but the truth is nobody really knows except for the lucky two at the heart of the trade association, and they have their fingers firmly on their lips. PM

Queso Arico

There are many reasons to visit the Canary Islands, from warm summers and beautiful beaches to sparkling seafood and some of the best places to gaze at the stars in Europe. But what's less well known is that it's also a great place for cheese.

Tenerife is the largest island of the Spanish archipelago off the coast of north-west Africa. It is known for its topography, with rugged hills leading to the dormant volcano Mount Teide and white sandy beaches popular with British pensioners. It is also home to a unique cheese called Arico. This hard goat's cheese, named after the town in the south of the island where it is made, was little known outside the Canaries until 2008, when an Arico cheese aged with *pimentón* (smoked paprika) and *gofio* (local flour made of toasted grains like corn, wheat or starchy plants) won the World Cheese Awards.

Queso Arico Curado al Pimentón wheels weigh around 500g (1lb 2oz) and are difficult to miss as the rind is covered with a deep red paste made of olive oil, *pimentón* and *gofio*. This treatment gives the cheese a distinct nutty flavour and dry mouthfeel.

Cheesemakers use milk from local goats originally introduced to the islands from Western Africa. The animals have adapted to the climate and local environment, thriving by eating small plants and brush, and producing a gorgeous fatty milk perfect for cheesemaking. The paste of the cheese is crumbly but firm, with some oiliness that is pleasant to the palate. The cheese is normally aged six months and the best pairing, according to locals, is the local wildflower honey that is harvested at the base of the volcano.

I spoke to Rafael Domínguez González, fellow judge and export manager for Chácon e Hijo, a wholesaler based in Tenerife, who knows more than a thing or two about cheeses from the Canaries. He served as a judge on the Super Jury in 2015, one of the few Spaniards to have done so, and helped me decipher a story I found by watching online videos of the 2008 competition in Ireland and reading the press releases and stories from the time. This was before social media documented everything in real time.

On the day of the competition there was a question about the cheese that was to be presented to the final jury. It seems as though the documents accompanying the samples had been mislabelled and in the translation from Spanish to English the origin of the cheese had been lost. Fortunately, among the visitors to the competition were the presidents of the regulatory bodies for other Canarian cheeses: Majorero, Palmero and Flor de Guía. They assessed the cheese by look, smell, texture and flavour and agreed it was an Arico. To the surprise of everyone, this was confirmed when the organisers rubbed off part of the red paste and found the word 'Tenerife' embossed on the cheese rind.

Since then, the Sociedad Cooperativa Quesería de Arico, the original makers of the award-winning cheese, have sadly gone out of business. We hope it soon returns, but for now gentrification and over-tourism have pushed up land prices and there is pressure to turn agricultural lands into high-end resorts and luxury apartments. It makes farming challenging, to say the least. This is also true in other agricultural areas around the world, but it is exacerbated in the Canary Islands, where land is limited, flights are cheap and the weather is nice.

According to the records, Queso Arico Curado al Pimentón competed in the last round against Cendré de Lune, made by Alexis de Portneuf, also maker of Le Cendrillon, 2009 World Champion in Gran Canaria (see page 62). Joining them in the final were previous World Champions including Le Gruyère, aged by Von Mühlenen (see page 31) and Fourme d'Ambert (see page 26). On this occasion a humble cheese from Tenerife rose to the top, impressing judges.

The original Arico may not exist anymore, but its place in world cheese history is secured. CY

ORIGIN: Tenerife, Canary Islands, Spain
PROTECTED STATUS: N/A
MILK: Pasteurised goat's milk
RENNET: Animal
AROMA: Earthy, herby
FLAVOUR: Lactic, toasted nuts, oil
TEXTURE: Compact, crumbly, dry
MATCH: There are three white grapes in this region – Malvasía, Marmajuelo and Listán Blanco – producing great wines to pair with this cheese. Also try honey or a compote made with sweet potato known as Dulce de Batata.

WORLD CHEESE AWARDS:
World Champion 2008 (Sociedad Cooperativa Quesería de Arico)

Beaufort

'Higher is always better' when it comes to Beaufort. That was the motto of Savoyard farmer Maxime Viallet, who helped save this unmistakable mountain cheese from extinction in the 1960s. More on that later.

His adage makes perfect sense when you witness Beaufort Chalet d'Alpage being made high up in the mountains of Savoie in France, where cheesemakers spend their summers in wooden chalets with little for company except free-roaming cows and views of Mont Blanc.

Jean-François Villiod is one such producer. I was lucky enough to visit Villiod's chalet high up on Col de la Bâthie in 2024 with a travel company called Cheese Journeys, set up by former cheesemonger Anna Juhl, who takes people on epic cheese holidays. It was an adventure that involved nearly an hour of traversing hair-pin bends in two vans full of excited American cheese-lovers (and an equally enthusiastic British cheese writer). Our ears popping at regular intervals as we snaked up the narrow mountain roads, we eventually reached the isolated chalet just as dawn was breaking, revealing an impossibly beautiful scene of cows grazing mountain pastures.

The 90-strong herd is walked up to this idyllic spot in early summer in a tradition known as *l'emmontagnée* (the climb), so they can access pastures that are like a potpourri of Alpine flowers and herbs. Only two or three 40kg (88lb) cheeses are made each day in the chalet, which are instantly recognisable as Beaufort thanks to their concave sides, which historically made them easier to strap to donkeys and carry back down the mountain in the autumn.

The animated chatter from the van soon gave way to a quiet reverence as we watched a young cheesemaker, wreathed in steam, quietly cut and stir warm curd in a copper cauldron. If it wasn't for the gas burner, rather than a wood fire, we could have been witnessing cheesemaking 200 years ago.

The wheels made by Villiod are aged for a year or more and are some of the most intense and nuanced cheeses I've ever tasted. A swirling mass of flavour that unravelled in stages, starting with roast beef and horseradish, before segueing into dried fruit, cooked butter, grass and flowers.

Chalet d'Alpage is peak Beaufort (excuse the pun). But there are other varieties under the cheese's PDO, which specifies that the cheese can only be made in Beaufortain, Val d'Arly, Maurienne and Tarentaise in the Savoie, using raw milk from two local cow breeds: Tarine and Abondance.

Cheeses labelled Beaufort are made from November to May, when the cows are housed in barns at lower altitudes and fed locally grown hay, while Beaufort d'Ete is made from June to October, when the cows graze mountain pastures at altitudes up to 1,500m (4,920 feet) above sea level. Both versions can be made with milk from more than one herd and are quite different in colour and flavour. Winter Beaufort has a lighter, ivory colour and mild flavour with warm, malted milk notes, while summer Beaufort is golden with complex herbaceous notes. Beaufort Chalet d'Alpage, meanwhile, represents a tiny fraction of production and can only be made from milk from a single herd that grazes pastures between 1,500 and 2,500m (4,920 and 8,200 feet).

The different classifications enable farmers and cheesemakers to make full use of the natural resources in the region. Meadows are maintained in a clever grass cultivation system that sees the cows moved up and down the mountain, fertilising the pastures with manure as they go, which in turn encourages a diverse plant life to grow the following year. Without the cows the landscape would return to scrubland and many of the unique flowers and herbs would be lost.

It wasn't always so rosy in the garden of Beaufort, however, which is where our friend Maxime Viallet comes in. The cheese, which dates back to the seventeenth century, fell on hard times in the 1960s when farm workers were lured away by the higher wages offered by construction jobs on ski resorts and hydroelectric dams. Production fell to less than 500 tonnes (492 tons) and there was a real danger the cheese could die out altogether.

Thankfully, a few passionate producers, led by the charismatic, beret-wearing farmer Maxime Viallet, had other ideas. They banded together to fight for Beaufort's future, overseeing innovations such as co-operative dairies and the introduction of mechanised milking and hay-making. They also set up the Beaufort Cheese Defence Union, securing protected status for the cheese in 1968.

The rear-guard action was highly effective, giving Beaufort a new lease of life, so that today there are more than 5,000 tonnes (4,920 tons) of Beaufort made each year, involving 335 farms and 34 producers.

The world is a more delicious place for it. 

ORIGIN: Savoie, France
PROTECTED STATUS: PDO
MILK: Raw cow's milk
RENNET: Animal
AROMA: Musky, floral, caramel
FLAVOUR: Beefy, herbaceous, brown butter
TEXTURE: Firm and smooth with some crystals
MATCH: Intense red wines, such as Mondeuse or Nebbiolo. Walnuts and dried apricots pick up on similar flavours in the cheese.

WORLD CHEESE AWARDS: Gold 2003 (Hennart)

HERO CHEESE

Camembert

Standing at the dairy window at Fromagerie Durand, one of the last *fermier* (farm-based) Camembert-makers in France, I find myself falling into a hypnotic state. Through the grimy plastic window a young cheesemaker in white wellies and a fetching blue hairnet is ladling curds into round plastic moulds, lined up in neat rows. With a deft flick of the wrist, each mould gets a scoop of the wobbly curds, before he moves on to the next. Once he's finished, he waits for around half an hour before starting again, topping up the moulds with another single scoop.

It's a process that will be repeated five times over several hours until each mould is full to the brim, but I'm oblivious to the passing of time. The patient, rhythmic action and the sound of cows gently mooing in the shed nearby lull me into a reverential trance. It's hard to keep your wits about you when witnessing one of the world's most famous cheeses being made just a few miles away from the village in France that it is named after.

If Camembert came for an interview for the position of One Cheese to Rule Them All, it would be hard not to give it the job. Loved around the world for its ripe flavour, plump texture and little round box, the cheese is inexorably intertwined with France's food culture, terroir and *savoir-faire*. In the land of fine *fromage*, Camembert is venerated like no other, which explains why its recent history has been a passionate story involving bitter court cases, protests on the streets of Paris, and a fight for the French way of life, no less.

According to legend, Camembert was first created by farmer's wife Marie Harel in Camembert in Normandy in 1791. Harel, whose picture appears on the labels on Durand's wooden cheese boxes, is said to have learned how to make the cheese from a priest, Charles-Jean Bonvoust, from the Brie region, who she sheltered at her farm during the upheaval of the French Revolution. There's a statue of Harel in Vimoutiers – a town near Camembert – and plenty of *rues* named in her honour across Normandy.

The only problem is that cheese historians have since found evidence that Camembert was being made in Normandy nearly 90 years before Harel was said to have invented it. There's even some doubt as to whether she actually ever met the priest Bonvoust at all. Cheese legends are notoriously unreliable.

Today Camembert has become a generic style of cheese, endlessly copied around the world, but if you want the authentic, original cheese, then Normandy is the place to visit. While the name 'Camembert' is not protected, 'Camembert de Normandie' is covered by a PDO, which specifies that the cheese must be made in the *département* using raw milk with at least 50 per cent coming from the traditional Normande breed of cow. The hand-ladling of curds into moulds (*moulé à la louche*) is also a key part of the designation.

There are only 14 Camembert de Normandie producers left, including five farm-based makers. Nicolas Durand is one of the most experienced. He's been making traditional Camembert for 40 years, using raw milk from his own herd of 100 cows, the majority of which are the traditional Normande breed (you can recognise them from their red-

pied coat and dark markings around the eyes that look like spectacles).

Once the norm, producers like Durand are few and far between in Normandy these days due to the rise of industrialised cheesemaking. Multinational dairy companies have abandoned the PDO in favour of using pasteurised milk and mechanised processes to make Camembert at scale. Unable to use the PDO-protected name, these cheaper alternatives are often confusingly labelled as *Camembert fabriqué en Normandie* (made in Normandy), a tactic that has been highly successful – around 60,000 tonnes (59,000 tons) are produced each year, compared to just 6,000 tonnes (5,900 tons) of PDO-label Camembert de Normandie.

Larger producers have also waged a lobbying campaign to alter the terms of the PDO to allow pasteurised milk, much to the fury of smaller producers. The so-called 'Camembert wars' have rumbled on for 30 years, with both sides fighting to come out on top, but in 2018 it looked like the game was up for traditional raw milk Camembert de Normandie when the association that represents producers finally caved into pressure and struck a deal to allow pasteurised milk with a separate sub-brand for authentic raw milk cheeses.

The agreement was front-page news across the country and led to a remarkable campaign to save Camembert de Normandie, involving a petition signed by more than 35,000 people. Lobby group Fromages de Terroirs, which branded the deal the 'death of Camembert de Normandie', even led a demonstration at the French parliament, with protestors posting raw milk cheeses in the letterboxes of MPs.

The fightback worked. At the last minute, Camembert de Normandie producers pulled out of the deal and as this book went to press an appeals court in Nantes had ruled that producers should not be able to use the term '*fabriqué en Normandie*', or indeed any reference to the word 'Normandie', to protect the PDO makers. Victory for David over Goliath, although the dairy giants are unlikely to give up the fight.

The huge outpouring of support for Camembert de Normandie reflects its special place in the nation's heart, not just as a cherished food, but also as a symbol of French culture, history and terroir. This was made clear to me when I visited the charming cheese museum in the village of Camembert, after waking from my curd-ladling reverie at Durand's.

There are some wonderful old bits of dairy equipment and displays of brightly illustrated cheese labels at the museum, housed in an eighteenth-century farmhouse, which tell the story of how Camembert became a national treasure. Its first step to immortality was the clever idea of putting the cheese in a wooden box. Until the end of the nineteenth century, Camembert's only protection on its journey to city cheesemongers was a thin paper wrapping. The soft cheeses would travel on a bed of straw and often arrive in a sorry state after long journeys by horse, cart and steam train. But at the end of the century an engineer called M. Ridel (his first name is lost to history) invented a game-changing machine for making small round boxes from poplar wood. Suddenly Camembert began arriving in Paris in perfect condition, but it was also exported across Europe and the Atlantic.

Just as importantly, the little boxes were also perfect for branding. Among the huge collection of cheese labels at the Camembert museum there are colourful illustrations of ripe cheeses and bucolic scenes of farm animals and dairymaids, but also pictures that reference war heroes, the latest fashions, political events, and historical figures from Joan of Arc to Napoleon. As Pierre Boisard wrote in his 1992 book *Camembert: A National Myth*, 'without its label, Camembert would not be what it is'.

The First World War was also a pivotal moment in Camembert's ascent to greatness, thanks to a marketing masterstroke from the association representing cheesemakers in Normandy, which agreed to supply the army with one day of its members' production each week at a reduced price. The cheese was included as part of the daily ration for soldiers on the front line, nicknamed *poilus* (hairies), who would often eat it with a swig of rustic red wine.

'The partaking of cheap red wine and Camembert served to remind the combatants of what they were fighting for: their land and its produce,' wrote Boisard. 'For men who had been at the front, Camembert was a part of the mythology of the Great War.'

The cheese remains an important part of French national identity today, adored by millions for it lustrous texture and punchy vegetal flavour. Camembert de Normandie is a star performer at the World Cheese Awards, regularly picking up category awards for Best Soft Cheese and Best French Cheese. It was also named World Champion in 2001 and 2004. Both winners were made by Isigny Sainte-Mère, one of the larger Camembert de

Normandie producers in the region, which sources milk from around 40 local farms and packages its cheese in boxes featuring a classic line drawing of a dairymaid carrying milk churns on a donkey.

But there are still challenges facing France's favourite *fromage*. The threat from big non-PDO producers making cheaper versions of the cheese is unlikely to go away, while increasingly onerous hygiene legislation in France is making life harder for all raw milk cheesemakers.

Back at Fromagerie Durand, the company's future has been made much more secure with a deal with supermarket chain Grand Frais, which buys and distributes most of the 800 or so cheeses the farm makes each day. The relationship has also allowed the business to increase the number of traditional Normande cows in its herd.

In other good news, the Camembert museum has expanded since my visit, with the opening of a working dairy next door, called Le Clos de Beaumoncel, which has viewing windows so visitors can be mesmerised by the dreamy movements of *moulé à la louche* as part of their tour. It also means that Camembert de Normandie is once again being made in the heart of the village where Marie Harel first invented the cheese – or didn't, depending on which cheese historian you talk to.

The future of France's national treasure looks assured, for now at least. PM

ORIGIN: Normandy, France

PROTECTED STATUS: PDO for Camembert de Normandie

MILK: Raw cow's milk for PDO cheeses

RENNET: Animal for PDO cheeses

AROMA: Dairy, vegetal, earthy

FLAVOUR: Brassica, mushrooms, buttery

TEXTURE: Soft, silky

MATCH: Cider is the recommended tipple in Normandy, but also try the local sweet apple liqueur called Pommeau. A blob of chilli jam is a superb side.

WORLD CHEESE AWARDS: Multiple awards, including World Champion 2001, 2004 (Isigny Sainte-Mère)

Cashel Blue

Some cheesemakers are like family. For me, this is true of the Furnos. Sarah and Sergio Furno have welcomed me into their house in Tipperary, Ireland, and we have shared time together in the USA and elsewhere in Europe. They are the cheesemakers and maturers of Cashel Blue, which also happens to be one of my favourite blues. Weighing around 1.5kg (3.3lb), with a soft paste and deep blue veins, it comes wrapped in gold foil like a priceless piece of treasure.

My cheese career started in Ireland in 2005, where I worked behind the counter at Sheridans Cheesemongers in Galway, under the management of Sarah Hennessy, now cheesemaker at Durrus Cheese in Cork. There was a time when I knew more about Irish farmhouse cheeses than those from my home country of Mexico.

Ever since I worked at Sheridans, I have loved Cashel Blue and its sheep's milk sister Crozier Blue. After moving to the USA, I was delighted to find both in New York stores; importers make seasonal orders to coincide with St Patrick's Day (there is also a lot of horrible, green-coloured Cheddar at this time of the year).

I met Sarah, Sergio and their kids on their farm during a trip to visit cheesemakers around Cork and Tipperary in 2011. Beforehand, I had committed to memory some facts about their operation, mostly from reading online and stories shared by cheesemongers from behind the counters. The company uses local, grass-fed milk from within a 25km (15.5-mile) radius of the farm and makes several different cheeses, including the sheep's milk Crozier

ORIGIN: Tipperary, Ireland
PROTECTED STATUS: N/A
MILK: Pasteurised cow's milk
RENNET: Vegetarian
AROMA: Herbaceous, earthy, piquant
FLAVOUR: Sweet, creamy, biscuity
TEXTURE: Soft and crumbly
MATCH: Have a Guinness. It always works. Red onion marmalade or pecans and chocolate pieces are great accompaniments.

WORLD CHEESE AWARDS: Multiple awards, including Best Irish Cheese 2009

Blue and a hard cheese named Shepherd's Store. The best part of my visit was listening to the account of how Cashel Blue cheese was invented.

Sarah's parents, Jane and Louis Grubb, started making cheese from the milk of their own herd of cows in the early 1980s. They started with quark- and Camembert-style cheeses, but soon started trialling a soft, creamy blue cheese. It was named after a local historic site, the Rock of Cashel, which dates back almost a thousand years and is said to be the place where Ireland's patron saint, St Patrick, began the conversion of the Irish to Christianity.

By 1984, the first wheels of Cashel Blue were ready to be sold, and soon afterwards the cheese started winning fans. The following year, Neal's Yard Dairy in London made the first order for the UK, helping with both recognition and sales. For the Grubbs, the most rewarding part of this relationship was connecting with other cheesemakers who were starting to make cheese in Ireland or reviving farmhouse cheese traditions in England.

The new generation joined in 2004, when Sarah and Sergio moved to Beechmount Farm and started focusing on cheese maturation, eventually taking over the business. During my most recent visit in 2024, I was happy to again see the distinctive shelving device they use to turn cheese. These ingenious rolling shelves hold the cheeses sideways, allowing them to be rotated periodically, ensuring they maintain their shape and have lovely smooth sides. This helps when it comes to wrapping them in gold foil, which not only looks pretty, but helps the cheese breathe and stops a crusty rind forming as the cheese matures for three to six months.

It is amazing that you can find this cheese made in rural Ireland as far away as Australia and California. This global distribution makes people think that the cheese is made by a large company. But the truth is that this is a farmhouse cheese made by a small family and a very dedicated team. CY

Le Cendrillon

It was a truly unique moment. Over 150 expert judges from all over the world gathered in Gran Canaria, the largest island in the Canaries archipelago, for a historic competition. The Super Jury in the final, of which I was a member for the first time, was deliberating on cheeses that could be named World Champion of the 2009 World Cheese Awards.

As the results were released, a sense of shock took hold as it became clear that the winning goat's cheese was to become the first non-European cheese to win the competition. What made the result even more surprising was that the cheese in question looked so French, but was actually made in Canada, in Quebec province to be precise

Among all the regular cheese heavyweights, such as Stilton and Cheddar, there was a modest little goat's cheese with an ash rind. We tasted a small amount and I was blown away. I even remember the French judge saying: 'This must be from France.'

Cendrillon (Cinderella) is a great name for the winning cheese, which is made by La Maison Alexis de Portneuf in Quebec. Just like the folktale character, the unassuming stepsister became the belle of the ball with a little help from a few fairy godmother judges. The small 125g (4.5oz) triangular-shaped log had made the journey from Canada to the Canary Islands, arriving in perfect condition.

The aroma was clean and milky; the flavour was light and lemony; and the texture was soft and delicate. Le Cendrillon first won over a panel of three judges and moved to the next round, before eventually arriving at the finals, where the dainty Quebecois cheese defeated some of the biggest names to be crowned the best cheese in the world.

The win was an unexpected victory for Saputo, one of the 10 largest dairy processors in the world, who had acquired La Maison Alexis de Portneuf in 2005.

Le Cendrillon continues to win medals, and remains iconic for having been the first non-European cheese to win the top honour at the WCAs. It wasn't until 10 years later that another cheese – Rogue River Blue from the US – managed the same feat (see page 143). It just goes to show that there is a world of good cheesemaking outside of Europe. CY

ORIGIN: Quebec, Canada
PROTECTED STATUS: N/A
MILK: Pasteurised goat's milk
RENNET: Vegetarian
AROMA: Lactic, sharp, mushroomy
FLAVOUR: Lemony, creamy, savoury
TEXTURE: Chalky when young; soft and creamy beneath the rind when more mature
MATCH: Sauvignon Blanc is a classic match. Nice with herby crackers, too.

WORLD CHEESE AWARDS: World Champion 2009

Comté

How do you eat cheese? Well, on one level the answer is simple. Chew, swallow and enjoy. Job done. But it's a lot more complicated when you go deeper into the world of professional cheese-tasting.

Systems designed to accurately describe and assess the quality of cheese have been occupying the minds of experts for decades, and they've come up with a confusing array of models and approaches.

At the World Cheese Awards, entries are judged on a 35-point scale, with points awarded or taken away for visual appearance, texture, aroma and flavour. To get a Gold medal you need over 30 points, which is no mean feat.

UK-based educational organisation the Academy of Cheese goes into even more depth with its own two-page system, called the Structured Approach to Tasting Cheese, which records everything from size, shape and texture to aroma, mouthfeel (how it feels when you eat it), and separate sections for simple and complex flavours. There are similar but significantly different approaches employed by the American Cheese Society, the Italian Culinary Institute and La Fédération des Fromagers in France.

Flavour is a particular focus for Comté-makers in the Jura region of eastern France. Made in hefty 40kg (88lb) wheels with raw cow's milk, this classic Alpine cheese is aged anywhere from 4 to 48 months and has multiple personalities. Sweet and milky with a bendy texture when young, it becomes increasingly crystalline with age, with roasted nut, caramel and dried fruit flavours that grow in intensity.

The Comité Interprofessionel du Comté, which represents the farmers, dairies and affineurs that make the cheese, has charted these diverse flavours in a handy flavour wheel. The Wheel of Aromas identifies 83 specific flavours in Comté, which are divided into six broad aromatic families: lactic, fruity, roasted, vegetal, animal and spicy.

It's a useful tool, but also a fascinating insight into just how complex and culturally specific flavours can be. There are plenty of words that you might expect, such as 'butter', 'hazelnut', 'wild mushrooms' and 'hay', but quite a few that feel decidedly French and unique to Comté. Hands up if you've ever tasted 'horse', 'brioche' or 'roasted onion' in cheese. What about 'leather', 'hard-boiled egg yolk' or 'cows at milking time'?

This wide spectrum of flavours is not surprising when you consider that the production of Comté involves a huge variety of producers in different parts of the region. There are around 2,400 small farms, 140 village dairies (*fruitières*) and 13 affineurs that collectively produce Comté in the Jura Massif, an elevated region that covers the *départements* of the Jura, Doubs and part of Ain. Under the terms of its PDO, Comté can only be made with raw milk from either Simmental or Montbéliarde cows, which graze diverse pastures in the summer and are fed hay cut from the same land in the winter.

There are common characteristics across all Comtés, such as a certain sweet nuttiness, but by the very nature of its co-operative model, involving thousands of small businesses across different landscapes, there is also great variation among the cheeses, influenced by the season and the micro-climate of the farms, but also due to subtle differences between

the cheesemakers and maturers. 'Every wheel has a story, and every story is different,' is how the Comté committee likes to put it. It's also fond of the phrase: 'No two wheels ever taste the same.'

This focus on terroir is relatively recent. As supermarkets became more dominant in France in the 1990s, Comté-makers came under pressure to centralise and standardise their cheeses, but they decided instead to take a stand and celebrate their small-scale collaborative approach and diverse flavours.

As part of this, food scientist Florence Bérodier began charting the different micro-regions of the Jura in terms of soil type, plant species and climatic conditions, as well as tasting Comté in a more professional way to see how the terroir was expressed in flavour. This grew into the Jury Terroir, a trained tasting panel of volunteers, who have met for more than 30 years to assess the flavours in Comté. The group, which includes farmers, cheesemakers, administrators and culinary instructors, gathers monthly at a special tasting room at the Centre Technique des Fromages Comtois in Poligny, where they taste Comté together under the guidance of Bérodier.

Cheeses from different *fruitières* are tasted individually, with each member of the panel making detailed notes on the flavour, before it opens into a group discussion. Each participant must only use four words to describe the flavour, which are then recorded and used to build up an agreed sensory profile. Tasters who try to dominate the process by using more words, or who try to influence other panellists with strong opinions, are quickly shut down by the moderator. The idea is to work together in an egalitarian and unified way to come to agreement, an approach that reflects the wider co-operative production model for Comté: the collective is prized over the individual.

There's a great report by anthropologist Christy Shields-Argelès on how the jury terroir operates and why it's so important to Comté. She was allowed to be present at several of the tastings, and the paper – 'A Cooperative Model of Tasting: Comté Cheese and the Jury Terroir' – is a fascinating read, not only because it deals with ideas around terroir, flavour and social cohesion, but also because there are detailed descriptions of how the tastings work with direct quotes from the panellists.

It's intriguing to read how people's backgrounds affect how they perceive flavour. A farmer will have a different vocabulary for describing a cheese compared to an office administrator because of their different life experiences, but they are still often able to come to agreement. Comté tasting is clearly a serious business, but there is also a fair amount of joking and banter around topics such as the difference between warm milk and vanilla milk, or what the hairs on udders smell like. First of all, it was news to me that udders are hairy. And secondly that they have a distinct aroma. Perhaps this is what the 'cows at milking time' description is getting at in the Wheel of Aromas.

Comté's focus on flavour and terroir in the 1990s turned out to be an inspired move. Each year the village cheesemakers in the Jura make around 65,000 tonnes (64,000 tons) of cheese, which equates to 1.75 million wheels, making it the largest PDO cheese in France. It also supports 14,000 jobs, including 4,500 farmers. There's eating cheese, and then there's tasting cheese. PM

ORIGIN: Franche-Comté, France
PROTECTED STATUS: PDO
MILK: Raw cow's milk
RENNET: Animal
AROMA: Fruity, nutty, creamy
FLAVOUR: Caramel, hazelnuts, umami
TEXTURE: Pliable to crystalline, depending on age
MATCH: Vin Jaune, a nutty, oxidative white wine from the Jura, is a sensational pairing. A few roasted hazelnuts or boozy cherries (*griottines*) are good on the side.

WORLD CHEESE AWARDS: Multiple awards, including Best Hard PDO Cheese 2007 (Entremont), Super Gold 2022 (Monts & Terroir)

Cornish Yarg

Wander the woodlands and hedgerows of Cornwall in early summer and you might bump into small groups of people busily hunting for an unusual botanical prize. These are pickers from Lynher Dairies, who spend early May and June combing the landscape close to the dairy in Ponsanooth for wild stinging nettles.

The reason why a cheesemaker needs nettles is immediately apparent when you meet Cornish Yarg. The iconic British cheese sports a beautiful green coat of nettle leaves, which are applied to the outside in concentric circles. As the cheese matures over a period of four weeks, a downy mist of white mould appears on the leaves, which makes the cheese look even prettier, and helps to soften the crumbly cheese beneath, creating a toothsome, herbaceous layer just beneath the foliage.

Nettle foraging is a precarious business. Gloves and a delicate touch are required so that the pickers are not stung and the leaves remain whole and unbruised. The size of the crop can also vary from season to season, depending on the elements. In a good year, the nimble-fingered team will pick 3 tonnes (2.9 tons) of nettles for the cheese, mainly from hedgerows, fields and woods. They also pluck around a tonne (0.9 tons) of wild garlic leaves for a sister cheese called Wild Garlic Yarg. These are carefully frozen back at the dairy, to be used when required throughout the year. Each leaf is sterilised before being placed on to the cheese using a paintbrush by a very skilled team nicknamed 'nettlers'.

For Lynher's owner, Catherine Mead, the annual fortunes of a wild plant that many people consider a weed play an astonishingly large part in determining how much cheese she can make each year. The dairy can only produce as much cheese as there are leaves, which is why Mead once tried to set up her own nettle farm, only to find that they are surprisingly hard to tame. Nettles are spiky characters in more ways than one.

Nettle farming is exactly the kind of entrepreneurial thinking that has made Catherine Mead a true hero of British cheese. Cornish Yarg was invented in the 1980s by Alan and Jenny Gray (Yarg is their surname spelled backwards), who were inspired by a 1615 recipe for a nettle-wrapped cheese found in an old book in their attic. Mead first got involved in the business in the 1990s, eventually taking it over altogether and settling production in Ponsanooth in the early 2000s. She has gone on to become a pioneering figurehead for British cheese and Cornish food, with a CV that includes stints as chair of both the Specialist Cheesemakers' Association and Cornwall Food Foundation. She was awarded an OBE for services to cheese in 2019 by Queen Elizabeth II.

Cornish Yarg has been a perennial winner at the World Cheese Awards, regularly picking up Gold medals down the decades, but it was a newer cheese from Lynher, called Cornish Kern, that achieved ultimate success in 2017, when it was named World Champion. The black waxed cheese is a kind of cross between a Gouda and a Gruyère, which is aged for 18 months until it is hard and crystalline, and has a wonderful mix of pineapple, butterscotch and savoury flavours.

Kern, which is Cornish for 'round', has become so successful that Mead invested in a herd of Ayrshire breed cows so that she can work with the farm to get the perfect milk

specifically for the long-ageing cheese. It's gone from strength to strength since it became World Champion, but we still think of Yarg as the original and best.

One last thing, which everybody always wants to know. Do you eat the rind of Cornish Yarg? The answer is, absolutely yes. The freezing process takes away the sting of the nettles, so there's no need to worry about sore lips. And there's a lovely herbaceous, green flavour from the leaves that adds to the experience. PM

ORIGIN: Cornwall, England
PROTECTED STATUS: N/A
MILK: Pasteurised cow's milk
RENNET: Vegetarian or animal
AROMA: Herbaceous, zesty, milky
FLAVOUR: Mushroomy, lemony, yoghurty
TEXTURE: Fudgy and dense near the rind, crumbly at its core
MATCH: A fruity IPA – the hops pick up on the nettle flavour. A sweet and tart apple chutney is a reliable sidekick.

WORLD CHEESE AWARDS: Multiple awards, including Gold 2009, 2018

Gorgonzola

Cheese made on a conveyor belt doesn't sound like it should be included in a list of the best in the world, but trust us, Gorgonzola is an iconic cheese worthy of the title. It is a triumph of tradition and innovation.

Originating in Lombardy in northern Italy, Gorgonzola is said to have been invented by mistake a thousand years ago when a cheesemaker left his curds unattended overnight to meet his lover. Upon returning the next morning and realising his mistake, he hastily mixed the curds from the previous day with fresh ones. Little did he know that blue mould spores had settled on the overnight curd, which he had unwittingly inoculated into the next day's make. It only became clear a few weeks later when the cheese started to turn blue in the maturing room – and turned out to be delicious.

It's a great story, much told by cheesemongers. The only problem is that there is literally no evidence to prove it, and it is remarkably similar to the myth explaining the discovery of Roquefort (see page 90).

Originally the cheese was called Stracchino di Gorgonzola, referring to cheeses made from the rich, creamy milk of tired cows (*stracca*, in the Lombard dialect) returning from Alpine pastures at the end of the summer.

Gorgonzola comes in two styles: *dolce* (sweet and mild) and *piccante* (more aged and piquant). *Dolce* is milder with less blue mould, and with the decadent sweetness of clotted cream, balanced by the minerality of the mould. *Piccante*, aged cheeses have more blue veins, and are more assertive, with zesty, peppery notes and a savoury finish.

The cheese is popular around the world, partly due to its commercialisation, made possible by the modernisation of its production. In 2018 I saw this first-hand with a visit to a large producer called Igor Gorgonzola in Piedmont in the company of Cathy Strange, fellow World Cheese Awards judge and Whole Foods Market Ambassador of Food Culture.

I was struck by the ingenuity of the production process, known as continuous coagulation. A long metal vat is lined with a type of plastic fabric that moves, like a conveyor belt, allowing for the process of cheesemaking to be automated. Milk, lactic cultures and rennet are poured into the vat on one side of the conveyor belt, with sections separated by metal dividers. As the milk ferments and coagulates, the belt moves forward until it reaches the next section where the curd is cut by automatic blades. Eventually the curds are moved to a draining machine that fills the 12kg (26.5lb) moulds.

The wheels of cheese are then turned by machine and placed on shelves by workers. The entire process takes a couple of hours to complete, during which humans touch nothing other than a couple of buttons.

Cheese tasters test batches between two and seven days after making, to determine if a cheese will be released quickly as *dolce*, or will be left for longer to become *piccante*. The younger version must be aged for a minimum of 50 days and a maximum of five months, while the *piccante* cheeses must be aged for a minimum of 80 days and up to nine months. Inside the facility, small cars move shelves stacked six levels high with cheeses, from making, to ageing, to packaging. I had only seen traffic like this in the late 1990s when I lived in Rome.

Gorgonzola is named after a small village near Milan, though nowadays much of the production takes place in the town of Novara. At the end of our tour of the Igor plant, we were greeted by Ivana Leonardi, an elegantly dressed older lady who, beyond being one of the matriarchs of the Leonardi family, the original owners of Igor Gorgonzola, also had expert knowledge of all things blue cheese and was eager to share with our group. One of her greatest pieces of advice was to top endive lettuce leaves with Gorgonzola and walnuts to make a delicious *aperitivo*.

There are other producers that have also started making versions with a slower fermentation process to appeal to new consumers interested in artisanal products. These are labelled as *naturale*. My favourite is made by Caseificio Angelo Croce in Casalpusterlengo.

Many producers around the world use the Gorgonzola recipe as a basis to create their own cheeses. I like Gorgonzola-style cheeses made by Hook's in Wisconsin and Patagonzola in Argentina (see page 190). CY

ORIGIN: Lombardy, Italy

PROTECTED STATUS: PDO

MILK: Pasteurised cow's milk

RENNET: Animal

AROMA: Creamy, tangy, hints of damp earth

FLAVOUR: Depending on the age, the cheese can be sweet and creamy when young, or firm, minerally and savoury as it matures

TEXTURE: Soft and velvety when young, firmer when aged

MATCH: Use in a blue cheese sauce and pair with gnocchi for a traditional dish of the region. Also enjoy with a gin and tonic.

WORLD CHEESE AWARDS: Multiple awards, including Best Italian 2004 (Vallebona Gorgonzola Naturale)

Graviera Kritis

By 2003 the World Cheese Awards were changing. Block Cheddars, Parmesans and Gruyères had dominated the early years, but the new millennium saw a shift in the kind of cheeses that were being entered. The big-hitters were still present as the awards evolved, but lesser-known cheeses from other countries started to pop up on the judging tables.

The World Champion in 2003 was a little-known goat's milk Camembert from the Loire, while there were Gold medals for Rogue River Blue from the US (see page 143), Serra da Estrela from Portugal, and a hard goat's cheese from Tenerife in the Canary Islands called Flor de Guía.

These showed how the awards were gaining traction internationally, but also reflected an increasingly globalised food world. The 2000s was the decade in which some chefs were more famous than rock stars, and securing a reservation at Noma, El Bulli or The Fat Duck was harder than getting a ticket to Glastonbury. The rise of low-cost airlines made the world a smaller place, creating a new generation of well-travelled foodies. People had tried Manchego in Madrid, Époisses in Burgundy and Mozzarella di Bufala in Naples, and wanted to be able to buy them back home.

Greek cheeses also started to make their mark at the awards around this time. Feta is undoubtedly the country's most famous dairy export – and there were plenty with Bronze and Silver medals in 2003 – but it was a cheese called Graviera Kritis that caught the judges' eyes, picking up both a Gold and Silver.

It's easy to understand why when you get your teeth into this hard cheese from the island of Crete. Made with sheep's milk, sometimes with a little added goat's milk (up to 20 per cent is allowed) in wheels weighing up to 25kg (55lb), it's matured for a minimum of three months. At this age it has a supple texture and buttery flavour, but it can be matured for much, much longer, becoming grainy and crumbly. Two-year-old versions are not uncommon and have a rich flavour that is a mix of caramel and dried fruit with an intensely savoury, perfumed finish.

While Graviera may have seemed exotic in the UK, it's an everyday sight on dining tables in Greece, where it is second only to Feta in popularity. According to legend, the cheese was first created in 1917 by a dairy scientist who took inspiration from the Swiss cheese Gruyère (Graviera roughly translates as Gruyère in Greek) but used sheep's rather than cow's milk. The recipe was shared with other dairies across the country and production of the cheese took off.

Graviera Kritis can only be made in Crete under the terms of its PDO, but there are plenty of other versions of the cheese made across the mainland and islands of Greece. PDO-protected Graviera Agrafon is made in the mountainous regions of Agrafa, while Graviera Naxou, also PDO protected, comes from the island of Naxos in the Cyclades and is made with cow's milk. There are countless other generic Gravieras made throughout Greece.

The two companies that won awards for their Cretan Gravieras back in 2003 are no longer making the cheeses, but there are still plenty of good alternatives out there. I am particularly fond of the aged Graviera Kritis made by Manousos Tsitsiridis in the remote mountains of Sfakia in western Greece. His 24-month cheeses, in strapping 16kg (35lb)

wheels, are made with sheep's milk collected from local shepherds whose flocks graze the native flora of this wild part of Greece, moving from the plains next to the sea in the winter to high mountain pastures in the summer. It's a singular cheese that is both sweet and savoury at the same time, with delicate herbaceous and sheepy notes. There's also an unmistakable hint of summer holidays and new horizons. PM

ORIGIN: Crete, Greece

PROTECTED STATUS: PDO

MILK: Raw or pasteurised sheep's milk; up to 20% goat's milk is allowed

RENNET: Animal

AROMA: Brown butter, nuts, exotic fruits

FLAVOUR: Caramel, dried pineapple, roasted lamb

TEXTURE: Pliable to grainy

MATCH: Assyrtiko grape wines with younger Gravieras; Xinomavro red wine with mature cheeses. Figs and melon are classic accompaniments.

WORLD CHEESE AWARDS: Gold 2003 (Cretalat), Silver 2003 (Fage)

Humboldt Fog

Mary Keehn, cheesemaker and founder of Cypress Grove, says the idea for Humboldt Fog came to her perfectly formed in a dream. A crystal-clear vision of how the cheese should look and taste, and how she would make it, was magically conjured up by her subconscious as she flew back from a trip to France where she had been visiting small *fromagers* (cheesemakers).

It must have been a lovely nap because Humboldt Fog is both delicious and stunning to look at. Made in snowy white wheels that have a striking dark black ash line running through the middle, the goat's cheese has a delicate texture and fresh floral aroma. If you find a slightly aged version, part of the paste under the rind will have become soft and silky.

The cheese is made by packing fresh curds into a mould and then sprinkling them with a layer of ash. More curds are packed on top to finish the cheese, which is matured for five weeks until a fuzzy white rind develops around the outside. Some restaurants and cheesemongers brûlée the top with sugar to create an instant dessert – the melted sugar balances the tanginess of the cheese in a delightfully decadent way.

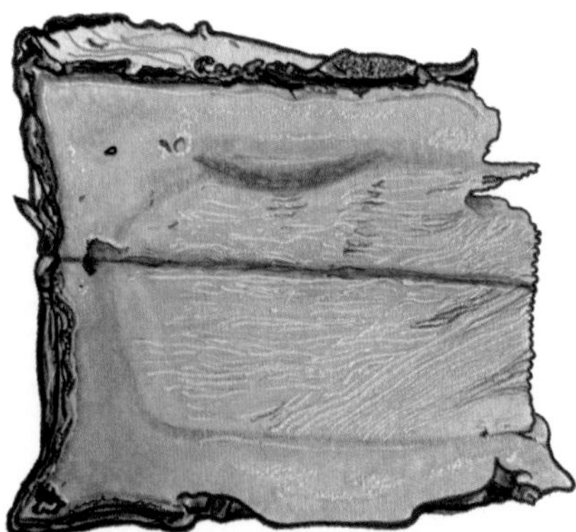

Humboldt Fog combines three cheese styles in one. It is a soft goat's milk cheese, with a bloomy rind like a Brie and an ash line like a Morbier. This mix of styles and techniques, along with the irreverent naming, is characteristic of American cheesemaking. Some say the name comes from the Californian fog that often rolls in from the Pacific Ocean, helping to cool the state's vineyards; others that it refers to the clouds of smoke from pot smokers living in Humboldt County. A self-proclaimed hippy, all of Keehn's cheese names reference California's laid-back attitude: Purple Haze, PsycheDillic and Bermuda Triangle are some of the others made by the company.

Keehn adopted two goats from her neighbours in the 1970s and started making cheese for her four children, selling locally around Arcata, California, before developing Humboldt Fog in 1992. She is part of a trailblazing group known as the 'goat ladies', a cohort of visionary women who saw a way forward from the overly processed cheeses that the US is better known for. They started making goat's milk cheeses in the 1970s and 80s, and turned the US into the artisanal cheesemaking heavyweight that it is today. Others in that group include Allison Hooper of Vermont Creamery, Laura Chenel of Laura Chenel's Chèvre, Judy Schad of Capriole Goat Cheese, and Jennifer Bice of Redwood Hill Farm. All except Judy have since sold their companies, and the cheeses they created can be found around the US and even in some Latin American countries.

Cheesemaking in the US is different to the rest of the world. While Europeans tend to stick to tradition, making cheeses that have been around for generations, US-based producers may borrow from history, but tend to rely more on innovation to create new products. This can be seen as an advantage, but presents a problem when the original cheesemaker retires, as they need to pass on their newly acquired expertise. Some cheesemakers are fortunate enough to have family members interested in continuing their enterprise, while others must look further afield. To be fair, this is starting to happen in France and Italy as well, but in the USA it is more evident.

Since the early 2010s there has been a frenzy of larger corporations buying smaller cheese companies in the US, including Cowgirl Creamery, Vermont Creamery and Rogue Creamery. Cypress Grove is now owned by Emmi, a Switzerland-based co-operative.

Humboldt Fog has long been one of my favourite cheeses. It symbolises the creativity and entrepreneurial spirit that has transformed artisan cheesemaking in the US. Whether it stays at the forefront of this movement under new ownership is another question. Do major multinationals dare to dream? CY

ORIGIN: California, USA

PROTECTED STATUS: N/A

MILK: Pasteurised goat's milk

RENNET: Vegetarian

AROMA: Floral, goaty, fresh

FLAVOUR: The young cheese has a bright, citrussy tang and distinctive creaminess, while aged wheels develop peppery notes

TEXTURE: Soft and chalky when young; as the cheese ages, part of the paste becomes gooey

MATCH: A cold, crisp lager and salted nuts are wonderful pairings.

WORLD CHEESE AWARDS: Multiple awards, including Gold 2008

Idiazabal

The town of Idiazabal in the Basque Country in Spain is a gorgeous location. The Atlantic breeze gives this hilly region a rugged feel, and it is the perfect place to keep sheep, especially the Latxa and Carranzana breeds used to make this delicious cheese. These breeds are known for being excellent mothers and for transforming grazing pasture into high-quality milk. Ultimately, this is the magic of small ruminants: they make milk from grass.

Modern shepherds follow the trails carved by their neolithic ancestors. From spring to autumn they live at the top of the mountains, then come back to the valleys during winter, a practice known as transhumance. Some work with their own milk to make cheese, while others pool milk from a couple of flocks.

Cheesemakers make wheels weighing 1–3kg (2–6.5lb) using only raw milk. The production time is limited by the natural milking cycle of the animals, during the months of February to June. Cheeses are normally aged for two months, but there are older versions. We prefer the younger versions, however, when the cheese is more nutty than gamey. Some producers use beechwood or oakwood to smoke their cheeses to give them that extra rustic flavour.

Cheeses made by shepherds using their own milk are known as *Artzai Gazta* and can be identified by the name *Baserrikoa*. Some shepherds work only with the milk of Latxa ewes, and those cheeses are known as *Latxa Gazta*. This may seem confusing at first, but it is a way in which shepherds have fought to differentiate themselves. Only about 35 per cent of Idiazabal is made by artisans; the rest is made industrially.

All Idiazabal is scored by a panel of experts who determine if a cheese has unique characteristics worth promoting. Those with the highest scores are normally found in black packaging and fetch a higher price. You instantly recognise an Idiazabal from its clean, polished exterior and pale-yellow paste, while the aroma has hints of green pastures.

Luisa Villegas, a visionary in the cheese world, is a fellow judge at the World Cheese Awards and founded the Instituto del Queso in San Sebastián. She worked for a shepherds' organisation and pushed to showcase their way of life – a project that would transform cheese in Spain, and the awards themselves.

ORIGIN: Basque Country, Spain

PROTECTED STATUS: PDO

MILK: Raw sheep's milk

RENNET: Animal

AROMA: Sheepy and rustic, with warm notes of whey

FLAVOUR: Gamey and nutty, sometimes smoky, with a balanced tanginess

TEXTURE: Soft and oily, with a semi-hard paste that can feel a bit granular

MATCH: Dry ciders make a great pairing, as well as the local Txakoli wine. Eat alongside a sweet chutney.

WORLD CHEESE AWARDS: Multiple awards, including 9 x Gold 2009 (Aizpea, Arazpe, Baztarrika, La Leza, Larte, Marti-Txiki, Otatza, Txurtxil, Uharte)

In 2016, her organisation hosted the awards in San Sebastián. The competition opened doors for dozens of Spanish producers to compete on home turf. Today, entries from Spain are among the most numerous. During the event in Donostia – the name for San Sebastián in Euskara, the Basque language – the Norwegian blue cheese Kraftkar (see page 130) won the World Champion title. Norwegian cheeses would go on to win another two world titles, and the country would twice become host of the awards. Villegas' charisma and tenacity was integral to the awards returning to Spain in 2021, to the city of Oviedo.

Idiazabal is cherished as a symbol of Basque identity. It is a common sight among *pintxos* – small appetisers served in bars – and as an accompaniment to grilled meat served at the famed *asadores* (grill restaurants) of the region; its sheepy flavour pairs well with the gamey notes of aged beef. Idiazabal is just one of the iconic sheep's milk cheeses from the Basque region. Others include Roncal, made east of the Navarre province, and Ossau-Iraty (see page 82), made on the French side of the Basque Country.

If you travel to San Sebastián or Bilbao to feast on Basque gastronomy you will understand how important this cheese is for the region. We have enjoyed a lot of this cheese on our trips to Euskadi – the Basque Country – always with a glass of crisp Txakoli, the local slightly sparkling wine that is poured from a great height into a flat-bottomed glass. Cheers! Or as they would say in the Basque Country, *topa*! CY

Manchego

Spain's most famous cheese is often misunderstood and undervalued. Mentioned in the tales of Don Quixote, with a history that stretches back to the Bronze Age, the sheep's milk cheese is easily recognisable by the herringbone pattern imprinted on the rind, and its straw-coloured paste with small eyes. The embossing of the rind was originally caused by the *esparto* grass baskets that served as moulds.

The wheels weigh roughly 3kg (6.5lb) and are sold primarily in three age profiles: *semi-curado* – two to four months; *curado* – six months plus; and *añejo* – over 12 months. Gaining recognition for this cheese was not easy. The PDO protections that limit its production to the Castile-La Mancha region using a specific breed of ewes named Manchega, were fought against by Manchego-style cheese producers in other regions of Spain. It wasn't until 1984 that the Spanish government enforced them, and 1996 when the European Union recognised them.

PDO designations are meant to guarantee tradition and authenticity, but increasingly conglomeration and mechanisation have translated into low-quality industrial cheeses. In Spain, large producers are allowed to push boundaries by making flavoured and average Manchegos, which undermine the cheeses made by artisan makers.

The Manchega ewes are rustic animals that transform low-quality pasture and brush from a semi-arid region into high-quality milk. The aromas and flavours of good-quality Manchegos are worth the fame, with herbaceous, nutty and eventually roasted notes.

One of the best Manchegos is made by Dehesa de los Llanos in Albacete, south-east of Madrid, which won the title of World Champion at the World Cheese Awards in 2012. A key part of the company's success is the careful management of its pastures and use of only traditional ingredients. Its Gran Reserva is made with raw milk from its own sheep and aged in its own maturation cellars.

To understand Manchego you need to understand a system of land management centred around *dehesas*. These enclosed areas of land are found across La Mancha and are the backbone of the region's sheep farming. A *dehesa* is a managed ecosystem that includes a diverse range of trees, plants and various animals, including birds, pigs and small ruminants like sheep and goats, which help maintain the landscape through grazing and fertilising the soil with their manure.

Dehesa de los Llanos's enclosure has been home to sheep since the seventeenth century and measures approximately 10,000 hectares (25,000 acres). This bucolic, self-sustaining environment results in happy, free-grazing sheep, producing rich milk that does not have to be pasteurised. Raw milk cheeses like this are labelled as *artesano* (a term to look out for when you are buying Manchego), which means it is made at a smaller scale and without the addition of egg lysozyme, an enzyme often used by larger producers to prevent spoilage.

There are lots of other Manchegos on the market, made industrially, some with rubs on the outside like olive oil, rosemary and even pork fat, and many more that are piquant and tangy. Unfortunately, for a long time there was little control over who made Manchego cheese and the standards for production. For this reason, it is possible to see many other cheeses using the same type of rind imprint. More recently the Spanish body tasked with enforcing the PDO rules has become stricter with producers and created new casein labels that allow for cut wedges to be easily identified as true Manchego.

In Mexico, where the EU's rules on protected cheeses are only recently partly recognised, Manchego has taken on a life of its own. Made with cow's milk, and with a creamy and pliable texture, it differs substantially from the Spanish original. The name Manchego has been used in Mexico for over 50 years and pre-dates the protections adopted by Spain.

This naming issue became a sticking point during the 2018 trade negotiations between Mexico and the European Union. Spain argued that the use of the term Manchego had to be stopped by the Mexican government, while on the other side of the Atlantic the argument was that the name was generic and had not been protected before the common use in Mexico.

While the trade negotiations were finally resolved, allowing Mexico to use the name, it was a compromise that all new producers will use 'Manchego style' (*Tipo Manchego*) to market their products. Producers in both Spain and Mexico are not happy with this arrangement, but the EU was not willing to stop a trade deal over cheese names. The resolution of this dispute has pushed Spain and other European countries to protect their cheese names before producers in other countries start using them. The issue continues to be a controversy between open-source advocates and traditional-knowledge champions. CY

ORIGIN: Castile-La Mancha, Spain

PROTECTED STATUS: PDO

MILK: Raw or pasteurised sheep's milk

RENNET: Animal

AROMA: Nutty and sweet, with piquant notes as it ages

FLAVOUR: Young versions are sweet and herbaceous; as the cheese ages it becomes zesty and roasted

TEXTURE: Granular when young, and flaky as it ages, with distinct oiliness

MATCH: Membrillo – quince fruit paste – is traditional. We also love it with wildflower honey and roasted Marcona almonds.

WORLD CHEESE AWARDS: Multiple awards, including Gold & Best Spanish Cheese 2009 (Villarejo), World Champion 2012 (Dehesa de los Llanos)

Mimolette

If the moon was actually made of cheese, it would probably be made of Mimolette. This spherical cheese from northern France has a spectacular craggy rind that is pitted and pockmarked like a lunar landscape. It wouldn't look out of place orbiting a small planet. And the astronomy similes don't end there. Slice into the hard cheese and the moon becomes a sun, thanks to a bright orange interior that glows like a ball of fire on a cheese counter.

The story behind this singular cheese is just as quirky as its appearance. It was first created during the Franco-Dutch war of 1672–78, when trade between the two countries came to a standstill. This was bad news for King Louis XIV, who was partial to a slice of Edam, so he instructed his minister Jean-Baptiste Colbert to commission a similar cheese to be made in France.

Colbert turned to the dairies around Lille in West Flanders, close to the Dutch border, who came up with a cannonball-shaped cow's milk cheese, which they coloured sunset orange with the pigment annatto (as a point of difference to Edam). To this day the cheese is still nicknamed *Boule de Lille*, after the city where it was first matured, and production is still largely concentrated in the same region, although it has also spread to Normandy and Lorraine (Mimolette is not PDO protected because of its wide geographical spread).

Mimolette is much more than a knock-off Edam. The cool, damp cellars of northern France provide the perfect environment for what is normally viewed as a troublesome pest in maturing rooms, but is the secret to Mimolette's dusty rind and fragrant flavour.

Cheese mites are microscopic insects that are part of the arachnid family. They are usually found in soil, where they break down fungi, but if they get into a cheese maturing room (it's almost impossible to stop them), they make merry on the rinds of hard cheeses, eating the mould and creating rough, rutted rinds.

ORIGIN: Lille, France
PROTECTED STATUS: N/A
MILK: Raw or pasteurised cow's milk
RENNET: Animal
AROMA: Caramel, earthy, nutty
FLAVOUR: Young: sweet, creamy; mature: roasted nuts, toffee, lemongrass
TEXTURE: Young: smooth, elastic; mature: brittle, glassy

MATCH: Belgian farmhouse ales, such as fruity saisons, are a refreshing choice, or lean into the sweetness with a measure of Bourbon. Roasted almonds and fennel crackers add crunch and fragrance.

WORLD CHEESE AWARDS: Multiple awards, including Gold 2004, 2009, 2011 (Isigny Sainte-Mère)

Most cheesemakers spend a lot of time and money trying to keep the little critters at bay using various techniques that centre around brushing and vacuuming. Affineurs of Gruyère and Comté in Switzerland and France have invested in robots that trundle up and down wooden shelves filled with cheese wheels, turning, brushing and flipping each one.

Others employ people with vacuum cleaners to hoover the cheeses by hand. It's a common sight in the store rooms of UK cloth-bound Cheddar-makers (Henry seems to be the brand of choice), although some are starting to invest in robots. Westcombe Cheddar in Somerset commissioned a cheese-turning robot from Switzerland for its stores, which it wittily christened Tina the Turner.

Mimolette is one of just a handful of cheeses where mites are welcome. Affineurs brush much less regularly, which gives the mites chance to create the bumpy rind by burrowing into the surface and allowing oxygen to change the flavour and texture of the cheese within. The older the cheese, the more potholed the rind is likely to be, which means a harder, drier texture and more intense, aromatic flavours.

If you like sweet, elastic cheese, then go for a three-month *Jeune* (young) cheese, while *Demi-Vieille* (semi-old) and *Vieille* (old) are taken to 6–9 months and 12–18 months, respectively. They tend to be nuttier and more caramelised, with a peppery kick, especially over 12 months. The daddy of them all, however, is *Extra-Vieille* (extra old), which is aged for over 24 months and has a glassy texture and flavours that remind me of toffee and lemongrass (the mites produce a molecule that has a lemony flavour).

If you are thinking that mites on cheese are not to your taste, it's worth pointing out that, whatever the age, Mimolette is one of the few cheeses where it's best not to eat the rind. Break up the interior into chunks with the tip of a knife and eat a bit like you would Parmesan.

That advice wasn't enough to convince the US's Food and Drug Administration (FDA), however, which banned imports of Mimolette in 2013, after mites were designated an allergen. Tests found that three-quarters of Mimolette imports contained more than the official limit of six mites per square inch. Over a tonne of the cheese was detained by customs, leading to a de facto ban.

The disappearance of Mimolette from US shelves caused a surprisingly large outcry in the country, albeit mainly from French immigrants, who took to social media in protest. Cécile Delarue, a French TV journalist, started up a 'Save the Mimolette!' campaign, while actor and comedian Jamel Debbouze recorded a video declaring the ban would mean 'the end of France and the end of the French community in the States'.

Thankfully, the FDA reversed its decision after just over a year, so that, at the time of writing, the pumpkin-coloured cheese is back on US cheese counters. PM

Mozzarella

One of the most popular cheeses in the world, yet so few know the joys of the original and best: Mozzarella di Bufala Campana.

There are multiple accounts of when water buffaloes were introduced to southern Italy. Some claim it was in the sixth century by the Goths during their invasions of the peninsula, or by subsequent Arab or Norman invaders. The animals were well suited to the marshy land around Naples, where they were used primarily as draught animals, but their milk was eventually used to make cheese.

Originally enjoyed by peasants, Mozzarella spread thanks to the implementation of annual contracts for milk producers in the town of Aversa in the nineteenth century, which secured a standard and fair price for their product. With the milk contracts, better working conditions were possible for farmers, which in turn allowed the cheese to be sold in larger amounts and in more distant markets, including Rome.

Mozzarella is made using a technique called *pasta filata*, or 'spun paste', in which hot water or whey is added to acidified curds to encourage partial melting. Once the curds soften, they are pulled and stretched until they take on a springy, elastic texture. This was historically done by hand: cheesemakers would plunge and manipulate the curd in extremely hot water and twist off balls of Mozzarella (from the Italian word *mozzare*, 'to cut off'), but today the job is mostly done by specialist machines.

There are many types of Mozzarella, each with their own name, such as *Aversana*, *bocconcini*, *ciliegine*, *ovoline* and *treccia*, all differing in size and format. There are other cheeses that use the same cheesemaking technique like Burrata (see page 110) and Caciocavallo (see page 112) from Italy; Quesillo de Hebra from Mexico; Queso Telita from Venezuela; Armenian Chechil; Polish Oscypek; and even Halloumi (see page 124). Buffalo Mozzarella is also made outside of Italy, but is not covered by the Mozzarella di Bufala Campana PDO. Noteworthy are those made by BUF in Colombia and available all over the USA, and Buffalicious in Somerset, available in the UK.

Cow's milk Mozzarella, known as *Fior di Latte* ('flower of milk') is the most common type of Mozzarella used today on pizzas or panini. There are artisanal producers making this type of cheese, but most cow's milk 'Mozz' is made by large dairy conglomerates, sometimes not even in balls, but in logs or available pre-shredded in most supermarkets. Some Italian delis in North America make their own Mozzarella cheeses using pre-packaged curd that is then formed into balls at the store. These taste fresher, but all of them pale in comparison to the authentic version made with buffalo milk.

In Italy, people get to their local *latteria* (dairy) early in the morning to buy balls of Mozzarella that have been made only a few hours before. The argument goes that the fresher the cheese, the better the texture and flavour. It's true that freshly made Mozzarella has a wonderful taut, elastic texture, and when you cut into a ball, it weeps tears of whey.

Mozzarella di Bufala Campana's delicate flavour makes it difficult for it to win top honours at the World Cheese Awards, where bold, aged cheeses tend to dominate the final panel. Mozzarella's subtle creamy notes are easy to overlook, yet to bite into a shiny white ball of buffalo Mozzarella is to taste the milk in its purest cheese form. CY

ORIGIN: Defined areas of the Puglia, Campania, Lazio and Molise regions, Italy

PROTECTED STATUS: Mozzarella is not protected, but Mozzarella di Bufala Campana carries a PDO

MILK: Raw or pasteurised buffalo milk

RENNET: Animal or vegetarian

AROMA: Milky and fresh

FLAVOUR: Subtle cream, salt

TEXTURE: Soft and elastic

MATCH: Olive oil, fresh ground black pepper and sea salt. It pairs well with Pilsner beers.

WORLD CHEESE AWARDS: Multiple awards, including Best Italian 2005 (Mozzarella di Bufala by Mandara)

Ossau-Iraty

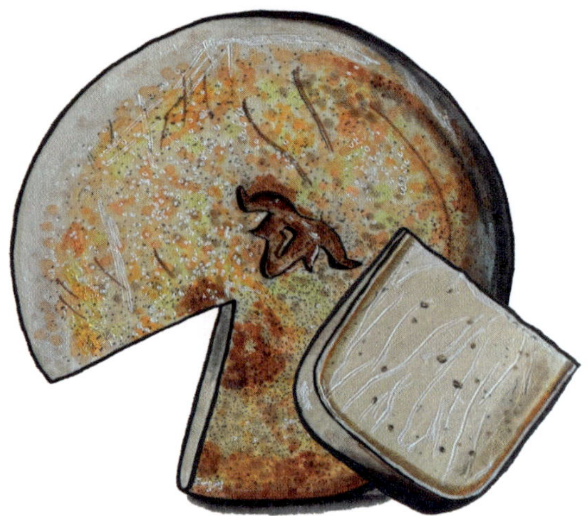

You can tell a lot about Ossau-Iraty just by looking at it. The hard sheep's milk Tomme is made across a large swathe of the western Pyrenees in France in a variety of different ways. There are co-operative dairies on the plains that pool milk from other farms, small *fermier* (farm-based) producers using their own milk, and *bergers* (shepherds) who take their flocks high up to mountain pastures in the summer to make *estive* (summer) cheeses.

Thankfully, the cheesemakers in this part of the world are an obliging bunch and have come up with a clever system for letting the cheese-buying public know which is which. If you spot the side-on profile of a curly horned sheep's head stamped on the rind, it's from a larger producer, which buys milk from multiple farms. If the sheep is looking directly at you with an 'F' built into the design, it's *fermier*. And if you see the *fermier* stamp alongside a mountain with an edelweiss flower inside, then you know it's one of the high-mountain summer cheeses.

The different faces of Ossau-Iraty are not surprising when you consider it's a cheese that has a history stretching back 700 years. It is named after the Ossau Valley in Béarn, and a beech forest called Iraty in the French Basque Country, two quite distinct parts of the Pyrenees, which just happen to have made sheep's milk cheeses in a similar way for centuries.

Historically, they were simply known as *fromage du brebis* in French, or *ardi gasna* in Basque, which translates simply as 'sheep's cheese'. The name Ossau-Iraty was a modern construct invented to give cheeses from the region a stronger regional brand. Ossau-Iraty was only recognised with an AOC in 1980 (and later a PDO in 1996), but there have always been important differences between cheeses from the two regions.

Basque cheeses tend to have sharper corners and are drier in texture, while those from Béarn are more rounded. The latter are also kept in more humid cellars and are washed with brine to create an orange rind and a more moist, supple texture.

The distinguished cheese writer Patrick Rance, author of *The French Cheese Book*, published in 1989, argued that the two regional cheeses were so different they should have kept their own identities, with Ossau sold as a separate cheese to Iraty. 'To group them together because both are made of ewes' milk ... is rather like lumping Chopin together with Tchaikovsky because both lived under Russian rule and both were composers,' he wrote with his trademark zeal.

He's not the only one who is unhappy with the all-encompassing PDO. Some of the *bergers* making *estive* mountain cheeses feel the appellation does not do enough to differentiate their unique, handmade cheeses from those made in large creameries down on the plains. Some have even withdrawn from the PDO altogether at various points in history.

In his excellent book *A Cheesemonger's Tour de France* (2024), another eminent British cheese writer, Ned Palmer, evocatively recounts a trip to one such *berger*, high up in the Pyrenees near the Spanish border. Stéphane Chetrit makes *estive* cheese in the remote and beautiful Soussoueou Valley using raw milk from his 200-strong flock of Bernais sheep (protected from bears and wolves by his dog).

But when Palmer visited him in his remote hut (*cabane*), he had withdrawn his cheeses from the PDO, calling it simply Ossau Fermier and Ossau d'Estives instead. His argument, explained while sharing slices of cheese with Palmer, is that there should be a separate category for industrial products that is clearly distinct from the cheeses made by small-scale producers, such as himself. In other words, the stamps on the rind are not enough.

For this reason, you won't find Chetrit's hut on the Ossau-Iraty PDO Cheese Route, which can be picked up at local tourist offices (or downloaded from the internet). The association that oversees the PDO has put together a map with 125 stops for visitors to the region, covering every aspect of the cheese, from *laiteries* (dairies), farms and summer huts, to the shops and restaurants that sell it. The good news is that Chetrit does offer separate tours of the unspoilt mountains where he makes his cheese. Either option sounds like a lovely way to spend a summer. PM

ORIGIN: Pyrenees, France
PROTECTED STATUS: PDO
MILK: Raw or pasteurised sheep's milk
RENNET: Animal
AROMA: Earthy, fruity
FLAVOUR: Floral, caramel, almondy
TEXTURE: Smooth, supple

MATCH: Cherry jam is a traditional match in the Basque Country. A honeyed Juraçon dry white wine is another good local pairing.

WORLD CHEESE AWARDS: Multiple awards, including World Champion 2006, 2011 (Agour)

Persian Fetta

There are no prizes for guessing where Feta comes from. Greece has been exporting it far and wide since antiquity, and it remains the most popular cheese in the country, eaten for breakfast, lunch and dinner, and every snack in between.

And yet the cheese that we are writing about is called Persian Fetta (with two 't's) and is actually made in the Yarra Valley in Australia. To untangle this confusing state of affairs we should probably take a few steps back into ancient history.

It's thought that Bronze Age cheesemakers across the Southern Levant used to pack salted sheep and goat's milk cheeses into ceramic pots so they would keep better and could be easily transported. The whey would naturally leak from the cheeses, mixing with the salt to create a brine, which would pickle the cheese. It didn't take too much for cheesemakers to start making their own brine to preserve the cheeses, and the idea spread. It's believed Greeks first started making an ancient prototype of Feta in at least the eighth century BCE, with ceramic pots being replaced with the tin containers and beechwood barrels used today.

But brined white cheeses also have a long history in Eastern Europe and other parts of the Balkans, while companies in Denmark and Germany started making Feta on a large scale in the 1980s and 90s. Not surprisingly, this upset the Greeks, who felt other countries were exploiting their national cheese, so the government applied to the EU to get PDO protection for the name Feta. After a lot of arguing with the Danish and the Germans, this was eventually rubber-stamped in 2002. It means that only cheeses from Greece, made with sheep's milk or a mix of sheep and goat's milk, can be labelled as Feta in Europe. That's why you see a lot of non-Greek Feta-style cheeses with names such as 'salad cheese'.

But outside of the EU is a different matter. Depending on the types of trade agreements signed between the EU and other countries, Feta might not always be protected in the same way. There are plenty of cheeses labelled as Feta made and sold in New Zealand and the US quite legally. And the same is true of Australia, where cheesemakers often call it Fetta – the second 't' added to differentiate it from the original.

ORIGIN: Victoria, Australia
PROTECTED STATUS: N/A
MILK: Pasteurised cow's milk
RENNET: Vegetarian
AROMA: Garlic, olive oil, butter
FLAVOUR: Creamy, salty, herbaceous
TEXTURE: Soft and curdy
MATCH: Yarra Valley Sauvignon Blanc, plus a few olives and artichoke hearts.

WORLD CHEESE AWARDS: Gold 2001

Australian Fetta is often made with cow's milk rather than sheep or goat's, and is submerged in oil flavoured with herbs and spices. The Yarra Valley Dairy just outside Melbourne was the first to come up with this kind of cheese in 1994, making a brined white cow's milk cheese, which is marinated in rapeseed and extra virgin olive oil with fresh thyme or rosemary, peppercorns and garlic. They called it Persian Fetta.

If you weren't confused already, Persia (modern-day Iran) doesn't actually have a tradition of preserving cheese in oil, but it was a clever way to market the cheese in Australia as being different from Greek Feta. Cow's milk has a creamier, milder flavour than sheep or goat's, which allows it to take on more of the flavour in the marinade, while the oil makes the texture softer and less crumbly.

Over the years, cow's milk Fetta has become a distinct Australian cheese in its own right, and has a loyal following not just in Australia. Yarra Valley exports its cheese all over the world, including to Asia and even the Middle East, where brined cheeses already have a long history.

The Greeks are not happy about this and there have long been arguments between the EU and Australia about whether cheesemakers should be allowed to use the name Feta/Fetta. It was one of the major stumbling blocks in a planned free-trade deal between the two countries, which collapsed in 2023, partly because the Australian government felt its food and drink producers should be able to continue using names such as Feta, Parmesan and Prosecco. Whether they will come to an agreement looks unlikely for now.

British cheese-lovers who don't want to fly halfway round the world to try some cheese can get a feel for what Persian Fetta tastes like by buying Graceburn, which is made in Kent by an Australian cheesemaker. David Holton worked at the Yarra Valley Dairy before moving to the UK, where he now makes a similar raw cow's milk cheese, marinated in extra virgin olive oil and rapeseed oil, infused with thyme, garlic, bay and pepper. It has an addictive melting texture and just the right balance of salt, cream and Mediterranean marinade. You can even use the leftover oil to make salad dressings and to marinate fish and meat.

Just don't call it Feta – or Fetta. 

Petite Breakfast Brie

Do you have a favourite breakfast cheese? To readers in the UK, US and Australia that might seem a strange question. But a few slices is the customary way to start the day everywhere from Scandinavia and Eastern Europe to Turkey and Latin America. High in protein with plenty of vitamins and salt, it sets you up for a hard day's work.

Jefferson Thompson, who founded Marin French Cheese Company in California, bet on dock workers' appetite for a protein-rich breakfast when he started selling Petite Breakfast Brie back in 1865.

The small 110g (4oz) cheese is made a little like a Brie, but it is not aged in a maturing room, so doesn't develop a fuzzy white coat. Think of it as a naked Brie.

The paste is still firm, but chewy, and the flavours are milky and fresh. It is a great snack or indeed a perfect breakfast cheese. I like to crumble it on a cherry tomato and rocket salad with an avocado oil dressing (though not for breakfast).

I visited Marin's dairy in Petaluma in 2019 with a group of Colombian cheesemakers on a technical trip to learn more about advances in dairy production in California. As we walked into the cheesemaking room, the warm smell of whey enveloped us, followed by chatter in Spanish. We quickly realised that almost everyone working on the production floor was originally from Mexico.

This is the reality of many cheese companies in the US, especially in the southern states bordering Mexico. Like restaurant kitchens in New York or Chicago, Mexican migrants are the backbone of cheese production in the US. The head cheesemaker told me that Petite Breakfast Brie reminded him of a cheese he ate when he was young, back in central Mexico – probably Panela Oreado (see page 141).

Petite Breakfast Brie is considered by the American Cheese Society (ACS), a US-based organisation, to be an 'American Original'. These are cheeses that have been developed in the US that do not squarely follow a single European recipe. Others are Colby, Cornerstone, Dry Monterey Jack (see page 138) and Teleme, to mention just a few. Judges at the ACS competition give medals to American Originals on their own merits, and while some are falling out of fashion, they have a devout following among knowledgeable cheesemongers.

All these American cheeses are mainly unknown outside of the US; some are even difficult to find outside of California or Wisconsin. The industrialisation of cheese production during the interwar period saw the development of highly processed cheeses, like Velvetta, while American singles were introduced to the market in the 1950s, marking the height of cheese industrialisation.

Dairy conglomerates like Kraft dominated the scene until the 1970s, when a new wave of cheesemakers started making cheeses like Humboldt Fog (see page 72). Along with producers of American Originals, new artisan cheese producers helped transform the US dairy landscape. Marin French also followed the fate of other trailblazing cheese companies by being bought up by a larger competitor: Jim Boyce bought the company from the original founders, the Thompson family, and eventually sold it to a French dairy company called Rians in 2011. However, the original commitment to quality and ethical farming remains undiminished.

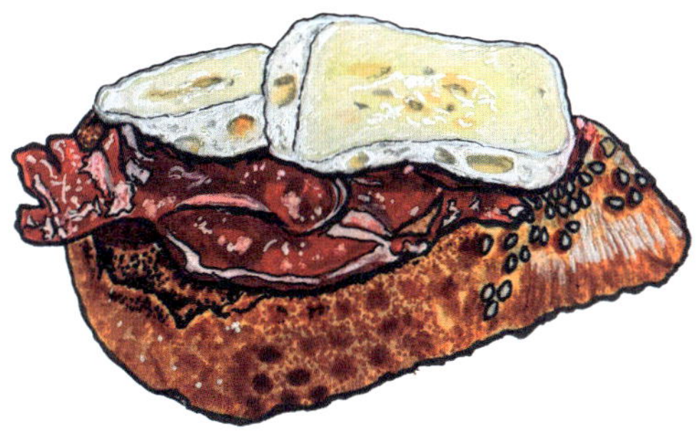

Petite Breakfast Brie won Best US Cheese at the World Cheese Awards in 2009, which was held in the Canary Islands. Previously, the company's Brie-style cheese had won best in category in 2005, marking the first time a non-French cheese had won that category.

From its humble beginnings selling cheese as a protein snack for hungry labourers to winning international awards and being part of the consolidation of US cheese, Marin's history is woven into American cheese culture. If you travel to the region, consider following the California Cheese Trail (there is such a thing!) and visiting the dairy in West Marin. CY

ORIGIN: California, USA
PROTECTED STATUS: N/A
MILK: Pasteurised cow's milk
RENNET: Vegetarian
AROMA: Milky and fresh
FLAVOUR: Tangy and creamy, almost of cheese curds, with slight saltiness
TEXTURE: Springy and chewable; softens easily when heated
MATCH: Crusty bread and a fruit jam. Kombucha or any other fermented drink.

WORLD CHEESE AWARDS: Best US Cheese 2009

Remeker

Most cheesemakers like to tell you what goes into their cheese, from the milk itself to the hard work and skill involved. But at De Groote Voort farm in the Gelderse Valley in the centre of the Netherlands, the van de Voort family prefer to list all the things they leave out of their cheese. It's a long list, including artificial fertilisers, pesticides and antibiotics, among many other things.

In fact, pretty much all the shortcuts taken by most dairy farms and cheesemakers to speed up production, reduce costs and make life easier have been rejected by the family in order to make a single cheese that is a pure expression of their farm.

Remeker is a hard aged cow's milk cheese, which is made a little bit like Gouda (see page 29), by replacing some of the whey with hot water during the cheesemaking process to create a pliable, sweeter curd. It's named after one of the fields at the farm, which is a mix of two old Dutch words *reem* (surrounded by) and *eker* (oak tree). But this doesn't tell half the story.

The farm, which has been owned by the van de Voorts since 1650, is made up of a series of meadows across 50 hectares (124 acres), which are home to a herd of around 90 Jersey cows. The breed famously provides incredibly rich milk; there's at least 25 per cent more cream in Jersey milk than there is in the milk from a standard black-and-white Holstein-Friesian, which is one of the reasons for Remeker's unique character.

Perhaps more importantly, the herd is raised organically and with the lightest of touches. The cows are not de-horned, and are housed in the winter in specially designed round barns (the van de Voorts believe square barns are too restrictive). And instead of using synthetic fertilisers, the fields are enriched with the farm's own fermented cow manure. The animals are also regularly rotated between different meadows so the soil and plant life have time to renew. This leads to diverse pastures of grass, clover and herbs, which results in healthier animals. The farm has not needed to give the cows antibiotics or worming medicine since 2004.

Things like rotational grazing, rejecting chemical fertilisers and pesticides, and enriching the soil naturally so that it remains healthy, are all features of an approach that has become known as 'regenerative farming'. It's a trendy phrase in farming circles, and a growing

number are embracing these methods as concerns about climate change and the cost of oil-based inputs have increased, but in many ways it's simply going back to less intensive farming methods that would have been used 70 years ago.

As well as being kinder to the cows and the land, these old-school farming techniques also result in excellent milk for cheese. To this end, the family does their best not to mess with it in any way. The milk is not pumped aggressively from the milking parlour to the dairy to help maintain the delicate structure of the fats, and there is no skimming, homogenising or pasteurising. It goes straight from the cow into the vat, so that all the natural micro-organisms from the farm and the animals are captured in the cheese, giving Remeker its deep flavour.

The cheese is pressed in 15kg (33lb) wheels, which are coated in clarified butter (ghee) made on the farm rather than the wax coating favoured by most Dutch cheesemakers. This creates a natural rind, which adds to the final flavour and texture as the cheeses mature in a specially designed cellar that uses groundwater to create natural humidity.

Young Remekers are only aged for two or three months so are buttery and pliable, while older cheeses (our favourites) reach 18 months and are crystalline with a delicate acidity and spice, plus brown butter and roasted hazelnut notes. More than that, it's the taste of the farm itself. PM

ORIGIN: Gelderland, the Netherlands
PROTECTED STATUS: N/A
MILK: Raw cow's milk
RENNET: Animal
AROMA: Nutty, buttery, herbaceous
FLAVOUR: Brown butter, roasted hazelnut, star anise
TEXTURE: Semi-soft and slightly crumbly when young, but older cheeses are harder and grainier
MATCH: White Port brings out the hazelnut flavour. Very nice with a fennel seed cracker.

WORLD CHEESE AWARDS: Best Dutch Cheese 2008

Roquefort

The legend of Roquefort's origin is one of whimsical romance. The story goes that a young shepherd was eating his simple lunch of bread and white sheep's curd, but abandoned it in a cave in order to chase after a beautiful girl. He came back weeks later only to find the cheese had been transformed by blue mould into something new and delicious. The tale is most likely apocryphal, but all of us who have worked behind a cheese counter have heard it and passed it on to our customers.

What is true is that in 1411, King Charles VI of France granted the residents of Roquefort-sur-Soulzon in the south of France the sole right to produce and age cheeses in the natural caves of the Combalou plateau. The royal decree was one of the earliest forms of protection for food production in a specific area, and would eventually evolve into the modern European Union system of PDOs and PGIs.

Roquefort is easily recognisable on a cheese counter. Its snowy white paste is speckled with pockets of blue-green veins. The wheels are short, about 8.5–11.5cm (3.5–4.5 inches) high, and weigh approximately 3kg (6.5lb).

The flavour is luxuriously creamy with a distinctive tang and saltiness, while the blue mould adds savoury umami depth. The companies making this cheese also sell pre-cut pieces in plastic trays, recognisable by the green label and the European Union PDO logo.

The cheese's iconic status is reflected in other blue cheeses, which are referred to as 'Roquefort-style'. Yet this cheese is truly unique because its ageing still takes place on wooden shelves in the caves of Combalou, which benefit from the perfect conditions of humidity, air flow and limestone walls. If you travel to southern France to see the caves, you will be surprised how little has changed over the years. This is a testament to the enduring importance of Roquefort. A definite contender to be the best cheese in the world.

Raw milk producers of this cheese are rapidly disappearing. We love the cheeses made by Maison Carles, the only independent company left, and those by Papillon, now owned by the French conglomerate Savencia. CY

ORIGIN: Roquefort-sur-Soulzon, France
PROTECTED STATUS: PDO
MILK: Raw sheep's milk
RENNET: Animal
AROMA: Milky, minerally
FLAVOUR: Creamy, salty, umami
TEXTURE: Creamy and moist
MATCH: Try it with dark chocolate, as well as with a drizzle of honey. A high-quality Canadian Ice Wine is a delicious pairing.

WORLD CHEESE AWARDS: Multiple awards, including Gold 2002, Best Blue Cheese 2004 (Société)

Selles-sur-Cher

If there was a job description for the position of cheese writer, one of the key requirements would be experience of matching cheese and wine. It's fair to say I've done my share of research over the years, and have come to a rather awkward conclusion: cheese and wine is not always the perfect pairing.

The tannins found in many red wines clash with the creaminess of cheese, especially softies such as Brie and Gorgonzola, in a rather disappointing way, while delicate white wines can be overpowered by strong, aged cheeses.

There's also huge variety in both wine and cheese, which makes it tricky to generalise. Wine made at one vineyard might taste completely different to another made down the road, even though they are part of the same appellation. Grape varieties, soil type and vintages all play a part, not to mention how they go about things in the winery. The same is true of cheese, which varies from batch to batch, depending on what the animals have been eating and how the cheese has been made and matured. Both are moving targets, so just when you think you have nailed down a killer wine and cheese match, the next time you try it one or both will have changed and it won't work in quite the same way.

That's not to say that wine and cheese don't go together. We've been enjoying the pairing since at least the Bronze Age, and when you get a good match it's transcendental, lifting the cheese and the wine to new heights. Cheese and wine nirvana, you might say.

This is a state of being that is particularly easy to attain in the Loire Valley in France, where cheese and wine have evolved together over centuries in a way that makes them easy bedfellows. It's a classic example of the old adage 'what grows together goes together'.

The Centre-Val de Loire is known as the Garden of France thanks to its sweeping rivers (including the majestic Loire), orchards and vineyards, as well as some of France's most beautiful châteaux. It's a hotbed of goat's-cheese making, best known for five PDO- protected cheeses that are a reference point for cheesemakers around the world.

Each has its own character, influenced by shape and maturation time. Sainte-Maure de Touraine is an ashed log; Crottin de Chavignol comes in a small button shape with a wrinkly rind; while Selles-sur-Cher is a little disc that is coated in ash and develops an impressive grey-blue mouldy rind. Then there are the pyramid-shaped Valençay and Pouligny-Saint-Pierre.

We could have picked any of them for the book. They've all won World Cheese Awards at one point or another over the years, but Selles-sur-Cher took the title of Best French Goat's cheese in 2004 (pipping many of its famous Loire rivals to the title).

Made in small hockey-puck-shaped rounds and weighing just 150g (5oz), Selles-sur-Cher is named after the village of the same name in the Loir-et-Cher *département*. As with the other goat's cheeses in this region, it's what is known as a lactic cheese, made by adding starter cultures to tubs of raw milk, with just a tiny amount of rennet. The milk is left to stand for anywhere from 24 to 48 hours, during which time the milk acidifies (thanks to the lactic-acid producing cultures) and creates the most delicate of curds. This is then hand-ladled into little round moulds, where it drains over another day or two before being turned out, salted and sprinkled with ash.

It's a slow process where not a lot happens for large stretches of time, before frantic bursts of activity around the ladling and salting stages. This was perfect for the farmers' wives who historically made the cheese in the nineteenth century because it allowed them to get on with all the other tasks that needed doing around the farm.

Selles-sur-Cher must be aged for at least 10 days. At this point it is still just a few steps away from milk, with a fragile, mousse-like texture and sharp, lemony flavour. But cheeses that are aged further to around 20 days develop a wrinkly, bluey-grey coat of moulds and yeasts, which break down the curd beneath into a silky goo, full of notes of hay and hazelnuts. Cheeses taken even further in the maturing process, up to 30 days, dry out and become crumblier, with spicy, goaty flavours.

Whatever condition you find Selles-sur-Cher, there's a very good chance it will match with one of the wines from the region. From the herbaceous, aromatic whites made with Sauvignon Blanc and Chenin Blanc, which are good with younger cheeses, to the light reds made with Pinot Noir and Cabernet Franc, which are low in tannins and have refreshing acidity, Loire wines have an almost symbiotic relationship with goat's cheese.

It is thought that the Moors first brought goats to the region in the eighth century, but goat farming really took off in the Loire in the nineteenth century when phylloxera (a sap-sucking insect) devastated vineyards across France. The thin sand and clay soils of the area, which are great for grape growing, were not rich enough for cultivating other crops, so winemakers pivoted to goat's cheese to get through the crisis. Goats are hardy souls that can thrive on poor soils, so were well suited to grazing the region's shrubby grasslands. Hay continues to make up the bulk of the goats' diet today, cut from the region's grassy fields during the summer.

Once grape growing was revived after the phylloxera crisis, the two industries evolved side by side across the Loire. Wine and cheese are both matured in similar limestone caves, while ash from burnt vines was sprinkled on Selles-sur-Cher to protect young *fromages* from flies. Food-grade vegetable ash is used today, which doesn't just look pretty, but also lowers the acidity of the rind to help the wrinkly yeasts and moulds to grow.

A young Selles-sur-Cher with a glass of dry or even sparkling Vouvray – a local appellation made from Chenin Blanc – is a fine pairing. There are notes of fresh apple and honey to the grape, which picks up on the lemony acidity and minerally flavour of the cheese. A more mature cheese with goaty, earthy flavours is very nice with a light red from nearby Chinon, made from Cabernet Franc. The firmer, saltier cheese softens the tannins, but there's also plenty of fresh acidity in the wine that cuts through the intensity of the cheese.

Of course, the fickle natures of wine and cheese mean they might not taste like that at all. Half the fun is tasting for yourself. PM

ORIGIN: Loire Valley, France

PROTECTED STATUS: PDO

MILK: Raw goat's milk

RENNET: Animal

AROMA: Young: grass, Greek yoghurt; mature: earthy, barnyardy

FLAVOUR: Young: lemony, minerally; mature: piquant, goaty

TEXTURE: Young: fluffy, mousse-like; mature: semi-hard, crumbly

MATCH: Chenin Blanc and Sauvignon Blanc are reliable foils. A young Selles-sur-Cher is delicious with asparagus.

WORLD CHEESE AWARDS: Multiple awards, including Best French Goat's Cheese 2004 (Fromagerie Pierre Jacquin & Fils)

Taleggio

There's no mistaking Taleggio. The soft cow's milk cheese from northern Italy has a distinctive square shape and eye-catching rind that ranges in colour from rose gold to deep sunset orange. It looks a little bit like a terracotta roof tile.

It's one of Italy's big four cheeses along with Parmigiano Reggiano, Pecorino and Mozzarella (see pages 38, 41 and 80), with a venerable history stretching back more than a thousand years. Originally made and matured in the Alpine valleys of Val Taleggio and Valsassina in Lombardy, today much of it is produced in state-of-the-art creameries on the lowland plains, which supply supermarkets around the world.

Taleggio is big business, with corresponding economies of scale and efficient manufacturing processes. But there is still a little bit of wild magic involved in the creation of its famous rind, wherever the cheese is made.

Milk can be pasteurised and starter culture strains bought from laboratories, but when it comes to nurturing the rind of Taleggio, makers large and small are reliant on the natural microflora in the dairy and maturing rooms. Affineurs smear the rind of young Taleggios with brine once a week to lay the ground for wild cultures in the air and on the wooden shelves to colonise the surface and create the pungent pinky-orange rind in a process that remains something of a mystery. Or as one affineur once told me: 'We don't know exactly why it is working, but we know it does so that's enough.'

Of course, scientists have tested Taleggio rinds over the years and have found remarkably diverse communities of micro-organisms, from bacteria to moulds and yeasts, that they are only just starting to understand. In a twist that is similar to the famous Irish washed-rind Gubbeen, they've even found a completely new type of mould, part of the *Penicillium commune* family, that seems to be specific to Taleggio.

Achieving the perfect rind might be more art than science, but specialist affineurs know just how much to wash and when, and can tinker with things such as temperature and humidity. One of the best in the business is CasArrigoni, which is based in Val Taleggio in Lombardy, where cheeses are kept in wooden crates in caves quarried from the mountainside. Director Adele Ravasio, whose family have been maturing Taleggio for over 40 years, once told me that the ideal rind should be thin with a rosy complexion, adding that it shouldn't be wet to the touch, but you should be able to feel the moisture when you take a bite. I always think a good Taleggio should also be pudgy and velvety with a fruity, almost woody flavour.

The history of Taleggio goes back to the practice of transhumance. In the nineteenth century, *bergamin* (herdsmen) would make large cheeses, such as Branzi, during the summer higher up in the foothills of the Alps, but would bring their cattle down to milder climes in the autumn ahead of the winter. The end-of-summer milk, especially from cows that were tired from hiking down mountains, was particularly creamy, which made it perfect for making soft cheese. Known as *stracchino* (from a Lombard word for 'tired': *strach*), this type of cheese could be made quickly and easily, and was matured in the cool limestone *grotte* (caves) of Valsassina and Val Taleggio.

Production moved further down onto the plains over time and Taleggio became the international behemoth it is today. But there are still small-scale raw milk producers, such as Sant'Antonio Cooperative in Val Taleggio, where the Locatelli brothers make cheese by hand.

Wherever it's made, under the rules of the PDO, every square of Taleggio must be embossed with the four-circle brand of the consortium that protects it. This contains three 'Ts' and the number of the dairy, although it's the rosy glow that really tells you when you have a well-cared-for cheese. PM

ORIGIN: Lombardy, Italy
PROTECTED STATUS: PDO
MILK: Raw or pasteurised cow's milk
RENNET: Animal
AROMA: Farmy, fruity, malty
FLAVOUR: Milky, earthy, fruity
TEXTURE: Silky and bulging
MATCH: The local tipple is Franciacorta sparkling wine, made with Chardonnay, Pinot Noir and Pinot Blanc grapes. Wonderful melted on a burger or in polenta.

WORLD CHEESE AWARDS: Multiple awards, including Best Italian Cheese 2002 (Cademartori), Gold 2023 (CasArrigoni)

Wensleydale and Cranberries

There may be some clutching of pearls at the fact that Wensleydale and Cranberries could even be considered for a book on the best cheeses in the world. Flavoured cheeses are like a red rag to a bull for cheese purists. There's nothing like a block cheese minced up with dried fruit, spices or chocolate chips to get cheese geeks into a froth of outrage and hand wringing about the state of food culture.

They've got a point. Much of the time, these kinds of cheeses are made with distinctly average base block Cheddars or Wensleydales, which are aggressively flavoured with bizarre ingredients. It's hard to mount a defence for a cream-tea-flavoured Cheddar (complete with added strawberry jam) or Espresso Martini Wensleydale. The less said about Parma Violet Cheshire, the better.

It's certainly very rare for these cheeses to be recognised at the World Cheese Awards. Judges tend to give them short shrift, viewing them as gimmicks. Too often flavoured cheeses are overpowered by the added ingredient, and the flavour of the cheese itself is lost, and if there's one thing judges really like it's the flavour of cheese.

That said, a Wensleydale and Cranberries, made by the Wensleydale Creamery, did win a Silver award in 2004. And there's no denying this type of cheese is hugely popular with the public, not just in the UK but in the US and Australia too, which have grown to be major export markets for British companies. The UK polished off more than 5,400 tonnes (5,300 tons) of Wensleydale with Cranberries in 2022, much of it bought around Christmas. There's a crowd-pleasing quality to the sharp, flaky cheese and the tartly sweet fruit. Put a slice on a digestive and you have instant cheesecake.

The Wensleydale Creamery in Hawes, Yorkshire, which claims it first came up with the idea of blending cranberries with cheese in 1996, makes around 1,000 tonnes (985 tons) of the cheese each year, accounting for around a quarter of the company's sales. I would never put it on a cheeseboard – it's too sweet for me – but millions of other people disagree, and its popular appeal is part of the reason why we've included it in this book.

There are various techniques for adding flavours to cheese. You can mix ingredients with the curd and mature the cheese with them already inside. This is how cumin or fenugreek seeds are added to Gouda in the Netherlands. The Italians, meanwhile, love to soak their cheeses in alcohol or even inject them with truffle paste (see Moliterno, page 132). There's also a huge family of cheeses that are smoked or coated in herbs, while cheesemakers often slice soft Brie horizontally in two so they can add a layer of truffle paste to the middle.

By far the most popular way of getting fruit (or indeed Parma violets) into cheese in the UK is to employ a process called remilling and extruding. This involves taking blocks of mature cheese and blitzing them into tiny pieces in a machine called a bowl chopper, which is basically a big blender. The 'milled' cheese is then mixed with cranberries (or whatever else you want to add) and fed into another impressive piece of kit called an extruder, which is a bit like a sausage machine.

ORIGIN: Yorkshire, England
PROTECTED STATUS: N/A
MILK: Pasteurised cow's milk
RENNET: Vegetarian
AROMA: Sweet, sour, milky
FLAVOUR: Yoghurty, candied, cranberry
TEXTURE: Semi-soft and flaky with chewy pieces of dried fruit
MATCH: Dry and fruity white wine, such as Picpoul, to cut through the sweetness, plus a digestive biscuit for the full cheesecake experience.

WORLD CHEESE AWARDS: Silver 2004 (Wensleydale Creamery)

The mixture is squished back together and forced through a round hole to form a long snake of cheese, which can be sliced into individual hockey puck truckles. Of course, you can change the die on the extruder to make different shapes, from hearts and stars to squares that can be sliced into wedges. There's something very impressive about the efficiency involved in the process of making remilled cheeses, from the speed of the bowl chopper that reduces 10kg (22lb) blocks of Wensleydale into grains of cheese in minutes, to the extruder squeezing out cheese like it's toothpaste.

Wensleydale and Cranberries is also part of a bigger story of how Wensleydale has been saved from extinction. The traditional farmhouse version of this crumbly, lactic cheese, which according to legend was first invented by monks 1,000 years ago, nearly died out in the twentieth century due to factors such as rationing, government-controlled milk prices and industrialisation.

The Wensleydale Creamery in Hawes managed to keep production going after the Second World War, making both block and more traditional cloth-bound versions of the cheese. It also helped secure PGI-protected status for Yorkshire Wensleydale in 2013.

This prepared the ground for a revival in artisan Wensleydale production, which has seen the launch of three new traditional versions of Wensleydale. Stonebeck (see page 222), Yoredale and Whin Yeats are made using methods that are very similar to those used on farms in Yorkshire before the War. They wouldn't dream of adding dried cranberries to their cheeses, but they would probably be very popular if they did. PM

Zamorano

It's usually easy to tell the difference between goat, sheep or cow's milk cheeses. But what about different breeds? Does a Jersey milk cheese taste different to one made with milk from Holstein cows? This is the kind of question that comes up in the various cheese exams I have contributed to over the years to help train cheesemongers on both sides of the Atlantic. These exams test knowledge of cheesemaking, affinage and culture, with a heavy dose of geography, as well as zootechnics balanced with sensory analysis and food science.

Zamorano could easily pop up as one of these questions. At first glance, it looks like a typical Spanish cheese. The zig-zag pattern on the rind resembles Manchego, and it has a straw-coloured paste similar to Iberico. But the nuances come from two key factors: animal breed and geography.

Zamorano is made with Churra and Castellana ewe's milk, instead of La Mancha ewes used for Manchego or a mix of cow, goat and ewe's milks for Iberico.

It's made in Castile and León, north-west of Madrid, while Manchego is made in Castile-La Mancha, south-east of the capital. These may seem like small differences, which shouldn't have much of an impact on cheese production. However, cheese experts recognise that these differences are precisely what makes cheese unique.

Castile and León is known for its hot summers and cold climate in winter. And the gastronomy of the region reflects that, with hearty dishes like *cochinillo* (suckling pig) and stews for the winter, and lighter dishes like *salmorejo*, a cold creamy tomato soup, in the summer.

Zamora is located in the most western part of the region, bordering Portugal and partly lying within the Duero river basin. With minimal rainfall, extensive agriculture is challenging. Shepherds in this region need animals that can withstand the changing environment. The two breeds reared there are robust and produce milk with high butterfat, perfect for making cheese. They are primarily used as dairy animals, but people do like the meat of Churras and use the wool of Castellanas.

The cheese is made following traditional methods. Most producers use raw milk, but the PDO allows for pasteurisation. The Consejo Regulador for this cheese recognises eight producers following PDO standards.

One of the best known Zamoranos is made by Quesería La Antigua in the town of Fuentesaúco. The cheese is aged for a minimum of 100 days and can be marketed as *curado* (aged for up to six months) or *añejo* (aged for more than nine months). Also look out for the younger Vellón de Fuentesaúco cheese, aged for three months and rubbed with olive oil. This helps the rind to develop slowly and gives a distinct herbaceous note to the cheese.

Another good name to look for is Vicente Pastor, which makes Zamorano with raw milk from carefully selected sheep of the Castellana breed in Morales del Vino. Aged for around six months, it's won multiple awards over the years and has a pleasant buttery flavour with hints of almonds.

Zamorano, like many other semi-hard sheep's milk cheeses, is sometimes seen as being a little old-fashioned. It is so traditional and consistent in its flavour that there's a danger it has become over-familiar to

shoppers. It's a problem many producers are worried about, so they are starting to innovate. Some are focusing on sustainability and making organic cheeses, while others are adding rubs and ingredients to the paste, from black garlic to truffle, with mixed results.

Winning medals at national and international competitions is also a strategy to keep cheese in the minds of buyers and consumers, and the city of Zamora hosts a biennial cheese festival that attracts 300,000 people over a weekend in September. The Fromago Cheese Experience comprises a 2km (1.25-mile) route through the city, which is lined with 300 cheesemakers showcasing more than 1,200 cheeses. Tastings, cooking demonstrations and a cheese tapas competition are all part of the festivities, as are exhibitions and art installations celebrating native sheep breeds. There's no substitute for good breeding. CY

ORIGIN: Castile and León, Spain
PROTECTED STATUS: PDO
MILK: Raw or pasteurised sheep's milk
RENNET: Animal
AROMA: Cooked butter, hay, almonds
FLAVOUR: Young: sweet, buttery, almondy; mature: tangy, sheepy, spicy
TEXTURE: Firm, but easy to crumble and cut
MATCH: Good with cured meats like jamon Iberico and full-bodied red wines from the Ribera del Duero.

WORLD CHEESE AWARDS: Multiple awards, including Best Spanish Cheese 2006 (Vicente Pastor)

2010s

Cheese goes global, reflecting a growing appetite for new foods as people travel further afield and discover different food cultures. Cheeses from Japan, Mexico and South Africa all win big at the awards. There's even a historic victory for a US blue in Italy, which controversially pips Parmigiano Reggiano in its own back yard.

Above: Montagnolo Affine (see page 136)

Anthill

If there was a cheese that captured the zeitgeist of the changing food scene in the 2010s, then you couldn't pick a better one than Anthill from Australia.

As we saw in the last decade, cheeses from outside the traditional powerhouses of France, Switzerland and Italy had started to make an impact at the World Cheese Awards in the 2000s, reflecting a wider hunger for new and exciting foods. But it was the 2010s when the trend fully blossomed, with entries from cheesemakers based everywhere from Norway and Japan to Mexico and Australia, which brings us back to Anthill.

Made by Woodside Cheese Wrights in the Adelaide Hills, this fresh goat's cheese won Super Gold in 2016 and made it to the final, where it became the talk of the awards, not just because it was from Australia, but because it was covered in a unique ingredient: green ants.

Woodside's dynamic owner Kris Lloyd came up with the idea when a chef friend – the late Jock Zonfrillo – turned up with a bucket of the insects one day. A native ingredient, harvested by hand by indigenous Australian communities in North Queensland, green ants have a bright and zesty citrus flavour that comes from the formic acid they produce as a defence weapon.

Lloyd took the bucket of ants as a challenge and set about scattering them on a fresh goat's cheese, which had been rolled in another native Australian ingredient, lemon myrtle, to create a completely new kind of cheese.

Entomophagy (eating insects) might sound strange to Western minds, but it's commonplace in many countries around the world, where insects are valued for their high protein content. There is a long history of ant-eating in Australia, China, India and across Latin America.

It makes perfect sense when you taste Anthill. The green ants, which are frozen beforehand so are no longer alive, pop in your mouth, releasing a fragrant flavour of lemongrass and lime. The insects also have a slight crunch, although it's probably best not to think about that too much and just enjoy the contrast with the soft, fluffy cheese beneath.

What makes the cheese really special is that rather than copying French Camembert or Italian Pecorino, as so many other cheesemakers around the world do, Kris Lloyd has created something that is uniquely Australian. Many of her other cheeses take a similar path, including cow, sheep and buffalo milk cheeses covered in native plants, such as the herb saltbush and the flowers from gum (eucalyptus) trees, which koalas reject in favour of the leaves. They also look fantastic. One of her best-sellers is Blackwood, a fresh *chèvre* (goat's cheese) rolled in a layer of ash, which is then covered in pink, yellow and red edible herbs and flowers, including the native bottlebrush. It looks more like a work of art than a cheese.

This attention to aesthetics makes sense when you meet Lloyd in person. When she isn't in white wellies and a hairnet in the dairy, she is about the most glamorous cheesemaker we know. She's often the most stylish person in the room at international cheese shows and awards, but also very down-to-earth and easy to chat to, with interesting thoughts about the cheese world, raw-milk production and regulations.

It helps that she had a life outside of cheese before she took over Woodside in 1999. Hailing from a Greek family, she previously worked in corporate development, while also doing the marketing for her family's winery, which has given her new perspectives on branding and innovation.

She didn't know how to make cheese when she bought the company, but quickly taught herself by visiting makers in France, Italy and the UK. Her travels also inspired her to set up CheeseFest in 2005, an annual cheese, food and wine festival in Adelaide that welcomes tens of thousands of visitors over a weekend in June. It's grown to become the biggest cheese festival in the country, but has remained loyal to its original mission to help educate people about food and drink from Australia.

It's exactly what you would expect from the woman who made Anthill. As she put it to me once, 'I want to make cheese that tells a story about my country.' PM

ORIGIN: Adelaide Hills, Australia
PROTECTED STATUS: N/A
MILK: Pasteurised goat's milk
RENNET: Vegetarian
AROMA: Milk, citrus, herbaceous
FLAVOUR: Lemongrass, yoghurt, sherbet
TEXTURE: Mousse-like, with a crunch from the ants
MATCH: Lloyd prefers the bubbles and freshness of Champagne. A drizzle of honey contrasts with the lemony acidity.

WORLD CHEESE AWARDS: Super Gold 2016, Best Australian Cheese 2022

HERO CHEESE

Bayley Hazen Blue

The view of Caspian Lake in the golden light of a summer morning is breathtaking. The air in this corner of Vermont's Northeast Kingdom feels impossibly pure. But I don't have long to gaze at the dreamy waterscape. I'm here on a mission to visit one of the most important cheesemakers in the US: Jasper Hill Farm.

Earlier, I had stopped at Willey's General Store, a small but perfectly formed local shop in Greensboro, which sits on the shores of the lake, where I found the shelves stocked with the full range of Jasper Hill's cheeses. In a town of only 800 residents and not a single stoplight, finding some of the best cheeses in the world in a local shop feels hopeful.

This is exactly the future the founders of Jasper Hill – the Kehler family – envision for every small town in America. Brothers Andy and Mateo, along with their wives Victoria and Angie, bought Jasper Hill Farm in 1998, driven by a desire to revitalise this rural community through sustainable farming and cheesemaking, and in the hope of providing a model for other parts of the US in the process.

Jasper Hill Farm is a couple of miles further on from the store, east of the lake, along a country lane. When I arrive it's as if I've stepped into a James Bond film. A massive concrete bunker, built into the hillside, looks like the lair of an evil master criminal, but is in fact a purpose-built complex of seven different maturing rooms designed to keep different cheeses in perfect condition. These are The Cellars at Jasper Hill Farm. A fortress for cheese.

Waiting for us at the entrance is Zoe Brickley, my long-time friend and teacher in the delicate craft of cheese ageing. She leads me inside to a reception area and changing room, where we suit up with white lab coats, hairnets and plastic boots, like a team of scientists heading into a secret lab.

The moment the metal gate opens, a rush of cold, damp air spills out, wrapping around us and sending a shiver down my spine. We begin in Vault 1, where young cheeses rest, then move back to the main hall and check out other rooms, each dedicated to a different stage of affinage or cheese style. We pause in awe before the cathedral-like vault where Cabot Clothbound Cheddar matures in meticulously arranged rows. But our destination lies deeper.

Vault 7 is where Bayley Hazen Blue ages. The air is thick with moisture and the floors glisten with water. The humidity is kept above 90 per cent, with constant oxygen exchange to encourage the inky blue veins to grow inside the cylindrical rounds of cheese. The atmosphere has an intensely mineral aroma, a blend of damp stone and earthy blue mould.

From back to front there are wheels at various stages of ageing. At the back are young cheeses without rind, but as we move forward we see the grey rind development, and also the light blue hue that takes over the cheese. The rinds become more rustic and the wheels more compact over time. The truckles weigh 3.2kg (7lb) and age for 8 to 10 weeks before reaching peak ripeness. When the cheese is about to be released, the interior is dense with a creamy texture. The flavour is nutty, grassy, and with hints of cocoa as well as a slight minerality from the blue mould.

Bayley Hazen Blue, which is named after a local landmark, has matured in tandem with Jasper Hill Farm's growth as a business. The Kehlers began making the cheese in the early 2000s, using milk from their small herd of 15 Ayrshire cows. From the start, they committed to using raw milk, a decision that was both a philosophical and political statement. At a time when American food safety regulations were becoming increasingly strict, this commitment reflected their unwavering dedication to traditional cheesemaking.

Their early success led to expansion, culminating in the opening of The Cellars in 2006. This 2,000-square-metre (21,500-square-foot) underground facility was designed not just to age their own cheeses, but also to aid small-scale producers by providing affinage and sales support.

Another turning point was their partnership with a local producer called Cabot Creamery Cooperative, which entrusted Jasper Hill with the ageing of its cloth-bound Cheddar. This collaboration provided financial stability and allowed the Kehlers to continue investing in research and development (R&D), as well as the building of the cheese caves.

Their open-minded approach to learning

ORIGIN: Vermont, USA
PROTECTED STATUS: N/A
MILK: Raw cow's milk
RENNET: Animal
AROMA: Earthy, nutty, toasted nuts
FLAVOUR: Sweet, nutty, grassy, anise spice
TEXTURE: Fudgy, dense, creamy
MATCH: Serve on rye bread with a drizzle of maple syrup. Pair with an imperial stout or an Ice Wine from the Finger Lakes of New York state.

WORLD CHEESE AWARDS:
Multiple awards, including Best Unpasteurised 2014, Gold 2023, Super Gold and Best American Cheese 2024

led to collaborations with academic researchers, helping to advance the study of microbial ecosystems in cheese rinds. Research conducted at The Cellars has contributed to a deeper understanding of microbial sequencing and the role of native bacteria in flavour development.

These milestones have helped establish Jasper Hill Farm as one of the most respected dairies in the USA, influencing other artisan producers. Professor Heather Paxson, an anthropologist at the Massachusetts Institute of Technology, describes this cohort of new cheesemakers as 'post-pastoral'. They are a group of dedicated artisans who seek to re-imagine rural life by blending traditional practices with scientific innovation. This vision is evident in Jasper Hill's commitment to low-intervention farming and a partial return to heritage production methods. From regenerative agriculture techniques, such as no tilling and rotational grazing, to the use of traditional starter cultures and the cultivation of their own native cheese moulds, Jasper Hill Farm embodies an approach that prioritises milk quality and natural microbial diversity, while maintaining a commitment to raw milk cheesemaking.

The US's Food and Drug Administration (FDA) regulates dairy products made and sold in the country. Because of the country's economic influence, FDA regulations shape food production worldwide. Since 1949, the government agency has enforced a 60-day minimum ageing rule for raw milk cheese, banning the sale of fresh, unaged cheeses made from raw milk. They argue that prolonged ageing may reduce potential pathogens.

But the rule is controversial. Researchers in the US have repeatedly challenged its scientific basis, arguing that it stems from flawed mid-twentieth-century experiments that do not reflect modern food safety advancements. Despite over seven decades of progress in microbiology and dairy science, the FDA has resisted changing the rule, insisting that more research is needed, even as global food safety standards evolve.

The FDA's position has led many cheesemakers to pasteurise their milk to avoid the regulatory risks and costs associated with long ageing periods. Pasteurisation equipment requires significant investment, but at times it appears to be the easier option compared to the costs of extended refrigeration and storage for cheese maturation. Mateo Kehler has worked closely with the FDA and state regulators, arguing that pasteurisation laws create barriers for new producers.

Jasper Hill Farm has expanded its R&D efforts, including the production of its own blue mould to inoculate the milk to make blue cheese. Historically, Roquefort producers placed loaves of rye bread in caves, allowing the mould to grow. The resulting mould was *Penicillium roqueforti*, responsible for blue veining in cheeses. Modern cheesemakers typically use lab-grown freeze-dried or liquid mould cultures, but since 2021 Jasper Hill Farm has periodically released Bayley Hazen Blue batches made using mould cultured in-house, a process it continues to refine. Along with using 'homemade' starter cultures, these methods aim to revive traditional cheesemaking practices, challenging industry standards that are overly dependent on commercial cultures.

By controlling their own milk, cultures and microbial ecosystems, Jasper Hill Farm ensures greater autonomy. The company shares this ethos with a nascent group of cheesemakers, often referred to as 'natural cheesemakers', who argue that their approach gives smaller producers the ability to make unique regional cheeses, rather than relying on the same standardised cultures used across the industry.

At the end of our tour of the network of underground caves, we have a final tasting of Bayley Hazen Blue, nibbling on tender slices of the crumbly, creamy cheese. Its sweet, toasty flavour is so evocative of where it is made that it's hard not to think again about the soft light and sparkling waters of Caspian Lake. Each wheel that leaves the building represents more than just outstanding craftsmanship. They are expressions of ideas, place and community. And as it evolves, Bayley continues to reshape the identity of American cheese. CY

Blu di Bufala

Italy is famous for its fresh buffalo milk cheeses, like Ricotta di Bufala and Mozzarella di Bufala Campana (see page 80), but aged cheeses made with this rich and creamy milk are a rare sight. Spotting a gap in the market, Alfio and Bruno Gritti of Quattro Portoni near Bergamo have, over the years, developed a range of *formaggi di bufala* that includes a Camembert-style, a Caciocavallo (see page 112), a washed-rind cheese, and what we consider to be the jewel of the crown, a blue.

Simply named Blu di Bufala, the cheese is visually striking. Made in a big 4kg (9lb) square with a rough rind scored with brush marks, the interior is snow white and marbled with blue veins running up and down. It looks like an elegant piece of Carrara marble. The smell is earthy towards the rind, while the paste is milky and minerally. Bite into a slice and the taste is sweet and tangy, with a nice piquant punch from the blue mould.

The Gritti family started rearing buffaloes in the 2000s. They saw an opportunity to move away from milking cows and into making distinctive products using buffalo milk. The milk is special as it is higher in proteins and fats that are good for cheesemaking, while having lower cholesterol when compared to cow's milk. Their first cheese was made in 2006, and six years later they won a Super Gold for Blu di Bufala.

In 2018 I had the pleasure of visiting the Grittis' farm. Amid the repurposed old buildings and barns, I saw curious baby buffaloes waiting to join their mothers after milking. Buffaloes are known for not easily releasing milk without their calves nearby, which means that herds are kept together for longer than cows. They are quiet animals, but can become agitated easily and charge at herders, so for this reason you need well-trained farm workers tending to them.

ORIGIN: Lombardy, Italy
PROTECTED STATUS: N/A
MILK: Pasteurised buffalo milk
RENNET: Animal
AROMA: Milky, minerally, earthy
FLAVOUR: Sweet, tangy, savoury
TEXTURE: Soft, crumbly, chalky when young

MATCH: Pair with Cabernet Sauvignon to balance the savoury notes of the cheese, or with a farmhouse ale to get extra umami notes. Eat it with a simple tomato salad or pears.

WORLD CHEESE AWARDS: Multiple awards, including Best Italian Cheese 2012, 2017

At Quattro Portoni most of the employees working with the animals are recent immigrants from India. It's a little-known fact, but Sikh migrants now form part of the backbone of the cheesemaking industry in the north of Italy and are recognised for their animal husbandry skills. Overall expansion of the Italian economy during the early 2000s meant that many farm jobs were opening up, as Italian nationals sought employment in higher-earning industries. Migrant workers filled the vacancies, using the skills they brought with them.

Water buffaloes (*Bubalus bubalis*), also known as Asian buffaloes, were native to Southeast Asia, but trade and conquest brought them to many parts of the world. I have seen buffaloes in rural Italy, the mountains of Colombia, and in the meadows of Chennai, India. They are still integral to agricultural communities in Southeast Asia, however, and formidable animals to work in warm climates. Their affinity for wet environments like rice paddies and muddy wetlands is partly because they need to regulate their body temperature by submerging in water.

During their stay in Sicily, beginning in 827 CE, Arab rulers introduced buffaloes to the island. Subsequently, Normans utilised them as draught animals in the marshy terrains of the southern Italian mainland, particularly to regions like Campania and Lazio. Their milk was eventually used to make the famous Mozzarella di Bufala Campana. These animals would adapt and become what we now know as Mediterranean buffaloes, and Quattro Portoni now has around 1,000 heads of cattle.

Over the centuries, buffaloes became part of the landscape and were used for many things, from draining swamps to providing meat and milk. Because of their usefulness they even became a target of Nazi extermination campaigns. Culling efforts by the occupation forces were officially aimed at eradicating malaria by clearing agricultural areas around Rome and Naples where buffaloes and the mosquitoes thrived. However, it is speculated that the policy was also designed to undermine anti-fascist peasants who depended on buffaloes for their livelihoods. Today, they are again cherished as part of the landscape and the gastronomic culture of Italy. CY

Burrata

We met Mozzarella earlier in the book (see page 80), but Italy's famous stretchy cheese has been upstaged by a younger, sexier cousin in recent years. Burrata is part of the same *pasta filata* (spun paste) family as Mozzarella, but is made in a slightly different way, so that it has an outrageously oozy centre. Slice into a glistening white Burrata and the cream filling flows out in a very seductive way.

It's a cheese that has certainly got chefs hot under the collar, knocking Mozzarella off the menu in restaurants around the world as the cheese of choice for salads, pasta and even desserts. Its mild milky character makes it a perfect vehicle for everything from tomatoes and spices to fresh fruit and honey.

Although it looks a little like Mozzarella, there are some important differences. Originally invented in Puglia on the heel of Italy, the cheese is made with cow's milk rather than buffalo. The process starts by making a Mozzarella-style cheese, stretching soft curd in hot water until it becomes supple and malleable. But rather than twisting it into balls, the elastic curd is fashioned into a kind of pouch. Much of the production is now mechanised, but there are still cheesemakers who do it manually - though they must have asbestos hands because the hot water used to stretch the cheese is 80°C (175°F) or even hotter.

The pouch is filled with a mix of double cream and scraps of Mozzarella (known as *stracciatella*) and tied at the top - historically with thin leaves from the asphodel plant, but now green plastic or raffia are more common. Sometimes the top of the pouch is simply gathered together and sealed with a knot.

ORIGIN: Puglia, Italy

PROTECTED STATUS: Not protected, though Burrata di Andria is covered by a PGI

MILK: Raw or pasteurised cow's milk

RENNET: Animal or vegetarian

AROMA: Warm milk, cream

FLAVOUR: Buttery, creamy, sweet

TEXTURE: Soft, creamy

MATCH: A fruity Italian white, such as Greco di Tufo, works well. Burrata is a natural partner for ripe tomatoes, with a drizzle of extra virgin olive oil and aged balsamic.

WORLD CHEESE AWARDS: Gold 2010 (Murgella)

Burrata, which takes its name from the Italian word for butter, *burro*, because of its rich flavour, is not protected, so can be made anywhere, although Burrata di Andria is covered by a PGI, meaning it can only be made in Puglia, where it was first invented.

The story goes that in the 1920s a dairy farmer in Andria called Lorenzo Bianchino was snowed in and unable to deliver milk to the local town. Rather than waste the cream that rose to the top, he instead fashioned Mozzarella pouches into a kind of storage vessel, adding shreds of any leftover cheese to the cream for good measure.

Whether this story is true is hard to verify. There are plenty of tall tales in cheese, with very little evidence to verify them. Snow in Puglia is pretty rare, although Andria is in the colder north, and there is a similar product made in the region called *mantèche*, which involves filling a hard, aged Mozzarella case with butter. Whatever the truth, it's a good story and one that is cemented as fact in the official PGI document that protects Burrata di Andria.

Like Mozzarella, the fresher the Burrata the better. If you can buy it straight from the cheesemaker, when the shell is still taut and smooth, and the filling is super fresh, it's a wonderful thing. Especially when you make that first cut and let the cream flow. PM

Caciocavallo

There's something rather jolly about the shape of this ancient Italian cheese. With its large, round bottom, pinched neck and little head on top, it looks for all the world like a giant pear or a dinky snowman. Put a whole cheese on the table and it rolls around in a comical fashion.

But Caciocavallo is no novelty cheese. The first reference to it was made by Hippocrates in 500 BCE, while the technique for making it was documented by Lucius Junius Moderatus Columella in his treatise *De re rustica* in 68 CE. Caciocavallo has serious pedigree.

The cheese is part of the *pasta filata* (spun paste) family, which includes Mozzarella (see page 80) and Provolone. These cheeses are made by plunging curd into very hot water and stretching it so that it becomes elastic and pliable, allowing it to be moulded into different shapes. Caciocavallo's distinctive shape is formed by tying string around the top of the cheese when it is soft so it can be hung up to dry. Caciocavallo roughly translates as 'horse cheese', in reference to the traditional maturation method where two cheeses were tied together at each end of a rope which was slung over a wooden beam, resembling a saddle on a horse.

The cheese was historically made with raw cow's milk and animal rennet, which gives it its distinctive piquant flavour. In 1993, the Italian government succeeded in gaining PDO protection for Caciocavallo Silano, made in five southern regions of the peninsula. This cheese is semi-hard and can be aged between 30 days during spring or 12 months for cheeses made in the winter. Spring and winter cheeses develop specific flavour profiles, but both have soured milk and buttery notes.

Two similar cheeses, Caciocavallo Podolico and Caciocavallo Irpino di Grotta, are considered a 'Traditional Italian Food Product' (PAT) by the Italian Ministry of Agriculture, but do not have European-wide recognition. Podolico is only made in spring and summer, when the Podolico cows graze on green pastures outdoors. The Irpino version is made with cows from the region near the town of Calitri and aged in natural caves, called *grotte*.

Most Caciocavallos are pale, and the exterior needs to be constantly cleaned to prevent dryness cracking the rind, leading to rancid notes. Younger cheeses will have cleaner, edible yellow rinds, while more aged cheeses will develop greyer skins from the natural moulds that grow on them. It is best to avoid the rind of the very aged cheeses as they will be too leathery.

Other *pasta filata formaggi* include the smoked cheese Scamorza, sausage-shaped Provolone, the egg-shaped Schiena d'Asino, and Ragusano, which looks like a house brick. These are simple cheeses enjoyed at every meal as part of an appetiser. They hold an important role in Italian cuisine, and for many early migrants to Canada and the USA they were a reminder of home; it is easy to find Caciocavallo and Provolone in shops in Little Italy neighbourhoods in New York City, Chicago and Toronto.

There are similar cheeses made in the Balkans and Eastern Europe, in particular in Albania, Bulgaria, Romania, Moldova, North Macedonia and Serbia, where they are sometimes called *kashkaval*. These are likely a legacy of the Roman Empire's expansion and interaction with nomadic tribes.

Caciocavallo's wobbly shape makes it an interesting cheese to serve. We recommend cutting it in half from top to bottom and then cutting wedges or slices. It's a fun cheese for a warm summer's day. CY

ORIGIN: Basilicata, Campania, Calabria, Molise and Puglia, Italy

PROTECTED STATUS: Not protected, but there is a PDO for Caciocavallo Silano

MILK: Raw or pasteurised cow's milk

RENNET: Animal

AROMA: Soured milk, buttery

FLAVOUR: Tangy, creamy, piquant

TEXTURE: Soft and springy when young; stringy as it ages

MATCH: A perfect accompaniment to fresh summer fruits and prosciutto crudo. It is also served melted on top of cooked vegetables and along with bruschetta and olive oil.

WORLD CHEESE AWARDS: Best Italian Cheese 2013 (Caseificio Di Nucci), Gold 2019 for di Grotta and Super Gold 2019 for Silano PDO (Delizia S.p.A.)

Celtic Promise

There can't be many office workers who haven't daydreamed about leaving the rat race behind for a simpler life in the country. But in the idealistic heyday of the 1970s there was an entire generation of people who turned their fantasies into reality by ditching modern life to live off the land. It turned out to be good news for British cheese, too.

Concerns about environmental issues, the threat of nuclear war, and industrialised food systems in the 1970s led to the birth of radical new ideas around living more simply and sustainably. The so-called self-sufficiency movement, which saw people set up their own smallholdings, was heavily influenced by one book: *The Complete Book of Self-Sufficiency* (1976), written by John Seymour, which was essentially a guide to dropping out to go off-grid.

While living in the Netherlands, John Savage-Onstwedder translated Seymour's book into Dutch, and was so inspired by its philosophy that in the early 1980s he decided to travel to Wales to meet the man himself. Not long afterwards he ended up relocating to Wales with his wife Patrice and their friend Paula van Werkhoven, with the aim of putting into practice some of the things they had learned from the book.

Land was relatively cheap in Wales at the time, so they were able to buy Glynhynod Farm ('Remarkable Valley' in Welsh) in Ceredigion's beautiful Teifi Valley, where they started farming organically. Caws Teifi Cheese was set up in 1982, using raw milk from their own tiny herd of cows. Patrice had trained under a famous raw milk Gouda producer in the Netherlands called Mrs Vermeer, so they started making cheeses in the same style, but also developed something a little different in the form of Celtic Promise.

Made like Caerphilly (see page 20), but in Gouda moulds so it has a rounded shape, the 500g (1 lb 2oz) cheese is washed in brine and cider as it matures, to help develop a moist rind that is sunset pink when it's young, becoming browner and increasingly pungent as it matures. It smells a little like a pile of apples fermenting in the corner of the farmyard, but the cheese beneath is buttery, milky and clean.

Celtic Promise has won pretty much every award going since those halcyon days, including the British Cheese Awards twice, and was named Best Welsh Cheese at the World Cheese Awards in 2018. And the future looks bright, with Savage-Onstwedder's sons taking over in recent years. John-James and Robert look after the farm and cheesemaking, as well as running a distillery making gin and whisky. The family have long attributed the success of their cheeses to the quality of the milk. Caws Teifi no longer has its own cows, but works with a small organic farm in Llanboidy, which has a herd of Jersey and Friesian cows.

By working organically, the farm has eliminated the need for synthetic fertilisers and other chemicals, while biodiversity is much richer. Caws Teifi has also long been a flag-bearer for raw milk, arguing that it is less energy-intensive and has a better nutritional profile. Most importantly, Savage-Onstwedder is adamant that raw milk cheeses taste better. Or as he put it to me several years ago: 'When God promised Abraham a land flowing with milk and honey, he wasn't talking about pasteurised milk. The flavour of raw milk cheeses takes you on a journey with a start, a middle and an end. You get the flavour of the land.'

The idealistic principles on which Caws Teifi was founded in the 1980s are still going strong today. PM

ORIGIN: Ceredigion, Wales
PROTECTED STATUS: N/A
MILK: Raw cow's milk
RENNET: Vegetarian
AROMA: Fruity, funky, farmyard
FLAVOUR: Buttery, fermented, brothy
TEXTURE: Semi-soft, slightly crumbly
MATCH: A glass of medium dry cider fits nicely, along with a few slices of fresh apple.

WORLD CHEESE AWARDS: Multiple awards, including Best Welsh Cheese 2018

Cheshire

It's hard to believe, but before Cheddar was king in Britain, Cheshire used to rule the country's cheese counters.

This crumbly regional cheese from the north-west of England is a tiny part of the British cheese market today, accounting for just a few per cent of sales, most of which is factory-produced block cheeses. In contrast, Cheddar represents more than half of all the cheese bought in the country.

But there was a time when it was the other way round. In the late seventeenth century, Cheshire was lusted after by cheese factors (buyers) for its buttery flavour and flaky texture. Walk into any self-respecting cheesemongers in London during the period and the shelves would have been full of Cheshire, with barely a Cheddar to be seen.

The story of Cheshire's rise and subsequent fall starts on a very specific date – 21 October 1650 – when the *James* cargo ship, chartered by an entrepreneurial London merchant called William Seaman, docked in London. The sail ship was filled with 20 tonnes (19 tons) of Cheshire – a huge amount for a cheese that was not well known in the capital, but Seaman had a hunch that its rich flavour would be a hit with Londoners.

He wasn't wrong. Up until this point, most of the city's butter and cheese had come by land from East Anglia, but the makers in that part of the country had gotten greedy over the years, skimming more and more cream from their milk to make butter, which resulted in increasingly thin and hard cheese. These low-fat 'flett' cheeses (from the word 'flotten', meaning skimmed) were disparagingly nick-named Suffolk Bang and became something of a laughing stock.

In his book *A Tour Through the Whole Island of Great Britain*, published in the 1720s, author Daniel Defoe described it as being 'perhaps the worst cheese in the world', while legend has it that the cheese had to be hung over the fire to soften before it could be eaten. There's also an old joke about a ship full of millstones and flett cheese that docks at a harbour, whereby it's discovered that the rats have eaten the stones rather than the cheese.

Cheshire, in contrast, was made with full-fat milk, which is why Seaman's gamble paid off. Despite costing nearly a third more than Suffolk Bang, the public were happy to pay for its rich flavour and tender texture. Suddenly everyone wanted Cheshire, and farms in the north went into overdrive to supply them in a kind of cheese gold rush. In 1729 more than 5,700 tonnes (5,610 tons) of the cheese arrived in London, brought down by beautiful, sleek sail ships called 'ketches'. It was a huge amount, more than five times that of tough old Suffolk Bang, which eventually died out completely.

Cheshire's remarkable rise to the top was matched by an equally rapid decline in the nineteenth and twentieth centuries, when newly built railways and the start of factory production saw Cheddar become the nation's favourite cheese. The number of farms producing Cheshire fell from more than 2,000 in 1900 to just 40 following the Second World War.

Yet the very first winner of the World Cheese Awards in 1988 was a Cheshire, made on a farm in Shropshire by Group Captain David Hutchinson Smith, who'd left a distinguished career in the RAF in 1970 to make cheese with his wife Jill, an agricultural scientist. After being named Best Cheese in the World, the company's distinctive Blue Cheshire (most Cheshire is white or has an orange hue from the addition of annatto) was promptly bought by a much bigger competitor, who ultimately decided to stop production to focus on another cheese.

This story of small Cheshire-makers closing down or being bought up by industrial creameries was a constant in the post-war years. Today most Cheshire is made in block form in factories and bears very little resemblance to the cheeses that came in on the *James*. It's usually only aged for a few weeks, vacuum-packed in plastic, and is super-sharp and milky. It's really not worth the time or the calories.

There are, however, two cheesemakers left still making Cheshire in the traditional way, and both have been serial winners at the World Cheese Awards, which just goes to show that seventeenth-century cheesemongers could spot a good cheese when they tasted one. Appleby's in Shropshire and HS Bourne in Cheshire both make cloth-bound cheeses with raw milk from cows that still graze on the Cheshire plain, which are bandaged in muslin and matured for three to four months.

Some are coloured orange with annatto (for some unknown reason southerners prefer Red Cheshire), while cheese for the north is generally left white. There is no real difference in flavour between the two, although Carlos disagrees. He says he can easily tell them

ORIGIN: Cheshire, England
PROTECTED STATUS: N/A
MILK: Pasteurised or raw cow's milk
RENNET: Animal or vegetarian
AROMA: Milky, lemony, minerally
FLAVOUR: Zesty, buttery, umami
TEXTURE: Tender and crumbly

MATCH: A steely Chablis meets the minerality of farmhouse Cheshire in a very pleasing way. A slice of juicy apple is a simple but effective accompaniment.

WORLD CHEESE AWARDS: Multiple awards, including Gold 2012 (HS Bourne), Super Gold 2012 (Appleby's)

apart, but we are yet to put his taste buds to the test. Proper Cheshire has a lovely mix of juicy, mouthwatering acidity, but also a creaminess and a beguiling savoury quality that always reminds me of roasted chicken. There's also a delicate mineral note that is often attributed to the salt deposits that run through the Cheshire plain, where the cows graze.

What happens next to farmhouse Cheshire is not clear. Appleby's has been making the cheese since 1952, and the third-generation owners, Paul and Sarah Appleby, still have many more years of cheesemaking left in them, plus five kids, which bodes well for the future. Likewise, John Bourne has passed on the cheesemaking torch to his son Hugo, who is keen to grow the business.

This is reassuring to an extent, but it would be nice if there were a few more farms making Cheshire, just to be on the safe side. It's a precious cheese jewel that needs to be safeguarded for the future. PM

Corra Linn

ORIGIN: Lanarkshire, Scotland
PROTECTED STATUS: N/A
MILK: Raw sheep's milk
RENNET: Animal
AROMA: Earthy, fruity
FLAVOUR: Fruity, brothy, lamby
TEXTURE: Close, slightly grainy
MATCH: The nutty notes of Amontillado sherry dovetail nicely with the savoury cheese. Rhubarb chutney cuts through the richness.

WORLD CHEESE AWARDS: Multiple awards, including Best Scottish Cheese 2019, Super Gold 2024

You'd be forgiven for feeling a bit sorry for Selina Cairns' sheep. Her flock of Lacaune ewes were historically bred to traverse the hot, rocky landscape of Aveyron in the south of France, where the milk is used to make Roquefort. It's a very different setting to the rugged hills of Lanarkshire, where her flock spend their days 300 metres (1,000 feet) above sea level in the Southern Uplands of Scotland. They are more likely to get soaked with rain than suffer from sunburn in this bracing part of the world.

But Lacaunes are surprisingly well suited to the chillier climes of Scotland. The breed's small hooves make them adept at navigating harsh terrain, and they are hardy in all types of weather, from the heat of southern France to the cold of southern Scotland.

It was Selina Cairns' father, Humphrey Errington, who first came up with the idea of milking French sheep in Scotland in the 1980s. A long-time lover of Roquefort, he decided to create a similar cheese using a recipe said to have been written in the 1820s by the famous Scottish poet and author Sir Walter Scott. After investing in a flock of Lacaune sheep from France, he set up Errington Cheese at Walston Braehead Farm and went about creating Lanark Blue – a soft, creamy cheese with a kick so spicy it was described as being a bit of a 'kilt lifter' (although it's much more approachable these days).

Errington Cheese is today run by Cairns and her husband Andrew, who have taken the business in exciting new directions beyond blue, from developing new goat's cheeses to opening a lovely farm shop and kitchen. But perhaps their biggest recent success was Corra Linn, named after a local waterfall.

Made in a similar way to Cheddar, but with raw sheep's milk, the cheese was created in 2008 as a way to store the excess of rich and creamy milk that comes in the spring. The 8kg (17lb 10oz) truckles of cheese are wrapped in muslin before being matured for anywhere from 6 to 24 months, which means there is cheese to sell all year round, even when the sheep have dried off in the winter.

It's gone on to be a huge hit, winning multiple awards and arguably eclipsing Lanark Blue in recent years thanks to its fruity, brothy flavours, and close, even texture, which are quite different to Continental sheep's milk cheeses such as Pecorino and Manchego. The more mature cheeses, aged for over a year, are particularly intense and delicious.

Corra Linn is a delight on a cheeseboard, but is also good in the kitchen. You can use it in cheese straws or grated over chargrilled broccoli. Cairns likes to make a pesto by blitzing wild garlic, roasted hazelnuts, olive oil and lemon juice with grated Corra Linn.

A true Scottish original. 

Fuoco

Cheese is not just a delicious thing to eat: it can also tell stories of exchange, migration, innovation and shared histories. This co-mingling of ideas and cultures is perfectly encapsulated in the Canadian washed-rind cheese Fuoco.

Canada has long embraced migration and new ways of thinking. The Fuoco family is part of that story. The parents, Egidio and Rosa, bought a farm in Saint-Lin–Laurentides, east of Montreal in Southern Quebec, and used it as a city escape. Over time, their sons Jason and Frank saw potential in the land and started taking care of buffaloes on the property, with the idea of making cheese. They now have around 80 animals.

Born in Canada, but deeply connected to his Italian heritage, Jason Fuoco embarked on a transformative trip to Campania in 2009 to master Mozzarella cheesemaking. Upon returning, he wasn't happy just replicating recipes. He eventually developed Fuoco, a washed-rind cheese that honours the local Québécois traditions, but offers something exciting and different.

Made in 125g (4oz) rounds with rich buffalo milk in the French-speaking province of Canada by an Italian-Canadian family, it's a cheese that feels French, Italian and Canadian all at the same time.

This confusing state of affairs is echoed by the eating experience. The washed rind has a powerful, funky flavour, but this belies a soft, melt-in-the-mouth interior that is delicate and floral. It's not one thing or the other, and it's all the better for it. Fuoco challenges not only your palate but also your perception of what makes an authentic cheese. I can only think of one other washed-rind buffalo milk cheese in the world: Quadrello di Bufala made by Quattro Portoni in Italy.

One of the most famous Canadian cheeses is a washed-rind cheese named Oka. First made by Trappist monks in Quebec province, this style became popular in the region and many others used the technique to make similar cheeses; the washing of the rind gives them a characteristic meaty flavour. Canada as a whole is probably best known for block Cheddars. Historically, the country had been a large producer of Cheddar, selling vast quantities to the UK up until the end of the Second World War.

The creation of the Canadian Dairy Commission, a government organisation, brought with it the implementation of strict production quotas in the 1970s to maintain a stable milk price. The rules also controlled inter-provincial cheese commerce, making it difficult to find cheeses made in Quebec in neighbouring provinces. Critics of the system argued that the rules discouraged smaller producers from setting up.

However, the same rules have allowed producers in Quebec to thrive as they have an assured share of the market. Some of the quotas and regulations changed during the 2010s to allow Canada to comply with international trade agreements, and opened the door for European imports.

Even though artisanal cheesemaking in Canada is small compared to that of the US or UK, there is a group of makers ensuring a supply of tasty cheeses in almost all provinces. Since 2022, there have been efforts to set up the Canadian Cheese Collective

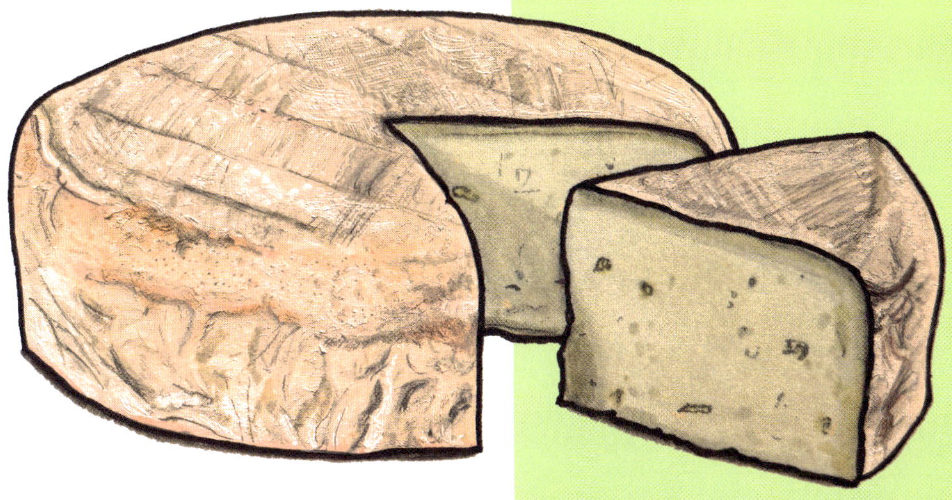

to bring producers, cheesemongers and experts under one umbrella to advocate for Canadian cheeses.

In fact, Canada is one to watch when it comes to new and innovative cheeses. One of my favourite cloth-bound Cheddars is Avonlea, made by COWS Creamery on Prince Edward Island, while British Columbia, on the other side of the country, also has an exciting cheesemaking culture, led by gorgeous goat's milk cheeses made by Salt Spring Island Cheese.

Fuoco is part of this new wave of Canadian cheeses, blending heritage and imagination. It shows that authenticity isn't just about tradition; it's also about creating your own path. CY

ORIGIN: Quebec, Canada
PROTECTED STATUS: N/A
MILK: Pasteurised buffalo milk
RENNET: Vegetarian
AROMA: Milky, floral, meaty
FLAVOUR: Sweet, funky, umami,
TEXTURE: Soft, creamy
MATCH: Maple syrup is a great pairing, or maybe try an Old Fashioned cocktail sweetened with it. Serve on French fries for an elevated *poutine*, a traditional Quebecois dish of French fries and cheese curds dripped in gravy.

WORLD CHEESE AWARDS:
Super Gold 2015

Gamalost

Unless you're seriously into Victorian cosplay, you're probably not tucking into kedgeree for breakfast and boiled beef for dinner. Which is to say that food fashions change. We're still eating Cheddar (Queen Victoria's favourite), along with Brie and Gruyère – cheeses that would have been familiar to people several hundred years ago – but there have been many that have fallen by the wayside down the decades. It's estimated that around 50 French *fromages* have died out in the last 50 years alone, while even modern creations regularly fall foul of changing tastes, new regulations and commercial pressures.

While it's not in danger of extinction quite yet, Gamalost from Norway feels like a cheese that is out of step with modern times. Its name is the first clue. Gamalost (sometimes spelled Gammalost or Gammelost) translates as 'old cheese' in Norwegian, which could be a reference to its long history or that it was historically matured for a long time. Alternatively, it might be because it looks like something that has been forgotten about at the back of a cupboard.

Gamalost is one of the oddest cheeses we know, with a challenging flavour to match. Brown, coarse and riddled with mould, it looks a little bit like an old loaf of bread, while the flavour is bracing. Bitter and sour, but also incredibly savoury, it's what you might politely call an acquired taste. In a time when sweet, creamy and nutty cheeses are all the rage, it's a throwback to another era.

Legend has it that the Vikings ate the cheese as an aphrodisiac, although the first reliable evidence of its existence dates back to the sixteenth century. The cheese was originally made on isolated farms and mountain chalets in the west of Norway during the summer. Cream would be skimmed from cow's milk to make butter, but rather than throw away what was left, the resourceful *budeia* (dairymaid) would allow the skimmed milk to curdle, before removing the whey to leave a low-fat, protein-rich curd. This would be formed into a cheese, cooked in the whey and then matured for weeks or months without any kind of salting. During this time the cheese would be colonised by natural grey and blue moulds, which would grow on the rind, but also throughout the crumbly interior.

Pretty much every part of this process is a seriously unusual way to make cheese, but makes sense in the context of small mountain farms trying to maximise the use of their milk. The point of Gamalost was not to make a rich, creamy cheese to sell, but to have a nutritious foodstuff to get you through the winter using milk that would have otherwise gone to waste.

As Norway modernised, production of the cheese moved to larger dairies, but these closed one by one as the flavour of Gamalost became less appealing to people who had discovered sweet, full-fat cheeses. There is now only one large dairy still making Gamalost, and just a handful of farm producers.

Dairy co-operative Tine, which makes Gamalost at its plant in Vik in Sogn, accounts for almost all of the country's production today, but it's an uphill battle to convince people that the intense cheese should be added to their shopping lists. Only around 65 tonnes (64 tons) of Gamalost are produced at the dairy each year, which is less than half of what it was at the beginning of the century. While older Norwegians still appreciate the flavour – typically serving it on thickly buttered bread or on salty crackers with jam – younger generations are much more likely to have a creamy blue or Camembert in their fridge.

But there are signs that perhaps all is not lost for Gamalost. The cheese won a Bronze medal at the World Cheese Awards in 2018, and Tine has been doing its bit to boost sales by highlighting its low fat content (less than 1 per cent) and high protein level (nearly 50 per cent), while also launching a new spreadable version. It also secured PGI status for Gamalost Frå Vik in 2006

At the same time, hardcore fans have been pulling together in an effort to get Norwegians to fall back in love with their unique cheese. A Gamalost appreciation society has been set up to campaign for what it describes as 'a Norwegian national treasure', and there is even an annual festival in Vik, which includes talks, tastings and concerts from the local choir.

One of those leading the charge is Kristin Glück-Evensen, who worked as a Gamalost *budeia* before becoming an advocate for the last remaining farm-made cheeses.

Glück-Evensen has a particular passion for using Gamalost as a seasoning. She argues that its deep savoury flavour adds a delicious kick to dishes – an opinion that is backed up by research she carried out with the Norsk Gardsost (Norwegian Farm Cheese Association). The organisation sent a 12-month Parmesan (famous for its umami flavour) and a five-month piece of Gamalost to a laboratory to analyse their glutamate levels (an amino acid that gives food savoury, umami flavours). The results came back showing that Gamalost had twice as much as Italy's finest.

Maybe grating Gamalost over pasta will be the next big thing in food. PM

ORIGIN: Hardanger, Voss and Sogn, Norway

PROTECTED STATUS: Not protected, though Gamalost Frå Vik is covered by a PGI

MILK: Pasteurised or raw cow's milk

RENNET: None

AROMA: Damp cellar, sour milk, rye bread

FLAVOUR: Earthy, sour, umami

TEXTURE: Coarse and grainy

MATCH: Raspberry juice is a popular pairing at the Tine café in Vik. Sour cream and lingonberry jam or cranberries are classic accompaniments in Norway.

WORLD CHEESE AWARDS: Bronze 2018 (Tine)

Halloumi

There's more to Halloumi than its famous squeak. The popular cheese, which makes an audible high-pitched noise when chewed, is an integral part of Cyprus's history, culture and economics, and has found itself at the centre of a fractious dispute about authenticity.

In some ways the cheese is a victim of its own success. Halloumi has become an essential ingredient on barbecues around the world, muscling its way onto the grill alongside steaks and burgers. According to Cyprus's official statistical service, exports of the cheese nearly doubled between 2017 and 2023, to countries such as the UK, Germany and Sweden. Brits love it so much they buy nearly half of all the Halloumi made on the island every year. It's become as British as pork pies and cucumber sandwiches.

Halloumi (or Hellim, as it is known in the Turkish north of the island) was historically made with a mix of sheep and/or goat's milk, plus fresh mint leaves, which were added for flavour and preservation (mint has antibacterial properties). But as demand has rocketed, so has the amount of more readily available cow's milk added to the blend. Much of the cheese that is exported is made on a large scale in square, salty blocks with a majority of cow's milk and a token sprinkle of dried mint. It does a job, but is not a patch on the sweet, handmade cheeses still enjoyed by Cypriots.

It's no surprise then that one of the most decorated Halloumis at the World Cheese Awards comes from a producer based on a farm that still does things in the old-fashioned way. The Polycarpou family has been making cheese in the village of Prastio in Limassol since the eighteenth century and has resisted the lure of industrial block cheeses. They

ORIGIN: Cyprus

PROTECTED STATUS: PDO

MILK: Raw or pasteurised sheep, goat and cow's milk

RENNET: Animal or vegetarian

AROMA: Milky, briny, animal

FLAVOUR: Salty, sheepy, steely

TEXTURE: Firm, springy

MATCH: Serving the fresh cheese with watermelon or grilled with honey is popular in Cyprus. A minerally white wine, such as Santorini made with Assyrtiko grapes, is a refreshing partner.

WORLD CHEESE AWARDS: Super Gold 2015, Gold 2016, Gold 2022 (Polycarpou)

continue to hand-fold discs of Halloumi in half to form a kind of pitta-bread-shaped cheese, using milk from their own flock to make 100 per cent sheep's milk cheeses. They also make goat's milk Halloumi and mixed-milk versions. Their cheeses have a rich flavour and a texture that is yielding rather than squeaky.

Halloumi has become such an important industry for Cyprus that the government secured a PDO from the EU in 2021 specifying that Halloumi can only be made on the island.

Happy days for Cypriot cheesemakers you might think, but the authorities were keen to preserve traditional Halloumi production, so the rules specify that the quantity of sheep and goat's milk used to make the cheese must be more than cow's milk. Cheesemakers that use more than 50 per cent cow's milk thus teamed up with representatives from the farming sector to sound dire warnings that there were simply not enough sheep and goats on the island to meet demand. There is currently a transitional period in place, which runs out in 2029, designed to give those cheesemakers time to switch over, but feelings still run high. Sheep and goat farmers have taken to the streets in protest at the delays, dumping milk and setting fire to hay bales. They argue that their more traditional Halloumi is being unfairly undermined by the cheaper cow's milk cheeses in the transitional period.

And just in case you were wondering . . . The noise that you get from Halloumi is due to its low acidity and high calcium content, which keeps the casein proteins firmly cemented together. This creates a dense, rubbery texture that not only stops the cheese from melting but also rubs against the enamel of your teeth, creating the famous squeak. PM

Huguenot

As we saw earlier with Selles-sur-Cher and Sauvignon Blanc from the Loire Valley (see page 91), when you're not sure which wine to serve with a cheese, it's a good idea to follow the principle of 'what grows together goes together'.

But why does this principle hold true? The explanation lies in terroir: the idea that geography and climate are responsible for the flavours found in the food and drink we love. However, there is an argument that terroir extends beyond purely environmental factors. Food scholars make the case that socio-political influences, such as migration, trade and cultural exchange, also leave their mark on a region's flavours.

Which brings us to South Africa, famous for its wine, and increasingly for its cheese. The Dutch colonised South Africa in 1652, when the Dutch East India Company established a trading post at the Cape of Good Hope, and they controlled the colony until 1795, when the British took over. Among the early European settlers were the Huguenots, French Protestants fleeing religious persecution. Between 1688 and the 1690s, around 300 Huguenots settled in the Franschhoek Valley, where they brought with them centuries-old viticultural expertise and agricultural knowledge. Their influence played a defining role in shaping South Africa's wine and dairy industries, which continues today.

Huguenot cheese was developed in the early 2000s by Rob and Petrina Visser at Dalewood Fromage, a 25-hectare (62-acre) second-generation estate in Klapmuts in the heart of South Africa's Cape Winelands. Rob, inspired by a visit to France's Haute-Savoie region, fell in love with the robust, nutty character of traditional mountain cheeses. Determined to craft a South African equivalent, he developed Huguenot, a 25kg (55lb) hard cheese made from rich Jersey cow's milk. Cheese judge Kobus Mulder, in his 2013 book *Cheeses of South Africa*, described it as 'something between an Abondance and a Beaufort'.

Huguenot develops butterscotch and nutty flavours, with distinctive umami depth, that intensify with maturation after just six months. Unlike its European counterparts, which often require longer ageing, Huguenot achieves complexity relatively quickly, due to the warmer climate of the Western Cape. Over the years it has become a modern South

African classic, winning multiple national dairy awards and earning a place on the shelves of Woolworths, the country's leading speciality supermarket.

Beyond cheesemaking, the Vissers are known for their commitment to regenerative farming. Their rotational grazing system ensures biodiverse pastures, and they have recorded 14 different plant species in their fields.

Can we call Huguenot a distinctly South African cheese? I believe so, not only because of the unique terroir of the Western Cape, but also because its story is shaped by more than just geography. This is where the socio-political realities of South Africa today play a role. The country's cheese industry has long incorporated international expertise, adapting techniques from European traditions while navigating the complexities of its past. Post-apartheid land reform and agricultural equity remain pressing issues, and South African cheesemakers operate within this evolving landscape. The tension between maintaining agricultural success and addressing historical injustices is a daily reality for food producers in the Rainbow Nation.

Huguenot cheese is proof that terroir is more than just soil and climate – it's also the history, people and cultural crossroads that define a place.

And if you were going to pair it? An oaked Chenin Blanc (a grape with its own French back story) from Stellenbosch would be perfect. CY

ORIGIN: Western Cape, South Africa
PROTECTED STATUS: N/A
MILK: Pasteurised cow's milk
RENNET: Vegetarian
AROMA: Buttery, earthy
FLAVOUR: Butterscotch, nutty, umami
TEXTURE: Smooth, firm, creamy
MATCH: South African Chenin Blanc works well, or a light red, such as Pinot Noir. Cured meats emphasise the cheese's savoury flavour. Pass the biltong!

WORLD CHEESE AWARDS: Super Gold 2010, 2014, 2017

Kilembe

We had spent the entire morning judging cheese. The first round had just concluded at the World Cheese Awards in Bergen, Norway, in 2018, but rather than stepping away, some judges lingered, eager to sample more. After tasting 50 cheeses each, you have to admire their stamina.

When someone encounters a remarkable cheese, word spreads quickly, and small samples are passed around. On this particular morning, one hard goat's cheese started to generate a buzz. Its rind featured the image of a Maasai figure in traditional attire against the backdrop of a vivid sunset. The questions on everyone's minds: could this cheese be from Africa? And if so, where exactly?

The Maasai are semi-nomadic people from Kenya and Tanzania, known for their ancient goat- and cattle-herding traditions. Over time, their way of life has faced challenges, as governments and settlers have encroached on their ancestral lands. And while Maasai gastronomy includes a fermented milk drink called *kule naoto* (a naturally soured milk), they do not traditionally produce rennet-set cheese. This only served to deepen my curiosity about the cheese in question. Determined to learn more, I made a mental note to investigate after the awards had concluded.

The cheese under such scrutiny was Kilembe, a 3kg (6.5lb) wheel crafted by Rina and Norman Belcher at Belnori Boutique Cheesery in South Africa. Its profile immediately brought to mind traditional Italian hard goat's milk cheeses like Sardinian Capra d'Oro, yet Kilembe carried a distinctive identity with buttery and nutty notes. Aged for six months, it developed a firm, crumbly texture, ideal for shaving.

Rina's personal history is based in East

ORIGIN: Gauteng, South Africa
PROTECTED STATUS: N/A
MILK: Pasteurised goat's milk
RENNET: Vegetarian
AROMA: Milky, buttery, toasted
FLAVOUR: Buttery, vegetable, nutty
TEXTURE: Crumbly, dry, firm

MATCH: Pinot Noir or red ale. Serve shaved over salads and grilled vegetables.

WORLD CHEESE AWARDS: Super Gold and Best South African 2018

Africa. She was born in Zambia, raised in Uganda, and educated in Kenya. When we spoke, she reflected on the breathtaking landscapes of her childhood and her desire to honour them. This vision materialised in a range of cheeses named after significant landmarks. Kilembe pays tribute to the historic mines near Lake Victoria, while the Serengeti and Kilimanjaro are immortalised in other cheeses. Norman, originally from South Africa, relocated the family to Gauteng province in 1979, where they ultimately built their cheesemaking legacy.

They started out in 2003, seeking a fresh start from corporate jobs. Now in their seventies, they continue to produce exceptional cheeses from their small herd of Saanen goats on their farm in Bapsfontein in north-east South Africa, between Pretoria and Johannesburg.

Belnori's range is impressive: they have 19 distinct products, including yoghurt and cheeses made from goat and cow's milk, a testament to Rina's boundless curiosity.

Their dedication has earned them international recognition, with multiple medals. At home, they are a dominant force in the Agri-Expo awards, consistently winning medals for many of their cheeses. With Kilembe's international success, it is evident that South Africa's cheesemaking potential is just beginning to be fully recognised. CY

Kraftkar

ORIGIN: Møre og Romsdal, Norway
PROTECTED STATUS: N/A
MILK: Pasteurised cow's milk
RENNET: Animal
AROMA: Creamy, earthy, mineral
FLAVOUR: Buttery, savoury, hint of blue mould
TEXTURE: Creamy, crumbly
MATCH: Serve with Norwegian flatbread, pickles and preserves for an easy lunch. Pairs nicely with coffee or a Bock-style beer.

WORLD CHEESE AWARDS: Multiple awards, including World Champion 2016

If you need proof of why the World Cheese Awards matter, then Gunnar Waagen's response as his Kraftkar cheese won the top prize says it all. The look of shock and joy on his face on that day in San Sebastián in 2016 was an unforgettable moment.

Kraftkar is a 1.8kg (4lb) blue cheese wheel made with pasteurised milk from Norwegian Red Cows and aged for a minimum of six months. The rind is mottled grey with a light blue hue, making it look like a fjord rock. The paste inside is cream in colour, with blue-greenish veins running from rind to rind. Its earthy and mineral aromas are matched by buttery and savoury notes on the palate, thanks to cream being added to the milk before curdling it, giving it an extra rich texture. It is a blue cheese that is easy to love.

It's made by Tingvollost, a family dairy in the village of Torjulvågen in northern Norway. Saghaug Farm has been here since 1303, and is now run by Waagen's daughter Kristin, alongside a hardworking group of female cheesemakers. The cheese was invented by Solvor Waagen, Kristin's mother, who in 2003 started making cheese from the farm's milk. By 2006, the demand for their cheese had convinced them to build a new dairy on their property.

But let's go back to the day Kraftkar won at the World Cheese Awards.

This was the first time a Norwegian cheese had won the competition, so there was a roar from the crowd in the hall. There was a particularly loud howl from one handsome older man, wearing a patterned *lusekofte* jumper, who came down the stairs from the audience towards the stage crying tears of joy. It was his cheese that had won! The moment was hugely emotional, immortalised in pictures of Gunnar Waagen holding his trophy aloft. The headlines around the world read 'Norwegian blue is the best in the world'.

Many small cheesemakers have mentioned Waagen's win as inspiring hope that their cheese could also win big one day. The pictures show him wearing a Basque beret presented to him by the local farmers, a simple act that speaks to the camaraderie between producers. At that moment Kraftkar was the best in the world. We all knew we had discovered a true gem.

Norway went on to host the World Cheese Awards twice after Kraftkar's win, in Bergen and Trondheim, and two other Norwegian cheeses have won the top honour since: Fanaost, a Gouda-style cheese, in 2018, and another blue, Nidelven Blå, in 2023. Now the country and its cheesemaking culture is recognised as world class.

Norway has a complex dairy history, with evidence of cheesemaking during the Viking

Age. The rough terrain and cool climate are suitable conditions for small cattle breeds, like the now endangered Vestlandsk Fjordfe or the Vestlandsk Raukolle. During the early 1900s, Norwegian breeders sought to improve cattle genetics by crossbreeding these and other native cattle with international breeds like Swedish Reds, Danish Reds and Ayrshires.

These efforts led to the development of the Norsk Rødt Fe (NRF) – the Norwegian Red breed – in 1935, which is now the dominant dairy cattle breed in the country, known for its high milk production, excellent fertility, and strong disease resistance.

Alongside these efforts, farmers realised they also needed better organisation for milk collection, processing and distribution. In 1928, small dairy co-operatives joined forces to create a larger organisation that would eventually rebrand as Tine, now Norway's largest dairy co-operative. Tine's best-selling product overseas is Jarlsberg, a semi-hard cheese with nutty flavours and big eyes. The company collects cow's milk from almost every dairy farm in the country willing to sell it, giving thousands of farmers a secure income.

Parallel to the system of ensured collection and standardised cheese production, there have always been *gårdsysteri* – farmstead cheesemakers that are a crucial part of rural life in many parts of the country. Artisan producers prioritise sustainability, while integrating modern technology and cheesemaking techniques. The recognition from the awards has shone a light on their hard work and encouraged others to start making their own cheeses.

Along with a group of female cheese professionals and guided by goat's cheese maker Kathrin Aslaksby, we toured a couple of farmstead cheese producers in the autumn of 2023 ahead of the competition in Trondheim. Our visit to Tingvollost was special, as we learnt about the support and recognition from the local community for Kristin Waagen's hard work and dedication to her small herd.

In this remote region of Norway, on a wall in the small café adjacent to their maturation facility, there is a large picture of Gunnar Waagen holding his trophy. He towers over the crowd, making him look rather like a *kraftkar* (strongman), the nickname given to the legendary Tore Nordbø, a medieval farmhand and Norwegian folklore hero, renowned for his extraordinary strength and size. And now for a blue cheese, named in his honour. CY

Moliterno al Tartufo

Flavoured cheeses have their critics, but there is one ingredient that seems to avoid the controversy. Truffle-infused cheeses are often the exception that proves the rule for people who would normally turn their nose up at cheese with added flavours.

This contradiction might be explained by truffle's reputation as an exclusive and expensive ingredient. Who can resist the story of truffle hunters and their keen-nosed dogs foraging in the earth for the prized fungus? Or perhaps it's just that truffle and cheese do go remarkably well together; there's something about the powerful perfume of truffle that fits with the savoury deliciousness of cheese.

This is evident when you slice into a wheel of Moliterno al Tartufo. From the outside this rustic cheese from Sardinia, which is made by Central Formaggi, looks like a traditional Pecorino, but the pale interior is laced with dramatic black veins of truffle paste. And the striking appearance is matched by its flavour. The sweet, semi-hard sheep's milk cheese, which is aged for around six months, is supercharged by the summer truffles, which bring intense notes of earth, wild mushrooms and garlic.

A decadent truffled Pecorino feels like something the Romans would have enjoyed as part of a Bacchanalian banquet, but Moliterno al Tartufo is actually a relative newcomer. Named after a town in Basilicata in southern Italy, the cheese has a history stretching back to the nineteenth century when it was made as a simple Pecorino without truffles. As the country industrialised, sheep numbers in the area fell and cheesemakers began searching further afield for milk.

One of these makers was the great-grandfather of the current owners of Central Formaggi, who sailed to Sardinia, where sheep outnumber people, in search of good milk.

ORIGIN: Sardinia, Italy
PROTECTED STATUS: N/A
MILK: Pasteurised sheep's milk
RENNET: Animal
AROMA: Buttery, earthy, piquant
FLAVOUR: Sharp, savoury, perfumed
TEXTURE: Fudgy, toothsome

MATCH: Full-bodied reds, such as Primitivo, stand up to the intensity of the cheese. A punchy accompaniment, such as spicy honey or wholegrain mustard, is required.

WORLD CHEESE AWARDS: Silver 2013, Bronze 2014, Gold 2015

He began producing Moliterno cheese on the island, where the company he founded continues to make it today in hand-woven *giunco* (reed) basket moulds, which leave a rustic imprint on the rind.

The clever idea of enriching Moliterno with black truffles didn't happen until much later, however, and relied heavily on a novel technique that is shrouded in mystery. Developed by Efisio Villecco (the father of current owners Piergiorgio and Jon Villecco) in the early 2000s, truffles from Abruzzo and Molise are blended to a paste, which is then injected into cheeses that have already been aged for around four months.

This sounds like a relatively simple process, but the black truffle veins that marble the interior of Moliterno al Tartufo are remarkably clear and distinct compared to other similar cheeses. There are usually two main ways of adding truffles to hard cheeses. You can sprinkle them into the curd and then make the cheese before ageing. Or you age the cheese with nothing in it and then break it up, add the flavouring and then reform it in a mould. Either way, the interior ends up being speckled with black flecks of truffle rather than a spider's web of veins.

The close texture of a four-month Pecorino leaves very little room for truffle paste to be injected, which suggests that perhaps the cheese is made in a way that leaves internal fissures that can be filled, or perhaps special machinery for piercing the cheese is involved.

The truth is that nobody knows apart from the Villecco family, and they are understandably keeping their cards close to their chest. Whatever their method, it's proved extremely profitable. Moliterno al Tartufo is sold by cheesemongers around the world, who would baulk at many flavoured cheeses, but are more than happy to make an exception for one with such defined veins of truffle. PM

Mont d'Or

If you've ever tasted Mont d'Or, you know it's more than just a cheese – it's an experience. Nestled in a wooden box, its aroma is seductive, earthy and unmistakable. Its luxurious, spoonable texture begs you to dip crusty bread in it, each bite a creamy indulgence. What's more, it's only available seasonally, making it feel all the more special.

Mont d'Or takes its name from a mountain in the Jura region, a stunning, forested stretch close to the Alps, spanning from Bourgogne-Franche-Comté in France to the Swiss cantons of Vaud, Jura and Neuchâtel. The elevation varies between 500 and 1,700 metres (1,640 and 5,575 feet), making the terrain rugged, hilly and deeply arboreal. For centuries, pastures at this high altitude served as summer grazing lands, freeing up valleys to grow seasonal crops. Once cooler temperatures started to settle in, cattle were brought down and fed dried hay. The milk of the summer is used to produce Alpine cheeses like Comté (see page 63), while autumn and winter milk is used to make smaller cheeses like Mont d'Or.

The mountain gave its name to Vacherin Mont D'Or. In 1981, France protected the name under its AOC (now PDO) regime, eliciting complaints from the Swiss, who argued that the cheese was also part of their heritage. France eventually amended its regulations and adopted two separate names for the cheese: Vacherin du Haut-Doubs, referring to a region near the border with Switzerland, and Mont D'Or after the mountain.

Meanwhile, the Swiss retained the name Vacherin Mont d'Or and were granted AOP status in 2003. While this distinction may seem minor, the protected designations carry significant differences. French PDO regulations require the use of raw milk, with production permitted from August 15 to March 15, and sales allowed between September 10 and May 10. Swiss AOP standards, on the other hand, allow for thermised milk and follow the same production timeline, though sales typically end in April. Despite these differences, both versions are exclusively made from Montbéliarde and Simmental cow's milk and aged for a minimum of 21 days.

This difference in milk treatment, alongside slight variations in the cheesemaking process, make the French cheese firmer, with more barnyard flavours and woody aromas. Both versions are made by wrapping spruce bark strips around the circular cheese to hold it together as it matures. As the cheese ages, the wood imbues the interior with a distinct smoky and resinous flavour. The washing of the rind encourages umami flavours to develop, making the cheese very meaty and animal.

The spruce bark strips, essential to Mont d'Or's signature flavour, are harvested by *sangliers d'écorce* (foresters), who specialise in managing the local spruce trees – in both the French Haut-Doubs area and in the Vaud canton in Switzerland. They carefully strip the cambium layer beneath the bark, not only for shaping the cheese but also to encourage sustainable tree growth. This delicate process takes place from spring to early summer, ensuring the bark is supple enough to wrap around the fresh cheese.

In 2022, I had one of the great moments of my cheese judging career, when I was invited to be a Supreme Judge of the Swiss Cheese Awards in Verbier, south-western Switzerland. My table included 12 samples of Vacherin Mont d'Or – a daunting but delicious exercise. Thankfully, my team was headed by a professor known for her expertise in this style. Each wheel we tasted was almost perfect, but we deducted points for rinds that were too moist, or when the bark was separating from the cheese, a sign it was drying too quickly. The rinds needed to be orange to golden in colour; little amounts of white mould were the mark of a cheese getting past its best. If the cheese rind was pinkish, it was close to its peak and should be consumed promptly. The interior should look bright. Dull or grey paste meant the cheese would be acrid. Little blue or green moulds on the bark were okay, but these should not be growing on the cheese itself.

These are all great tell-tale signs to look for the next time you choose Mont d'Or, whether it's French or Swiss. A true seasonal treat. CY

ORIGIN: Jura region, France and Switzerland

PROTECTED STATUS: PDO France, AOP Switzerland

MILK: Raw or unpasteurised cow's milk

RENNET: Animal

AROMA: Woodsy, earthy, pungent

FLAVOUR: Creamy, grassy, meaty

TEXTURE: Soft, gooey, silky

MATCH: Pair with a Sancerre or Gewürztraminer. Best served slightly warm with roasted potatoes and crusty bread.

WORLD CHEESE AWARDS: Multiple awards, including Super Gold 2016

Montagnolo Affine

I love creamy, bloomy-rind cheeses, and can't live without blue cheese. The makers of Montagnolo Affine know that I am not alone and invented this cheese to appeal to all of our desires. It's a cheese designed to be loved, just like its more famous sibling: Cambozola.

Montagnolo Affine was developed in 1990 by the Champignon-Hofmeister Group, a family-owned company focusing on commercial cheeses for speciality retailers. Their operation is large, sourcing milk from 1,000 farms in Bavaria and Saxony in south-east Germany. The 2kg (4.5lb) cheese has a buttery soft texture and mineral-umami flavour, a light grey rind and bright-white interior dotted with blue mould. Its rich flavour is due in large part to the fact that double cream is added to the whole milk, making it what is known as a triple cream cheese.

At the World Cheese Awards every cheese is judged blind, but some are easily recognisable. There's no mistaking a Parmigiano Reggiano or a round of Stilton. When judges do recognise a cheese, it is important they give an unbiased score. Still, some flavour profiles appeal to judges from specific regions more than others. There's a good chance that a judge from Portugal will know and love the *torta*-style sheep's milk cheeses, such as Serra da Estrela (see page 196), that they have been raised on, but might find a hunk of farmhouse Cheddar a strange and mysterious thing, and vice versa.

Other personal factors may also come into play. Studies show that taste buds deteriorate with age and, along with the effects of lifestyle choices like smoking or drinking, some judges may have a more nuanced palate than others. Similarly, the professional background of each judge determines the way they approach the task. A trained chef may judge based on how a cheese could be used in a recipe, while a dairy

scientist may look for flaws and attributes in the cheesemaking technique. For this reason it is important to have balanced teams of judges, whose areas of expertise complement each other. Award-winning cheeses are those that appeal to many different palates. Large commercial dairy companies understand this and consider it during their research and development (R&D) of new products. It is a competitive market out there for new cheese styles.

This brings us back to Montagnolo Affine, which won the World Champion title in Birmingham, UK, in 2013, and also the top prize at the International Cheese Awards the year before. When it won at the World Cheese Awards, there were 2,777 cheeses from 30 countries in the competition. A couple of dozen or so were selected as candidates to win the top award by the first panels of judges. The Super Jury then tasted these final cheeses and found two of them remarkably similar. We voted, and once the results were out, Montagnolo Affine had won first and second place. The producer had entered the cheese in two different categories. This is a remarkable feat. Not once, but twice, the cheese had convinced judges that it was the best cheese in the competition. We don't remember any other cheese performing this well at the awards. In fact, the rules changed after this event to prevent producers entering the same cheese in different categories. Having conquered the competition in such a resounding way, this cheese is considered an example of what good R&D can achieve. CY

ORIGIN: Bavaria, Germany
PROTECTED STATUS: N/A
MILK: Pasteurised cow's milk
RENNET: Vegetarian
AROMA: Earthy, mineral
FLAVOUR: Creamy, buttery, light tanginess
TEXTURE: Soft and gooey
MATCH: We prefer it with a dessert wine or a malt-forward beer. Enjoy it melted on a burger.

WORLD CHEESE AWARDS:
Multiple awards, including World Champion 2013

Monterey Jack

American cheese tends to have a bad reputation for being over-processed. And there's certainly no denying that the US is home to the Kraft Single and Velveeta, the famously processed products that stretch the definition of 'cheese' to its very limit. But there are other cheeses that sometimes get lumped in with these plasticky inventions that deserve our attention.

This is especially true of Monterey Jack. This cheese has many origin stories, but it would seem as though it was first made by Spanish settlers living in California in the 1700s, during the colonial period. Records indicate that the cheese was made in a Franciscan monastery in the town of Monterey in northern California.

It was sold fresh and without a rind and may have got its name from a Scottish businessman, David Jacks, who started selling the cheese commercially and exporting it out of northern California. Records show that in 1882, Jacks sold cheeses labelled 'Jack's Monterey'. However, there were also other sellers, including Andrew Molera, who had a production plant in Big Sur.

Monterey Jack is pale white with a buttery and aromatic paste – very much like a young Mahón from the Balearic Islands. It is now mostly sold pre-sliced for sandwiches, but can be found in 5kg (11lb) wheels or 2.5kg (5.5lb) rectangular blocks. There are also variants such as Pepper Jack, flavoured with chillies, peppers and herbs, and blended cheeses, including Colby Jack (Monterey Jack marbled with the orange Cheddar-like cheese Colby) and Cheddar Jack. As the cheese ages it becomes more nutty and can resemble a young Parmigiano Reggiano, but with a sharp finish almost like a commercial Cheddar. This aged version is known as Dry Jack.

The story of the 'dry' version dates back to 1915 when D.F. DeBernardi, a San Francisco-

based cheese wholesaler, started selling an aged version to his mostly Italian-American clientele. Legend has it that he stumbled across the idea after forgetting about a few wheels of Monterey Jack cheeses at the back of his store for several months, which turned out to be delicious. The First World War had disrupted shipments from Europe to the US and there was the need for a grana-style cheese, such as Grana Padano or Parmigiano Reggiano. DeBernardi covered the aged cheeses in a mix of oil, pepper and an ebony pigment made from soot from oil lamps, called lamp black, presumably to make the cheese look and taste more rustic and piquant.

Thankfully, oil lamp soot is no longer used today. A more modern version of Dry Jack was developed by the Vella family in Sonoma, California, around the 1910s. Their aged cheese is rubbed with a paste made of unsweetened cocoa powder and black pepper, then matured for up to a year by placing it sideways and rotating it often. There's also an extra-aged version called Golden Bear that is aged for two to four years until it is hard, brittle and crystalline. It's a very different beast to standard Monterey Jack, which spends just a couple of months in the maturing room and is supple and buttery.

Monterey Jack is regarded as an American Original, crafted in the US without adhering to any specific European tradition. Young cheeses melt into a velvety puddle on burgers and steaks, while Dry Jack works a treat shaved over salad or grated on pasta, just as DeBernardi's customers would have enjoyed it over 100 years ago. CY

ORIGIN: California, USA
PROTECTED STATUS: N/A
MILK: Pasteurised cow's milk
RENNET: Vegetarian
AROMA: Monterey Jack: buttery, aromatic; Dry Jack: earthy, nutty
FLAVOUR: Creamy, nutty, sweet
TEXTURE: Monterey Jack: firm, creamy; Dry Jack: hard, oily
MATCH: Pair with a California Chardonnay or an IPA beer. You can shave the aged version on top of pasta and salads, or CalMex food.

WORLD CHEESE AWARDS: Gold 2013 (Dry Jack from Vella Cheese Company)

Panela

For my first book, *Quesos Mexicanos*, I researched over 30 Mexican cheeses. It took over three years to complete and was a wonderful way to understand my country of origin. The hardest cheese to document was Panela. It is such a ubiquitous cheese in Mexican cuisine, especially in the Bajío region, Morelos and Tlaxcala states, and Mexico City, that there are no specific records of its origin.

The cheese is pale white, fresh and crumbly. There are wheels as small as 250g (9oz) and as big as 5kg (11lb), made using skimmed or full-fat cow's milk, but also goat's milk. It is delicious grilled, as a stuffing in *chiles rellenos*, and by itself as a snack. Many dietitians recommend it in Mexico for folks trying to lose weight, as it is high in protein and low in fat.

In my research, I found that Mexican revolutionaries ate Panela as part of their rations. It was easy to make near the front lines or in towns where trains would move goods closer to the troops. During the early decades of the twentieth century most Panela was made with goat's milk in the states of Guanajuato and Queretaro, in the Bajío region north of Mexico City. After the revolution, the cheese became popular in the centre of the country, and it started being produced with cow's milk. Today it is a staple, along with another famous cheese called Quesillo de Hebra, also known as Queso Oaxaca.

When I was growing up, my maternal grandmother would keep a piece of Panela under a fabric napkin outside of the fridge. After a couple of days, the cheese would start developing a soft, orange rind with savoury notes. When I close my eyes, I can hear my grandmother making food and cutting a small piece of cheese to let it soften on top of a warm tortilla.

The process of letting this cheese air dry is known as *oreado*, a traditional method of

ORIGIN: Bajío region, Mexico
PROTECTED STATUS: N/A
MILK: Pasteurised cow's and goat's milk
RENNET: Animal or vegetarian
AROMA: Fresh milk, briny
FLAVOUR: Citrussy, creamy, umami
TEXTURE: Chewy, soft, crumbly

MATCH: Brings freshness to spicy dishes and sauces. Pair it with mezcal or a lager.

WORLD CHEESE AWARDS: Bronze 2016 (La Consentida), Super Gold 2017 (Quesos Navarro)

preserving cheeses. Airing cheeses this way is not an uncommon technique in other regions too, where refrigeration is limited or not necessary. I have also seen cheeses treated in similar ways in India and Peru, as well as in Italy and France. In Mexico, Panela Oreado has fallen out of favour, as most people prefer it fresh; the more industrialised versions become bitter from the enzymes used if left to age.

I missed the cheese from my youth, so I helped Judith Flores, a producer in Guanajuato state, to make something similar. Her company, La Consentida, won a Bronze medal at the World Cheese Awards in 2016. The next year another Panela made by Quesos Navarro won a Super Gold and competed in the last 16 cheeses.

While these two cheeses are wonderful, there is a lot of bad-quality Panela sold in Mexico and the US. For a cheese this fresh – normally eaten five days after making without any maturation – cheesemakers need very high-quality milk. It's such a pure cheese that there is nowhere to hide if the milk isn't up to scratch. This translates into higher farming costs, which many consumers are unwilling to pay for an everyday cheese.

Panela, along with other fresh cheeses, has a hard time competing at international competitions because it is so subtle that it is often drowned out when compared to the bold flavours of blue and aged cheeses. But the Guild of Fine Food has tried to give this style of cheese a fighting chance. Since 2010, there has been a consolidation point in Mexico City for entries from across the country. This ensures that cheese travels in the proper conditions and is in the best shape possible when it arrives to be judged.

We are including Panela here to shed a light on both the cheese and on Mexican cheesemaking culture. Like many other countries in Latin America, the country has a diverse cheese industry with recipes as old as 200 years. I am convinced a Latin American cheese will one day win the World Champion title – and maybe the One Cheese to Rule Them All will be from Mexico. CY

Paški Sir

ORIGIN: Pag, Croatia
PROTECTED STATUS: PDO
MILK: Raw and pasteurised sheep's milk
RENNET: Animal or vegetarian
AROMA: Animal, herbaceous, acidic
FLAVOUR: Roasted lamb, dried sage, piquant
TEXTURE: Crumbly, grainy
MATCH: Full-bodied Croatian reds work well, such as those made from native Plavac Mali grapes. Serve with quince jam or grate over pasta.

WORLD CHEESE AWARDS: Multiple awards, including Best New Cheese 2010, Super Gold 2018 (Gligora Dairy)

The Croatian island of Pag in the Adriatic is picture-postcard beautiful thanks to pristine beaches, azure waters and a rugged interior that is home to a cornucopia of wild flowers and herbs. But before you book your summer holiday, spare a thought for the farmers there.

While the landscape is idyllic, its poor limestone soil makes it a tough place to grow crops, while the fierce Bora wind can be so strong that it is said to blow fish from the sea onto the island. The rocky terrain is not a problem, however, for a particularly hardy breed of sheep that has evolved over centuries to suit the island's conditions. Shaggy white Pag sheep are so tough they can survive on tiny amounts of food and by drinking salt water. They're a common sight on the island as they pick their way through the barren rocks to nibble on yarrow, fennel, mint and sage; more than 330 different plant species have been recorded in Pag, which are seasoned with salt blown in from the surrounding sea.

This combination of climate, breed and diet create an exceptionally creamy, aromatic milk, used to make Croatia's most famous cheese, Paški Sir (pronounced 'Pashki Seer' and meaning 'cheese from Pag'), protected by a PDO in 2019. Made in 3.5kg (8lb) wheels, the outside of the hard cheese is often rubbed in olive oil (another success story on the island), before being aged between 2 to 24 months.

Young cheeses have a flexible texture and mild, sweet flavour, but it's in the hard, grainy aged cheeses that Paški Sir really comes into its own. Some of the sweetness remains, but there's also a spicy tang to the cheese, plus salty and roasted lamb notes, and a wonderful aromatic herby flavour that comes straight from the rocks of Pag.

According to the PDO, the cheese never has the 'barnyard' aroma that you find in other sheep's milk cheeses because the animals graze outdoors all year round (most livestock are housed in barns in the winter). The cheese also has a distinct umami flavour thanks to a compound called succinic acid, derived from the herbs eaten by the sheep – a flavour that is not found in other sheep's cheese made in Croatia. Roasted Pag lamb is also a delicacy on the island for many of the same flavourful reasons. PM

Rogue River Blue

Wine aficionados have probably heard of the 1976 Judgment of Paris. To celebrate the United States' Bicentennial, a group of merchants organised a blind tasting for French wine experts in Paris to compare wines from France and the US. The results shook the wine world, when two Napa Valley wines were selected as winners of the competition ahead of their French counterparts.

A similar seismic shift occurred in the world of cheese in 2019, when an American cheese claimed the title of World Champion at the World Cheese Awards.

That cheese was Rogue River Blue – a blue cheese wrapped in Syrah grape leaves soaked in pear spirit – made by Rogue Creamery in Oregon. Each 2.25kg (5lb) wheel is aged for a minimum of nine months and released annually around the autumnal equinox. Over time, the blue mould transforms the interior to a fudgy paste, and the long ageing period helps create small crystals that give the cheese a unique crunch. The combination of the grape leaves and pear spirit provides a deep earthy and boozy aroma to the cheese.

The grape leaves, sourced from nearby vineyards, are applied just as the cheese is to be released. Hand-wrapping it in this way is the final step in a meticulous process designed to create a cheese with a true vintage. Each year, the cheese develops subtle variations, shaped by changes in the organic milk, the ageing process, and the way it absorbs flavours from the leaves and spirit.

The atmosphere in Bergamo on competition day in 2019 was electric. Italy was hosting for the first time, and local producers were eager to claim victory on home soil. Outside the judging hall, a busy trade show had stalls from Italy's biggest cheese brands, with public tastings and business meetings – everyone waiting for the final results to be announced.

As the Super Jury tasted the cheeses in the final, a flawless sample of Parmigiano Reggiano arrived (although cheeses are judged blind, there is no mistaking real Parmigiano Reggiano). It was a cheese so perfect in structure and aroma that it seemed destined to take the top prize. Indeed, the cheese was leading the final until the very last sample was tasted. Then along came a bold blue cheese, championed by judge Bruno Cabral of Brazil. The panel tasted and the scores were tallied. The room fell silent. There was a tie for first place.

After a tie in 2001 resulted in two winners, the competition's rules had been changed. Now, the final decision rested in the hands of Nigel Barden, a long-time judge and charismatic presenter of the awards. He walked off stage to taste both cheeses, considered the choice before him and, like the rest of the panel, was delighted by the blue cheese, voting for the blue over the Parmigiano Reggiano – a brave move considering the hundreds of expectant Italian cheese-lovers in the audience.

He went back on stage to reveal his decision and the official announcement was made: Rogue River Blue was the winner. A blue cheese from the US had just defeated one of the most revered cheeses in Italy and the world. There was a stunned silence in the hall before Italian flags were quickly folded up and put away, and the room emptied in double quick time. It was as if Italy had just lost the football World Cup Final to the US on penalties.

ORIGIN: Oregon, USA
PROTECTED STATUS: N/A
MILK: Pasteurised cow's milk
RENNET: Vegetarian
AROMA: Boozy, creamy, earthy
FLAVOUR: Toffee, savoury, mineral
TEXTURE: Fudgy and soft, with small crystals that give it a light, crunchy feel
MATCH: Pair with Viognier or a bourbon-based cocktail. Serve with hazelnuts and honey.

WORLD CHEESE AWARDS: Multiple awards, including World Champion 2019

Cathy Strange, another member of the Super Jury representing the US, was not deterred, calling winner David Gremmels on the phone to tell him the good news, thereby creating a new tradition where the winning cheesemaker is contacted immediately. Gremmels was bailing hay on the farm in the early morning darkness when he got the call, mistaking it for a prank at first. The result was headline news in Italy and the US the next day, with the story going viral in the weeks and months after, helping to put American cheese in the spotlight internationally.

Rogue Creamery traces its origins to 1933 and was owned for many years by the Vella family. Ignazio 'Ig' Vella, who took over the reins from his father in 1998, was committed to craft skills and became a key figure in the renaissance of cheesemaking in the US. Known as 'the godfather of artisan cheese', Vella sold the business to David Gremmels in 2002 and mentored him in the art of cheesemaking. Gremmels was obviously a quick learner because the newly created Rogue River Blue, made to highlight the terroir of the Rogue Valley, was named the Best Blue Cheese at the World Cheese Awards in 2003.

The original recipe called for raw seasonal milk, a decision that set the cheese apart, and Gremmels' commitment to raw milk cheese production was key to the early success of his company. His advocacy, however, made the company a target of US regulators, who have often discouraged raw milk cheese production during the past 70 years. Facing mounting regulatory pressure and the need to expand market access, the company ultimately transitioned to using pasteurised milk for broader distribution.

In an ironic twist, the cheese that won in 2019 had been made with pasteurised milk and inadvertently submitted to the competition. Gremmels' original intention was to enter the raw milk version, but a mix-up in the shipping department would change the course of events. And while it was still possible to find raw milk versions in the US after the win, the conglomerate Savencia, which had purchased a controlling share of the company in 2018, decided to make the cheese using only pasteurised milk following Gremmels' retirement in 2023.

Rogue Creamery is a leading example of sustainable and ethical growth, becoming the first public benefit corporation (B Corp) in Oregon in 2014, and certified humane and USDA organic since 2016. The company's commitment comes from a mission to protect Southern Oregon's Rogue River Valley, part of the Klamath-Siskiyou region, recognised as one of the most diverse temperate coniferous forests globally.

Rogue River Blue paved the way for a new wave of boozy cheeses. Since 2019, we have seen a lot of innovation in this category, with cheesemakers experimenting with a range of spirits. More cheeses are being washed in beer and ciders, others submerged in wine or coated in grape must, while some even incorporate alcohol directly into the paste. As consumers seek bolder, more complex flavours, boozy cheeses are finding new fans. CY

St Tola Ash

As we saw with Milleens (see page 36) and Cashel Blue (see page 60), Irish cheese has undergone an extraordinary revival in the past 40 years. Farmhouse cheesemaking had died out completely in the post-war years, but thanks to pioneering producers such as Veronica Steele and the Grubb family, a new generation of artisan cheeses flourished, aided by a similarly dynamic restaurant scene.

Ireland was known as the Celtic Tiger in the late 1990s as its economy boomed on the back of foreign investment, which helped fuel an explosion of new restaurants. The period was marked by a new-found confidence in Irish food, led by the hugely influential Ballymaloe Cookery School in Cork, with chefs reinterpreting traditional Irish recipes using locally sourced ingredients.

It was great news for Irish cheesemakers, especially St Tola Farmhouse Cheese in County Clare. Former school teacher Siobhán Ní Ghháirbhith took over the business in 1999 at the peak of the boom and her zingy, lactic goat's logs were just what chefs and cheesemongers were looking for.

Made in easy-to-slice 1kg (2lb 3oz) and 600g (1lb 5oz) logs, St Tola Ash has a dark, wrinkly rind and smooth, creamy body that sings with citrus and yoghurt notes. A non-ash version is also made, simply called St Tola, which has a slightly more moist texture and golden rind.

Smear either on a slice of warm soda bread with a dollop of chutney and you have an instant gourmet snack. But they are also star ingredients in the kitchen, and can be used to add a fresh, creamy lift to all sorts of recipes. Ní Gháirbhith recommends stirring her cheese into pasta, as a filling for omelettes or in salads. She even uses it to make cheesecakes and chocolate mousse.

A fluent Irish speaker and advocate of Irish culture, who was brought up on the farm in Inagh, Clare, where the business is based today, Ní Gháirbhith is a charismatic force of nature with seemingly boundless levels of energy. A natural networker, she has that canny knack of being able to get round a room in no time, and have a legion of new friends at the end of it.

On top of making one of Ireland's most loved cheeses, she is also part of the organising committee of the country's farmhouse cheese association, Cáis, and helped found the Burren Food Trail and the Slow Food chapter in County Clare. She was quite rightly recognised with a Local Food Hero award from the Restaurant Association of Ireland in 2024.

When I visited her farm to meet her herd of goats and to see how her lactic cheeses are made, she explained to me that her love of local food and culture has always been fundamental to what she does. 'I'm a proud Clare woman with a strong sense of where I'm from,' she explained as we patted the downy white Saanen, Toggenburg and Alpine goats. 'I wanted a future for the farm and I could see the demand and potential for regional foods was growing.'

This local focus is clear to see at the farm (it's open for public visits). While intensively reared goat herds are often kept indoors their whole lives and given feed bought in from far and wide, the goats at St Tola graze 26 hectares (65 acres) of natural pastures during the summer, which are sprinkled with buttercups, meadow sweet and wild garlic.

They return to airy, straw-lined sheds in the winter where they are fed hay produced on the farm. It's this natural, home-grown diet that gives the milk and the final cheese its pure, clean flavour.

It's a similar approach in the dairy where the curds are formed in open vats and drained of whey in muslin bags – a simple method of cheesemaking that stretches back thousands of years. The maze-like mould that grows on the rind during maturation is also completely natural. Rather than adding ripening cultures to the milk, natural yeasts in the air colonise the surface over three weeks.

Watching Ní Gháirbhith delicately turn her cheeses to make sure the crinkly rind formed properly was to witness a true artisan at work. As she deftly rotated the wrinkly grey logs, she also explained how the cheese got its name. Apparently, St Tola is the eighth-century patron saint of Clare, also known as the 'saint of toothaches'. Legend has it that people would take a piece of stone from a local Celtic cross, dedicated to St Tola, and hold it against their mouths to cure toothache.

We'd rather have some smooth, creamy goat's cheese on a hunk of soda bread. PM

ORIGIN: County Clare, Ireland
PROTECTED STATUS: N/A
MILK: Raw and pasteurised goat's milk
RENNET: Animal or vegetarian
AROMA: Citrussy, floral, milky
FLAVOUR: Honey, milk, savoury
TEXTURE: Smooth, creamy
MATCH: A saline dry white wine, such as Muscadet Sèvre-et-Maine sur Lie, is a winner, or go for dry Irish cider. Beetroot and rhubarb are natural bedfellows.

WORLD CHEESE AWARDS:
Multiple awards, including Best Irish Cheese 2012, 2017

Takara no Takara

It was when Narumitsu Saito was learning to make cheese in the Jura in France that the penny dropped. The Japanese cheesemaker had visited this mountainous region of eastern France to learn more about its most famous cheese, Comté. He was immediately struck by how similar the rolling hills and valleys of the Jura Massif were to his home back in Hokkaido, where the family farm sits at the foot of the snow-capped volcano Mount Yōtei.

So when Saito returned to Japan to set up Takara Cheese Dairy in 2007, a Comté-style cheese was an obvious choice. Named after the farm in the beautiful Kimobetsu area, Takara no Takara (it means 'to nurture dreams') is a hard cheese made with milk from a herd of just 50 Holstein and Jersey cows, which are tended by Saito's older brother.

As in the Jura, the animals have plenty of space to roam and graze diverse pastures on the 20-hectare (50-acre) farm (there's a sign at the dairy proclaiming 'milk from happy cows'), while the cheese is made in a similar way to Comté in a copper vat with raw milk and the dairy's own starter cultures, which it makes in-house by fermenting leftover whey.

Saito has even built a clever maturing 'cave' cooled with around 35 tonnes (34 tons) of ice made by freezing huge trays of water during the winter. As the ice slowly melts during the warmer months, the cold water is piped into a cooling system to maintain a constant temperature in the maturing room.

But Takara no Takara is not Comté. The climate, geography and local flora of Kimobetsu are different to the Jura, as are the cows (Comté is made with milk from Montbéliarde and Simmental breeds). It means the cheese has its own distinct personality, according to Japanese cheese writer, educator and judge Kanako Mathys, who lives in England and is a mine of information on all things cheese.

ORIGIN: Hokkaido, Japan
PROTECTED STATUS: N/A
MILK: Raw cow's milk
RENNET: Animal
AROMA: Cooked milk, butter, toasted nuts
FLAVOUR: Caramel, umami, bonito flakes
TEXTURE: Smooth, silky
MATCH: Black coffee is a popular match in Japan, or go for an earthy Pinot Noir. Dried apricots work well with this style, but Saito likes to grate his cheese over rice with a few bonito flakes.

WORLD CHEESE AWARDS: Gold 2019

'It's a silkier version of a really good 18-month Comté,' she told me after returning from a trip to Japan. 'It isn't powerful at all, but there are layers of flavour that are well-balanced. Buttery with the sweetness of cooked milk and a toasty note. Sweet and umami come together, plus a subtle nuance of bonito flakes. It's a very elegant, magnificent cheese!'

For the uninitiated, bonito flakes, also known as katsuobushi, are shaved slivers of smoked and fermented skipjack tuna which are packed full of umami. It's an integral ingredient, along with kombu (dried kelp), in dashi, a broth that is used in Japanese sauces and soups. It's also a brilliant way to describe the savoury deliciousness you find in these kinds of Alpine cheeses.

Mathys' insightful tasting notes came after she tried Takara no Takara as a judge at the Japan Cheese Awards in 2024, where the cheese was named Supreme Champion. It also scooped a Gold medal at the World Cheese Awards in 2019.

Japanese success is no surprise when you discover how the country has embraced artisan cheesemaking in recent years. The number of small cheesemakers in the country has tripled to more than 350 since 2000, with a corresponding surge in entries to the World Cheese Awards, many of which have picked up awards.

Japan has eaten processed cheese since the 1950s as a legacy of the US occupation after the Second World War, when a school-lunch programme was introduced that included milk and cheese. But production of what is called 'natural cheese' has only really taken off since the millennium as Japanese diets have become more Westernised.

The growing interest was reflected by a cheese festival called 'Cheese Fun! Fan! Fun!', which ran alongside the Japan Cheese Awards in 2024. It was attended by more than 4,500 people in just a few days, who met cheesemakers, took part in workshops and tasted more than 200 cheeses while the results of the awards were eagerly awaited.

It's a sign of just how much the country's cheeses are evolving that many of the entries were inspired by Japanese ingredients and food culture, rather than just mimicking French *fromages*. Cheeses wrapped in cherry leaves, sprinkled with blossom or washed in sake were just some of those tasted by the cheese-loving public, although none was quite as 'elegant' or 'magnificent' as Takara no Takara. PM

Taupinette

ORIGIN: Poitou-Charentes, France
PROTECTED STATUS: N/A
MILK: Raw goat's milk
RENNET: Animal
AROMA: Fresh, earthy, minerally
FLAVOUR: Tangy, soured milk, grassy
TEXTURE: Soft and dense, turning runny and gooey
MATCH: Strawberries and raspberries are decadent pairings for this cheese. Enjoy with a glass of sparkling wine or a sour beer.

WORLD CHEESE AWARDS: Best Unpasteurised Cheese 2018

I remember the first time I walked into a *fromagerie* in Paris. The sight of so many cheeses was exciting, and also overwhelming. Some were easily recognisable, others totally new, yet the most exhilarating part for me was the soft goat's cheese section.

Depending on the time of year, you will find cheeses from the Loire Valley like Sainte-Maure-de-Touraine and Selles-sur-Cher (see page 91); from the Poitou-Charentes region like Chabichou du Poitou; or from the Auvergne such as Gaperon. Most of them are made with raw milk, although there is a growing trend to use thermised milk.

If you are lucky, you may also find Taupinette or her bigger sister Taupinière, both made by siblings and third-generation goat herders and cheesemakers Alain and Béatrice Jousseaume at Chèvrerie Jousseaume in Roullet-Saint-Estèphe in south-west France. Taupinette (which translates as 'small mole mound') is made with the milk of Alpine breed goats, and the small, half-sphere cheese resembles the earth mounds left behind by burrowing moles. It is a delicate cheese that ages rapidly, becoming gooey and silky with time. The flavour is earthy and tangy, with slight soured milk notes. A perfect cheese to eat on crusty bread or toss on top of grilled vegetables in the spring, or salads in the summer.

Compared to other soft goat's milk cheeses, Taupinette is a modern cheese. First crafted in 1998, it has won many awards, including Super Gold in 2018.

The only problem is that you are unlikely to see it in the US. That's because regulations over raw milk cheese production and sale in the country prohibit those made with unpasteurised milk if they have not been previously aged for a minimum of 60 days. It is an outdated rule that means Americans only ever get to taste pasteurised versions of France's most famous soft cheeses, unless they travel to Europe. But their nuances and differences can really only be tasted when the milk is left raw and the terroir of the cheese is left intact.

There are some US alternatives made with pasteurised milk that are similar in style. Wabash Cannonball made by Judy Schad and her team at Capriole Goat Cheese in Indiana is a particularly good one. It's a lovely wrinkly ball of zingy goat's cheese that always draws my eye on a cheese counter. CY

Torta del Casar

A cheese that speaks of western Spain's history and traditions, where sheep-rearing has been a practice for centuries. Before cotton production became widespread in the 1700s, sheep's wool and skins were the most common materials used to make fabric and clothes.

In Extremadura, shepherds reared Merino and Entrefino sheep to produce high-quality wool and suede leather from their skins. As other materials gained favour, prices for wool and leather fell and shepherds turned to milk production to make ends meet. Although records show that Torta del Casar was already being made in 1791, there was a sharp increase in milk production to make cheese once those socio-cultural aspects changed. Today, the cheese can only be made with the milk of these two breeds of ewes.

The cheese is made using thistle flower stems to curdle milk and give a distinct texture and flavour. The wheels are between 200g (7oz) and 1kg (2lb 3oz), depending on the producer, with a leathery exterior that has been created by rubbing with salt or submerging in brine. Sheep's milk cheeses made with thistle rennet are integral to the food culture of Spain and Portugal, collectively known as *tortas* because their round shape resembles a cake (*torta* in Spanish).

Torta del Casar originates from the Cáceres region in southern Extremadura. On the other side of the border, Portuguese *torta* cheeses like Amanteigado, Serra da Estrela (see page 196) and Azeitão use similar techniques.

The popularisation of thistle as a coagulant is credited to Iberian peninsula Jews, who, following kosher laws, sought to make dairy products without the use of animal rennet. Cheesemakers prepare a tea-like substance with the purple crowns of cardoon flowers (*Cynara cardunculus*) and add it to the fresh milk, which then magically transforms into curd. The thistle gives the final cheese a delicate herbal bitterness and breaks down the interior very quickly into a silky soup.

Slice the top off a Torta del Casar and you have instant cheese fondue, for scooping out with a spoon or bread. The fabric trade's loss is the cheese world's gain. CY

ORIGIN: Extremadura, Spain
PROTECTED STATUS: PDO
MILK: Raw sheep's milk
RENNET: Vegetarian (thistle)
AROMA: Sweet, vegetal, acidic
FLAVOUR: Buttery, herbal, artichoke
TEXTURE: Silky, soft, very runny
MATCH: Rioja and *guindillas* (pickled yellow chillies) are firm friends.

WORLD CHEESE AWARDS: Best Spanish 2019

La Tur

Wherever you are in Piedmont you are surrounded by good food and drink. The hills of this hilly north-west region of Italy are carpeted with vineyards and hazelnut groves, while a patchwork of paddy fields explains why risotto is a speciality of the region. Most famous of all are the white truffles that lie hidden underground like buried treasure in the rolling woodlands, waiting to be unearthed by *trifolau* (truffle hunters) and their expertly trained dogs.

There's plenty of reasons for cheese-lovers to visit, too. The campaign group Slow Food, which fights to protect and preserve traditional foods around the world, holds a spectacular cheese festival in its home town of Bra every two years, where the streets are lined with artisan cheesemakers.

There are also some lovely PDO-protected cheeses made in the region, including springy wheels of Bra, the crumbly blue Castelmagno, and soft, fluffy discs of Robiola di Roccaverano, made high up in the foothills of the Maritime Alps near the border with France.

All three allow for the addition of different milks. Robiola is mainly goat's milk, but cow and sheep's milk from local breeds are sometimes mixed in, while Bra and Castelmagno are predominantly cow's milk cheeses, but goat and sheep's milk can also be added.

This *laissez faire* approach to milk is a quirk of history and geography. Small farms would typically have a mix of animals to make the most of different types of pasture and to ensure they were not overly reliant on a single species. The farms were not big enough to make separate cheeses with the different milks, so would have just poured whatever they had from day to day into the same vat to make one cheese. The ratios would have changed depending on the season, with a higher percentage of sheep and goat's milk in the spring and summer when their milk is in full flow, but perhaps none at all in the late autumn when the animals had dried off and the cows were still producing.

La Tur, made by Caseificio dell'Alta Langa, close to the vineyards of Barolo and the famous truffle trading town of Alba, follows the same Piedmontese tradition. Similar in style to a Robiola, but not part of the PDO, this dainty and delicate soft cheese with a wiggly rind is made with a mix of all three milks in equal quantities. And they each bring something different to the party: buttery richness from the cow's milk, sweetness from the sheep, and bite from the goat. The texture is important, too. Beneath the rind there's a layer like liquid satin, while the heart of La Tur is plush and velvety. US cheesemonger Murray's describes it perfectly as 'a scoop of decadent ice cream melting from the outside in'.

Caseificio dell'Alta Langa was set up in 1991 by the Merlo family, who decided to stand out from the crowd by making soft cheeses under their own brand, rather than as part of the collective PDO. La Tur takes its name from the Piedmontese word for 'tower', in reference to its cylindrical shape, which also looks a little like a cupcake. It was a clever business move. Around half of all sales come from exports to countries including the US, UK, Germany, Netherlands and Japan.

That's not to say that life is easy as a mixed-milk cheesemaker. One of the directors told me that they have 'three times the problems than if we just used one type of milk' when I went to visit in 2022. That's because the composition of the milks changes throughout the year, with varying fat and protein levels depending on what the animals are eating and where they are in their lactation cycle. The solution? To add more or less cow's milk cream to help balance the changes, which also explains La Tur's luscious flavour and texture. For the full Piedmont experience, serve it with a sliver of white truffle and a glass of the local Roero white wine. PM

ORIGIN: Piedmont, Italy

PROTECTED STATUS: N/A

MILK: Thermised or pasteurised cow, goat and sheep's milk

RENNET: Animal

AROMA: Yoghurty, yeasty, lemony

FLAVOUR: Double cream, lemons, mushrooms

TEXTURE: Silky, velvety

MATCH: The floral, peachy flavours of Roero white wines from Piedmont, made with Arneis grapes, are a great foil. Cherry jam or even a sliver of truffle are excellent companions.

WORLD CHEESE AWARDS: Gold 2012

Vacherin Fribourgeois

Ask a room full of Swiss people for their favourite fondue recipes and you'll get as many answers as there are people. The country's most famous dish is made in many different ways with various combinations and ratios of Swiss cheeses. Some swear by 100 per cent Gruyère; others argue that Emmentaler is an essential part of the mix; while Sbrinz and Appenzeller are sometimes touted as the secret ingredient (especially in the regions where those cheeses are made). But perhaps the most famous version is Moitié-Moitié – a recipe made with equal parts Gruyère and a lesser-known cheese called Vacherin Fribourgeois.

A semi-hard, buttery cheese from western Switzerland, Vacherin Fribourgeois is made in large 10kg (22lb) wheels with a rugged rind, partly washed to develop animal umami aromas. The cows graze outdoors for most of the year and their milk is kept unpasteurised to preserve the complex flavours that come from the meadows in which the animals live.

Like other cheeses from Switzerland, there are large-scale producers of Vacherin Fribourgeois, but also more traditional versions made by small producers in the valleys and high up in the Alps. While these cheeses may seem generic, the differences come in the complexity and nuance of its production – how it is made and aged, the environment in which the cows live and what they eat.

The name *vacherin* can be traced back to 1420, originally referring to the personal allowance given to *vaccarinus* (herdsmen) as part of their payment for taking care of the animals in the mountains. Legend has it that a monk from the Montserrat monastery

in Catalonia passed on the recipe of this cheese to the local *vaccarinus* after learning it while abroad.

While often overlooked as just an easy-to-melt cheese, it has a strong tradition as a table cheese in western Switzerland, where producers are proud of their work and continue to maintain their traditions.

Svetlana Kukharchuk, fellow judge and owner of The Cheese Lady stores in Scotland, recommends pairing Vacherin Fribourgeois with whisky. We both interned at Murray's Cheese in New York City in the early 2000s when we were enrolled on an affinage apprenticeship at the famous cheese shop's caves. Hervé Mons helped set up the affinage programme at the iconic NYC store before the entire company was bought by Kroger Supermarkets. Those years were foundational for me, and also marked an era in the US cheese industry. Other Murray's alumni would go on to open stores around the country, become export managers and buyers, and some would even end up running US cheese companies. Good cheese stores have the power to change the industry and shape public perception.

I remember tasting Vacherin Fribourgeois during a class at Murray's. Its creamy, savoury flavours still linger in my mind. Though I still fumble over its pronunciation (I say 'vash-eran free-bor-zhwah'), the cheese itself is unforgettable. CY

ORIGIN: Fribourg, Switzerland
PROTECTED STATUS: AOP
MILK: Raw and thermised cow's milk
RENNET: Animal
AROMA: Buttery, animal
FLAVOUR: Creamy, savoury, umami
TEXTURE: Firm, pliable, melty
MATCH: Pair with a robust Syrah or a whisky. Beyond fondue, it's great melted on potatoes.

WORLD CHEESE AWARDS: Super Gold 2012 for Vacherin Fribourgeois Rustic (Cremo)

2020s

A period of creativity among the world's cheesemakers, who bend time, science and tradition to forge unique new products. From cheeses shaped like mountains or sprinkled with olive-stone ash to others coated in coffee or wine, boundaries are pushed in wildly different directions. But there are also important wins for historic cheeses made using time-honoured methods.

Above: C2 (see page 166)

Almnäs Tegel

If you need a stepping stone into the world of Swedish cheese and a new decade of the World Cheese Awards, then Almnäs Tegel provides the perfect launch pad. The giant 25kg (55lb) cheese, which is made by Almnäs Bruk on the shores of Lake Vättern in the south of the country, is shaped like a square paving slab and even has four footprints stamped on the rind. It also tells the story of how a nation found its cheese mojo again.

Almnäs Tegel is one of Sweden's best-known cheeses, partly because of its distinctive appearance and sweet, savoury flavour that is reminiscent of Alpine cheeses, but also because it has a great back story to go with it. Launched in 2008, the cheese was inspired by the history of the estate in central-southern Sweden where it is made, while simultaneously telling the story of how Swedish cheese has reinvented itself.

Almnäs Bruk is a 2,425-hectare (6,000-acre) farming estate that has a history stretching back to 1225. It's been run by French Cistercian monks, the Swedish Crown and a series of noble families down the centuries, with cheese made there since at least 1830. That was until the 1960s, when the dairy closed down as small-scale farmhouse production became increasingly uneconomical in the face of a national drive towards industrial dairy production. Hundreds of small farms stopped making cheese across the country in what is known as the *mejeridöden* ('dairy death').

The estate's dairy remained closed until 2008 when the current owner, Thomas Berglund, decided to return the property to its former cheesemaking glory, setting up what is called 'the cheesery' in a former distillery, and developing several new and traditional cheeses. Almnäs Tegel was inspired by the local brick factory (*tegel* means 'brick'), which in the eighteenth century would leave freshly made clay bricks in the sun to dry. This was too tempting for the farm workers' children, who could not resist running across the soft bricks, leaving perfectly formed footprints in their wake. Many of the estate's outbuildings were built with the bricks, and you can still see ghostly footprints on the attic floor of the manor house today.

Inspired by the story, Berglund decided to make a square cheese, stamped with the image of children's footprints. Made in a similar way to Gruyère or Comté in a copper vat, the cheese is washed in brine during maturation to create a dark terracotta rind, which makes it look perfect for building walls. There's something reassuringly solid about the flavour too, which is immediate and satisfying, with big hits of dried orange and pineapple, butterscotch and meat stock.

Much of the intensity comes from the washed rind and the long ageing time, which can be up to 22 months, but Berglund's approach to farming also brings complexity. The herd of Brown Swiss and Holstein cows are reared organically with access to diverse pastures and home-grown cereals, while the farm avoids artificial fertilisers and chemical pesticides.

As well as Almnäs Tegel, Berglund also makes a traditional Swedish cheese called Wrångebäck – the only one in the country to be protected by a PDO – as well as several other innovative new cheeses that are rooted in tradition. He's part of a growing number of small cheesemakers that have rejected the large-scale industrial methods that came to characterise the Swedish dairy industry in the second half of the twentieth century. The country has rediscovered many of its traditional cheeses, such as crusty, cellar-aged goat's cheese from Jämtland in central Sweden, and raw cow's milk Svedjan Gårdsost (Swedish farmhouse cheese) in the northern Västerbotten region.

There are now courses for artisan cheese production, organised by the National Center for Artisan Food, and an annual cheese festival at the Nordic Museum in Stockholm every year. There's even an association of artisan cheesemakers: Sveriges Gårdsmejerister (the Swedish Dairy Farmers' Association), which was founded in 1998 and has more than 100 members. It feels like something special is being built in Swedish cheese, and Almnäs Tegel is an important brick in its foundation.

In case you were wondering, the footprints on the cheese are not made by children these days (there are laws against that sort of thing), but with a square plate embossed with four footprints that is pressed into the soft surface of freshly made cheeses. PM

ORIGIN: Västra Götaland, Sweden
PROTECTED STATUS: N/A
MILK: Raw cow's milk
RENNET: Animal
AROMA: Sweet, fruity, earthy
FLAVOUR: Butterscotch, pineapple, roasted nuts
TEXTURE: Hard, granular
MATCH: The fruity, nutty tones work well with beer, especially amber ales. A shard of hazelnut brittle adds to the sweet nuttiness.

WORLD CHEESE AWARDS: Super Gold 2018, 2021

Basajo

There are plenty of wonderful cheese stalls to catch the eye at London's famous Borough Market, but there's one that really makes people stop and stare. L'Ubriaco is piled high with what at first glance look like elaborately decorated cakes, but on closer inspection turn out to be brightly coloured cheeses soaked in wine and topped with fruit, nuts and chocolate.

The affable cheesemongers that run the stall are quick to hand out titbits for transfixed shoppers to taste, as they explain that *ubriaco* means 'drunk' in Italian, and that all their products are made using an old Venetian tradition of soaking cheeses in alcohol.

It's not just the public that are mesmerised by the cheeses either. World Cheese Awards judges have found these drunken cheeses irresistible over the years, especially one particular raw sheep's milk blue that is soaked in sweet wine. Basajo, which is made in Treviso by La Casearia Carpenedo, is a serial award winner, most notably picking up Super Gold medals in 2021 and 2023.

Made in 2.8kg (6lb) rounds, the cheese is decorated with plump, wine-soaked golden raisins, which sit on top like a fruity crown, while the soft paste is porcelain white with pastel blue veins and has a heady, boozy aroma from being matured in the Sicilian dessert wine Passito di Pantelleria. It brings an ambrosial sweetness to the creamy, spicy blue that is almost intoxicating.

The alchemist behind this meeting of curd and grape is Antonio Carpenedo, who comes from a long line of cheesemakers in Italy's north-west. He set up La Casearia Carpenedo in 1976 using a local technique that involves soaking cheese in different types of wine and grapes as they mature.

The story goes that the tradition started during the First World War when hungry

ORIGIN: Veneto, Italy
PROTECTED STATUS: N/A
MILK: Raw sheep's milk
RENNET: Animal
AROMA: Alcoholic, fruity, spicy
FLAVOUR: Sweet, boozy, creamy
TEXTURE: Soft, fondant-like

MATCH: A glass of dessert wine, preferably Passito di Pantelleria, is the obvious choice. Fresh pears or figs help cut through the richness.

WORLD CHEESE AWARDS:
Multiple awards, including Super Gold 2021, 2023

Austro-Hungarian soldiers would launch raids into Treviso to forcibly take food from farms. Fatigued and hungry themselves, the farmers took to hiding the fruits of their labour, resulting in one bright spark deciding to conceal a few wheels of cheese underneath his fermenting grapes. Once the soldiers had moved on, the cheese was retrieved and turned out to be rather delicious.

Carpenedo took the idea and ran with it, inebriating different cheeses with various alcohols, which helped to revive the drunken cheese tradition and create a new category of flavoured cheeses known as *ubriaco*.

The company's first cheese, Ubriaco di Raboso, was a semi-hard cow's milk cheese soaked in the local Raboso red wine and piled with grape must, but Carpenedo and his sons Ernesto and Alessandro, who run the business today, have gone much further, developing a huge array of different Ubriaco cheeses soaked in Prosecco, beer and gin. Basajo was created by Ernesto, under his father's watchful eye, and is named in honour of his one-year-old daughter whose attempts to say '*formaggio*' came out as '*basajo*'.

Different techniques are used in the maturing room, from literally submerging whole cheeses in wine and burying them under grape must to maturing them in wine barrels, but key to the whole operation is a method based on the acronym TUTA: *Tempo* (time), *Umidità* (humidity), *Temperatura* (temperature) and *Ambiente* (environment).

By controlling and adjusting these four parameters in the maturing room, the family are able to make cheeses that maintain a balance between the flavour of the cheese and the alcohol, which is exactly what World Cheese Awards judges are looking for when they assess a flavoured cheese.

Basajo is a case in point. Aged for six months, including three months in wine, the creamy and salty blue cheese is delicious in its own right, but the dessert wine and golden raisins bring a contrasting sweetness that tempers the spice of the cheese, rather than overpowering it. It's a cheese and wine course in one bite.

No wonder the drunk cheese stall at Borough Market is so busy. PM

Bergkäse

Bergkäse is a cheese with multiple personalities. Made across the Alps in Germany, Austria, Switzerland and Italy, it can be seen as a generic 'mountain cheese' (the English translation from German for *Bergkäse*), but in fact it has distinct regional variations, each shaped by the differing socio-cultural characteristics of their place of origin.

Overall, the cheese is fruity with herbal aromas. It has a distinctive interior with a golden, hay-coloured paste dotted with small, perfectly rounded eyes, but the best part is the balance of soft and firm textures, creating a pleasant mouthfeel and making it the perfect snacking cheese.

Since 1997, Allgäuer Bergkäse from Germany, and Vorarlberger Bergkäse and Tiroler Bergkäse from Austria have been protected by a PDO. While Swiss Bergkäse follows strict regional rules, it does not have PDO status. All varieties are made using the milk of Braunvieh (brown cow) breeds. German Bergkäse producers favour using the milk of Allgäu brown cows, an earlier descendant of Alpine cattle reared for their meat and milk. The Austrian and Swiss varieties are made using the raw milk of Brown Swiss cows, a Braunvieh breed developed in Switzerland for its high milk yield. Swiss producers are allowed to pasteurise their milk.

Allgäuer Bergkäse originates from Bavaria and Baden-Württemberg in southern Germany. During the eighth century, Benedictine monastic traditions helped shape the region, and this was followed by Wittelsbach dynasty rule (1180–1918), which played a key role in consolidating Bavaria's economy and influence. Under Bavarian governance, cheese production became a strategic economic asset – both for export and as a way to collect taxes. The tradition of centralised control followed German unification in 1871; Bismarck's government encouraged agro-industrial expansion, prioritising large-scale commercial dairies to support an export-driven industry.

Across the border, Vorarlberger Bergkäse hails from the Bregenzerwald and Großes Walsertal regions of western Austria. This region was settled by Walser herders and dairy farmers emigrating from the Swiss canton of Valais between the twelfth and fourteenth centuries. They brought with them Alpine traditions, including the transhumance system. Unlike their German counterparts, Austrian cheesemakers maintained a tradition of small-scale, co-operative cheesemaking, inspired by Swiss dairy practices. Further east, Tiroler Bergkäse is produced in the Tyrol region under the same principles. Each one differs in size, starting with smaller Tiroler Bergkäse wheels weighing 12kg (26lb), followed by Allgäuer Bergkäse wheels ranging from 15kg (33lb) to an uncommon 50kg (110lb) pieces, and Vorarlberger Bergkäse's 35kg (77lb) wheels.

Swiss cheesemakers in South Tyrol sometimes incorporate cream into the curd to enhance the richness of their cheese. This is particularly relevant as many US-based cheese producers also add cream to their Bergkäse-style cheeses, presumably to match the original full-fat flavour. German and Swiss-made cheeses are widely available in the international markets, as the focus is on exports. Austrian Bergkäse remains largely a regional speciality.

One of the most recognised Bergkäse is made by Alma Vorarlberger in Austria. Washed frequently to create a thicker rind, and with strong microbial cultures that impart flavour to the interior, this process develops umami notes and a subtle smokiness in the cheese, which has won Super Gold several times.

The name 'Alma', meaning 'nourishing' in Latin, was traditionally given to the highest-yielding cow in the herd. In 1921 the name became a brand when a group of independent farmers decided to transform their *Landwirtschaftlicher Käseverein Bezau* (Agricultural Cheese Association of Bezau) into a co-operative. The association was initially set up to fight the monopolistic practices of a commercial group known as the *Käsegrafen* (cheese lords), who controlled much of the production, sale and export of cheese during the Austro-Hungarian Empire.

The Alma co-operative would grow over the next 87 years into an independent business with a brand identity central to Austrian gastronomic culture – the dairymaid dressed in traditional Alpine clothes became a symbol of heritage and quality. Eventually, the business was bought by food conglomerate Rupp AG in 2008.

Bergkäse is practically unknown in the UK and the US, especially in regard to other mountain cheeses from Switzerland. Often compared to Appenzeller (see page 50), it shares many attributes, including milk source, size, flavour profile and texture, but without the secret herbal wash that gives Appenzeller its flavour.

Bergkäse is a style of cheese that is a testament to how socio-cultural influences shape the cheeses we cherish. CY

ORIGIN: Austria, Germany, Italy and Switzerland

PROTECTED STATUS: 3 separate PDOs (1 in Germany; 2 in Austria)

MILK: Raw and pasteurised cow's milk

RENNET: Animal

AROMA: Roasted nuts, herbal, fruity

FLAVOUR: Umami, meaty, slight smokiness

TEXTURE: Firm, pliable

MATCH: Viognier or English bitters. Serve in traditional Käsespätzle, an egg noodle and cheese dish with caramelised onions.

WORLD CHEESE AWARDS: Multiple awards, including Super Gold 2023 (Alma Vorarlberger), Super Gold 2021 (Dorfsennerei Schlins)

Brunost

ORIGIN: Gudbrandsdalen, Norway
PROTECTED STATUS: N/A
MILK: Pasteurised cow's milk
RENNET: None
AROMA: Sweet, caramel, milky
FLAVOUR: Caramel, tangy, brothy
TEXTURE: Smooth, melty, sticky
MATCH: Black coffee and bread. Pair with aquavit or sake for a dessert.

WORLD CHEESE AWARDS: Multiple awards, including Bronze 2019, 2022 (Nakashima Farm), Super Gold 2023 (Eleftheria), Silver 2024 (Heidal Ysteri)

What is cheese? It may seem like a straightforward question, but there are grey areas between the great lactic families of milk, cream, butter, yoghurt and cheese that spark heated debates among dairy nerds. Brunost is a good example. It's Norway's favourite cheese, but there is an argument to say that it's not cheese at all.

Broadly speaking, cheese is made of the proteins and fats found in milk. Brunost ('brown cheese') is made from whey – the watery liquid left over from processing curds during cheesemaking. This by-product is sometimes fed to pigs, or sprayed on the land as a fertiliser. It can also be churned into whey butter, dried to create protein powders for fortifying other foods and drinks, or heated to extract the remaining proteins and sugars to make a secondary cheese. Many cultures have their own versions of whey cheese, from Anari in Cyprus and Ricotta in Italy, to Requesón in Spain, Requeijão in Portugal and Lor in Turkey.

In Norway, they take it a step further, boiling whey for up to 12 hours until most of the moisture evaporates, leaving the proteins and sugars to caramelise into a sweet, fudge-like substance called Brunost, which looks a little like modelling clay. No rennet or starter cultures are used, and it's not technically made from curd, hence the question: should it even be considered cheese at all?

Early cheesemakers discovered that prolonged boiling of whey led to caramelisation, producing the soft and crumbly Mysost. There is no clear reference as to how this cheese was first developed, but presumably peasant farmers made Gamalost (see page 122) and Pultost cheeses with skimmed soured milk. They had an abundance of skimmed milk as most of the cream would have been separated to make butter. Farmers also had an abundance of wood to feed fires and could maintain whey boiling for at least eight hours. Some later enhanced the process by adding cream, giving rise to Brunost. In 1863, Anne Hov, a Norwegian dairymaid, is credited with perfecting the recipe for Brunost. Having whey as its base, all varieties of Brunost are slightly tangy. Often described as tasting like caramel, it is never cloyingly sweet, but rather has a pleasant brothiness.

Brunost is typically made with cow's milk whey and cream, creating a firm, fudgy texture. In central Norway's Gudbrandsdalen region, adding goat's milk whey to Brunost is common, resulting in the variety known as Gudbrandsdalsost. During the winter, you can also find a cardamom-infused version named Julebrunost. While for a milder taste, try Geitost, made from goat's milk whey. Or if you prefer creamier cheeses, Fløtemysost is made by adding double cream to the whey.

Brunost is the overall name given to this Norwegian staple. Most of it is produced industrially by Tine, a Norwegian dairy conglomerate, using controlled heating systems to monitor sugar concentration and viscosity. However, there are artisanal products like those made by Stordalen Gardsbruk, as well as Heidal Ysteri with their beautifully shaped medieval-looking prisms.

For those unfamiliar with its sweet-salty balance, brown cheese can be an acquired taste. However, its popularity has spread far, finding enthusiastic audiences in Japan and India, where cheesemakers are producing local varieties. While in South Korea and the Philippines, imported Norwegian-made cheeses are used as a pizza topping.

The quality of cheeses made in Japan and India is indisputable. After spending three years perfecting his cheese, Hirotaka Nakashima entered the Japan Cheese Awards, winning the Mixed Cheese category in 2018. Before he began making Brunost, Nakashima had no prior connection to Norway. His motivation came from a desire to use leftover whey from the other products made by Nakashima Farm in Saga prefecture located on the southern island of Kyushu. In an ingenious adaptation, he repurposed an *anko* (あんこ / red bean paste) machine to aid in brown cheese production. Following local success, he entered the World Cheese Awards, earning a Bronze medal in both 2019 and 2020.

Like Nakashima, Mausam Narang based in Mumbai had no prior ties to Norway when she launched her cheesemaking business in 2015. Having lived and studied in Germany, she returned home and was struck by the limited range of cheeses available. Determined to introduce new styles to India, she began making varieties that she believed would appeal to local tastes, and named her business Eleftheria ('freedom' in Greek). Her instincts proved correct, and her Brunost captivated locals and wowed international judges, earning a Super Gold medal in 2023 at the awards hosted in Trondheim, Norway. This was not only the highest honour ever awarded to an India-made cheese at the World Cheese Awards, but also a groundbreaking achievement for brown cheeses. Eleftheria's block is striking as it features the words एल एफ (EL EF) written in Devanagari (Hindi script).

Whether crafted in Norway, Japan or India, Brunost is a cheese worth experiencing. Try cutting thin slices with a cheese plane and eating with rye bread and berry jams for breakfast. Its caramelised flavours might just bring a touch of hygge into your life. CY

C2

Yes, you read that right. C2 is the name of a raw milk cheese from Australia, not a new plastic explosive. That's not to say that the debate over raw milk cheese production has not been volatile at times.

C2 was the first modern raw milk cheese made in Australia. Nick Haddow, founder of Bruny Island Cheese Co. in Tasmania, created this Alpine-style cheese with a dense texture and caramel notes, first made in 2003. Each wheel weighs around 8kg (18lb) and is aged from four to eight months. The rind is developed by constant brushing to encourage a robust barrier to protect the gorgeous bright hay-coloured interior with characteristic small eyes and buttery smell. It is a cheese so rooted in its terroir that it has helped pioneer a movement in Australia.

Haddow learnt how to make cheese in Europe and Australia, and is based on Bruny Island, a tiny landmass off the south coast of the much larger island of Tasmania in southern Australia. His ethos is to showcase the best of Tasmania, working hand in hand with local farms to ensure the milk for his cheeses is the very best quality.

The company also brews beer, bakes bread, makes condiments, and sources wines and liquors from other Tasmanian producers, all of which are sold online. Haddow runs a very successful hamper club, with boxes of Tasmanian produce shipped all over Australia. In part, this business model, selling direct to consumers, is a response to how remote Tasmania is from other parts of the country, but it also stems from a deep pride for the local land. This independent spirit, plus Haddow's advocacy for raw milk cheese production, has gained him recognition around the world.

Regulators worldwide have wrestled with the commercialisation of raw milk cheese for over 70 years. In Australia, health authorities have long restricted the import of fresh raw milk cheeses, permitting only aged varieties. Initially, regulations allowed only cheeses matured for at least 120 days, based on the assumption that ageing reduces the risk of harmful pathogens. However, in 2015, Food Standards Australia New Zealand (FSANZ) revised these rules, allowing the production and importation of certain raw milk cheeses aged for 60 days, aligning more closely with international standards.

The debate over raw milk cheese in Australia has been nothing short of explosive. In a notorious 2003 incident, the Australian government seized and later ordered the destruction of a shipment of Roquefort, claiming it failed to meet local food safety standards. The move was widely seen as an overreach. Will Studd, a cheesemonger and one of Australia's most vocal raw milk cheese advocates, staged a protest, loading the banned cheese into a hearse and draping it in the French flag, before filming its burial in a landfill. He was called a 'cheese terrorist' by one dairy industry magazine, a label that served to amplify public interest. The backlash, combined with pressure from French officials and Australian food producers, eventually forced regulators to reconsider their stance on raw milk cheese.

Since then, despite the loosening of some restrictions, the rules remain a complex patchwork. Now certain aged European raw milk cheeses can be imported under strict conditions, while on the domestic front, FSANZ introduced highly controlled production standards, enabling local cheesemakers to legally produce and sell aged raw milk cheeses, but only after navigating rigorous safety protocols.

Haddow was the first to succeed with C2 in an impressive feat of patience, although it cost a pretty penny. Deep pockets were needed to comply with the complicated rules, which at times feel like they have been designed to be so onerous as to discourage production of raw milk cheese entirely.

In a recent turn of events, in 2022 the Australian government approved the importation of select British raw milk cheeses following the UK's decision to leave the EU. Perhaps raw milk cheese disputes are as much to do with trade as health and safety.

And if you were wondering, C2 simply refers to the fact that this was the second style of cheese he made: 'Cheese Two'. CY

ORIGIN: Tasmania, Australia
PROTECTED STATUS: N/A
MILK: Raw cow's milk
RENNET: Animal
AROMA: Sweet, fresh, buttery
FLAVOUR: Milky, earthy when young; sweeter, more caramelised notes as it ages
TEXTURE: Firm, malleable
MATCH: Tasmanian Pinot Noir or an oaky Chardonnay from Australia. Pair with Bruny's own Bread and Butter Pickles.

WORLD CHEESE AWARDS:
Super Gold 2023

Cabrales

Visiting one of the world's best Cabrales producers is not for the faint-hearted. Pepe Bada has dedicated his life to the spicy blue cheese, which he matures in a lofty limestone cave high up in the Picos de Europa mountains of Asturias in Spain. Getting there requires stamina.

I found this out in 2021 when the World Cheese Awards was held in Oviedo, the capital of Asturias. Monika Linton, the thoughtful and generous owner of pioneering Spanish food company Brindisa, invited me along with her team to visit her old friend, who has long supplied her shops and restaurants in London with top-notch Cabrales. It was an epic pilgrimage.

We started by driving to the tiny mountain village of Tielve, nearly 700 metres (2,295 feet) above sea level, on a long, winding road that rose steadily, becoming increasingly narrow with hairpin bends, sheer drops and rocky overhangs. We were greeted by a strong handshake and a slap on the back by Bada – a compact, wiry man with sharp eyes behind little round glasses – before we all piled into a 4x4 and roared off along a dirt track for a further 3km (1.9 miles) up into the limestone peaks.

At the end of the track was not a cave but several rucksacks filled with 2kg (4.5lb) rounds of young cheeses, made by Andrea Fernández Gutiérrez (Bada's partner's daughter) in the Arangas dairy in Rozagás. There's no road linking the dairy to the mountain cave. The only way to get the cheeses up there is the old-fashioned way – on your back.

The final leg of the journey involved Bada leading us up steep slopes and along barely visible mud paths with cheese strapped to our backs, only stopping to admire views of the slopes and valleys that have been sculpted by the snow, wind, rain and sun for millennia.

Eventually we reached a plum tree just beneath a battered steel door in the rock face, which was yanked open by Bada, who ushered us into his famous cave, known as El Teyedu. As we ventured inside, the light from his head torch illuminated giant calciferous stalactites, slick wet rocks and row upon row of wooden shelves filled with pale white cheeses that seemed to glisten in the humid gloom.

As we unloaded our young cheeses, Bada immediately set about choosing others that he deemed ripe and ready to take back down the mountain. Cutting a triangular wedge from the top of the cheeses, he peered at the mottled greeny-blue interior and tasted a little at the same time, earmarking those ready to be sold and those that needed a little longer. All the while there was a rhythmic drip of water from the cave ceiling as it hit the rudimentary corrugated roof above the cheeses.

Cabrales is aged for anywhere from two to six months, becoming progressively soft and buttery in texture as the blue veins within slowly release enzymes that break down the fats and the proteins in the paste. The flavour is like nothing else. It starts with a sharp, almost alcoholic burst, mixed in with sour milk and rich cream, before it heads off into smoke and steel. The experience is as intense as downing a shot of tequila or slurping an oyster. You can do nothing except ride the wave of flavours that fizz and crackle on your tongue.

Much of this electrifying flavour is to do with the wild yeasts, moulds and bacteria that thrive in the damp caves, but the milk itself is also important. Made with cow's

milk and the possible addition of sheep and goat's milk, Cabrales has been made in the Picos de Europa for at least 200 years, with locals combining their livestock into larger communal herds, which would be taken up into the mountains to graze the summer pastures by a few of the villagers, while the rest focused on harvesting and making hay.

This co-operative model would see the herdsmen make the cheese up in the mountains where the cool, humid natural limestone caves were the obvious place to store the wheels. When they were ready to be taken back to the village at the end of the season, they would be wrapped in sycamore leaves to make handling the sticky cheeses easier (foil with a leaf design is now standard).

The PDO covering Cabrales today sets out strict requirements for the maturing caves, specifying that the entrance must be north-facing and there must be at least one other opening for ventilation to create a breeze known as *soplado*. Flowing water, humidity over 90 per cent and a constant temperature of 6–10°C (43–50°F) are also set out in the legal document protecting the cheese.

All these boxes are ticked by Bada's cave, which at 1,200 metres (3,940 feet) above sea level is one of the highest in the region. The higher the cave, the better the Cabrales, according to locals, which might explain why Bada's Cabrales, named El Teyedu after his cave, is so feted. In 2023, a single wheel of El Teyedu set a Guinness World Record when it was sold to a restaurant at a charity auction for €30,000. It was also named as one of the best blue cheeses in the world at the 2016 World Cheese Awards.

ORIGIN: Asturias, Spain

PROTECTED STATUS: PDO

MILK: Raw cow's milk; raw sheep and/ or goat's milk can also be added

RENNET: Animal

AROMA: Sharp, earthy, yeasty

FLAVOUR: Fiery, creamy, steely

TEXTURE: Crumbly when young; buttery when mature

MATCH: Pedro Ximénez sherry tempers the spice, while pressed figs and nuts pick up on its fruity savoury tones.

WORLD CHEESE AWARDS: Multiple awards, including Super Gold 2016 (El Teyedu & Los Mazos), Gold 2021 (Rojo Prieto & Maestro), Gold 2023 (Cueva de Molin)

But El Teyedu is not the only Cabrales to win big at the awards. Throughout the 2020s, several other Cabrales producers have picked up Gold and Super Gold medals, making it one of the most decorated blues in the competition.

On the long walk back down the mountain range to Tielve (there was no 4x4 to help us this time), Bada and Linton chatted amiably in Spanish, pointing out unusual flowers, trees and rock formations with their sturdy hiking staffs. We even came across a shepherd with a herd of shaggy goats who eyed us warily from a distance, the sure-footed animals elegantly hopping from rock to rock.

Tasting different ages of Cabrales back in the village, Bada passed around slices on a stubby paring knife. Surprisingly, it was the four-month cheese, labelled Pepe Bada, that was most powerful, full of fire and spice that almost burned my tongue, while the six-month El Teyedu cheese had mellowed in the cave with a texture like butter. Not that either could ever be described as mild. If you like punchy cheese, then you must go a few rounds with Cabrales. PM

Barely Buzzed Cheddar

You might have heard of a mother dough in sourdough bread baking, but what about a mother cheese? Beehive Cheese in Utah builds many of its creations on a base cheese called Promontory – a creamy, sweet American Cheddar made with Jersey cow's milk – which serves as the parent for numerous flavoured varieties. These are made by coating the outside in unique rubs.

The most famous of Beehive's many daughters is Barely Buzzed. Crafted using the traditional Cheddaring technique, where curds are stacked to expel whey before being milled and pressed, the cheese is coated in a blend of espresso coffee and lavender, a rub that infuses it with deep, roasted notes and subtle floral undertones.

Cheese maturers learnt early on that moving the young wheels between two humidity-controlled facilities to age them allowed temperature changes to develop caramel and butterscotch flavours, balanced by aromatic complexity. After three initial weeks when the cheese is kept at a low temperature to control flavour development, the young wheels are rubbed and further matured at higher temperatures, promoting the development of cultures that give the cheese its characteristic creamy flavour.

Beehive Cheese was founded in 2005 by brothers-in-law Tim Welsh and Pat Ford in Ogden, in the northern part of the state of Utah ('Beehive' is taken from the state's nick-name). The area is known for its rough, natural beauty as part of the Ogden Canyon. With no prior experience in cheesemaking, Welsh and Ford enrolled in a course at the Utah State University before launching the dairy. Their groundbreaking idea was to cover their 9kg (20lb) wheels with unique flavours, including tea, porcini mushrooms, honey and sea salt, and chilli peppers.

In the world of flavoured cheeses, rubbed cheeses are often favoured over those with flavourings added to the paste, as the surface treatments enhance the flavour rather than overwhelm the cheese. Adding flavours to the curd can turn a cheese sour or bitter early in the maturing process or can overpower the cheeses. When melted over a warm slice of apple pie, Barely Buzzed transforms a familiar dessert into a gourmet experience, marrying the cheese's caramelised richness with the tart sweetness of baked fruit.

We dug deep into the world of Cheddar earlier in the book (see page 22), highlighting the differences between block, cloth-bound and re-milled versions of the iconic cheese. In truth, much of the Cheddar made and sold around the world is of the first type: big blocks, made at scale and vacuum-packed in plastic.

Beehive Cheddars are different, based on a company ethos of responsibility and family support. Katie Welsh and Corinne Ford encouraged their husbands in their venture and soon got involved in all aspects of the company. Over time, the entire family joined in, and as of 2024, the next generation is leading the way. Tim's son, Britton Welsh, now oversees operations, while Pat's son, Oliver Ford, heads sales. These family and community values translated in 2023 into the company becoming B Corp accredited – a business certification scoring companies' social and environmental commitments. The certification is often sought out by more conscious consumers seeking to support companies that seem to balance profit with purpose.

After the COVID-19 pandemic many things have changed for Beehive Cheese. Its focus before the emergency was supplying restaurants and hotels, but when lockdowns hit, sales disappeared overnight. This made the family re-evaluate their priorities and further partner up with their long-term milk supplier. In 2024, instead of building a new creamery to make more cheese, they transferred production to Gossner Foods in Idaho, though still following Beehive's proprietary recipe of the mother cheese.

This has allowed them to shift focus to maturation. Now the wheels are transported to Utah after the initial three weeks, to be rubbed and aged in-house and released after eight months.

Mother would be proud. 

ORIGIN: Utah, USA
PROTECTED STATUS: N/A
MILK: Pasteurised cow's milk
RENNET: Vegetarian
AROMA: Coffee, floral, creamy
FLAVOUR: Caramel, butterscotch, roasted
TEXTURE: Creamy, smooth, pliable
MATCH: Porter beers or Zinfandel red wines. Serve alongside pieces of chocolate or mix in with popcorn.

WORLD CHEESE AWARDS: Multiple awards, including Gold 2019, Silver 2024

Džiugas

Examine the label of almost any cheese and it will list milk, cultures, rennet and salt. But you could argue there's one very important ingredient that is missing: time.

How long a cheese is matured for can have radical consequences for its flavour and texture, as is well demonstrated by a cheese from Lithuania called Džiugas (pronounced 'djogas'). Made by a company called Žemaitijos Pienas in the north-west city of Telšiai, it's one of the country's proudest food exports, similar in style to Parmigiano Reggiano with a hard, crystalline texture and intense fruity flavour. Quite how crystalline and intense depends on the age of the cheese. Entry-level cheeses are matured for 12 months, but there are also 18-, 24- and 36-month versions that are progressively more powerful in flavour and crunchy in texture.

The science of what happens to a cheese over time is complicated, but essentially proteins and fats are broken down and metabolised by enzymes, while moisture also evaporates. The crystals in hard, aged cheeses like Džiugas are formed during this process by amino acids called tyrosine, or the bonding together of calcium and lactic acid.

Žemaitijos Pienas takes all of this to extraordinary lengths with its 'exceptional ripening' cheeses that are aged for 48 to 120 months. We've not yet managed to lay hands on a 10-year-old Džiugas (they are rare birds costing 700 euros per wheel), but even the difference between the 12- and 36-month cheeses is marked. The younger 'mild' cheese is supple and pleasantly fruity, but by three years it has grown into a much more confident toddler with a big personality that demands

your attention. Think dried pineapple, beef stock and a pleasant hot tang. Perhaps the 10-year-old cheese is more like a moody pre-teen, although Žemaitijos Pienas describes it as having 'gentle milky elegance and the sweetness of nuts and dried fruit'.

Not all cheeses can be aged for these huge stretches of time. A very low moisture content and a sturdy rind to stop the interior drying out are essential. The Lithuanian cheese is also only made in the summer when the cows are at pasture, which helps when it comes to long ageing. Feeding preserved feed, such as silage, to cows can introduce bacteria to the milk, which can lead to problems with cheeses 'blowing' (puffing up with gas) and cracking in the maturing room.

The other secret to Džiugas's long-lived existence is how it is matured. The 4.5kg (10lb) wheels are kept in temperature-controlled maturing rooms where they are placed on their sides on racks with rotating rods and gently turned 60 degrees twice a week to smooth the sides and create a strong rind.

This work in the maturing room feels rather appropriate considering Džiugas is named after a fierce and ancient warlord, who lived in a hill fort in Telšiai (an illustration of him with flowing locks and clutching a cheese adorns the cheese's packaging). Legend has it that the secret of his strength was a well-aged cheese he kept in the cellar of his farmhouse. PM

ORIGIN: Telšiai, Lithuania
PROTECTED STATUS: PGI
MILK: Pasteurised cow's milk
RENNET: Vegetarian
AROMA: Tropical fruit, sour cream, broth
FLAVOUR: Dried pineapple, roasted nuts, beef stock
TEXTURE: Waxy, crystalline

MATCH: Try with a fruity IPA and a handful of roasted almonds, which pick up on pineapple and nutty notes in the cheese.

WORLD CHEESE AWARDS: Gold 2021 (24 months)

Époisses

ORIGIN: Burgundy, France

PROTECTED STATUS: PDO

MILK TYPE: Raw and pasteurised cow's milk

RENNET: Animal

AROMA: Meaty, earthy, fruity

FLAVOUR: Smoked bacon, farmyard, double cream

TEXTURE: Springy when young; custardy goo as it ages

MATCH: Burgundy wine is the classic combo, especially meaty Pinot Noir and buttery Chardonnay. Crusty bread and onion marmalade are suitably rustic sides.

WORLD CHEESE AWARDS: Multiple awards, including Best French Cheese 2021 (Berthaut)

A cheese that splits the room. Literally, in some cases. Break out a ripe Époisses at a party and you'll find hardcore cheese-lovers drawn inexorably to its sticky orange rind and glossy interior, while the rest back away in terror.

The reason? Époisses is part of a particularly fragrant family called washed-rind cheeses, whereby the outside is washed in brine, or brine with alcohol, in the maturing room to encourage a smelly orange bacteria to grow. This bacteria is also found on human skin, so it's not uncommon to detect a strangely familiar pungent aroma.

Époisses is at the stinkier end of the washed-rind spectrum, partly because it's washed in Marc de Bourgogne, a rustic French brandy made with the crushed grapes left over from Burgundy wine production. It gives the cheese an eye-watering whiff. The story goes that Époisses is so powerful that it's illegal to carry it on the Paris Metro, although we can find no actual evidence of the law. Not that this has ever stopped cheesemongers telling customers the tale.

The thing to remember with Époisses is that its bark is worse than its bite. It might have an unholy pong, but the flavour is often rather agreeable: rich, meaty, and with hints of roasted peanuts and booze.

In 2021, Indian cheesemaker and judge Mansi Jasani championed the cheese in the final of the World Cheese Awards in Asturias, Spain, extolling its aromatic virtues with great élan. She described it to us as 'the taste of France itself: elegant, complex, and a bit funky'.

That particular cheese was made by a dairy called Fromagerie Berthaut, which is based in the village of Époisses in Burgundy, where the cheese was first invented in the Middle Ages. Husband and wife Robert and Simone Berthaut set up the company in 1956 to save the cheese after it was threatened with extinction following the two world wars.

They did such a good job of reviving its fortunes that the cheese was protected under French law in 1991 (and later by a PDO), meaning it can only be made in specific *departéments* of Bourgogne-Franche-Comté and Grand Est. There are now nearly 40 Époisses-makers in the region and Berthaut was so successful that the business was bought by multinational Savencia in 2013.

Most Époisses are pasteurised or made in larger creameries. But there is one *fermier* (farm-based) producer still working in the traditional way. The cheese made by GAEC des Marronniers is intense, even by Époisses' standards: smoky, fruity, and full of umami notes.

Just don't be worried by the whiff. 

L'Etivaz

They like to do things their own way in L'Etivaz – the tiny Swiss town so high up in the Vaud Alps that it has ski stations for neighbours and is part of a former district called Pays-d'Enhaut, 'the land above'. This lofty position in the world, away from the big cities of Switzerland, is reflected in a fiercely independent identity and steely determination among locals.

It is also deliciously expressed in their cheese, named after the town, which was born in the 1930s in defiance of central government dictates as a way to preserve and promote mountain culture. Back then Swiss cheese production was centralised under the government-funded Swiss Cheese Union, which had been set up in 1919 to secure the industry during uncertain times. The Union controlled everything, from the price of milk and cheese to how it was sold and marketed, and was focused almost exclusively on Switzerland's big three: Gruyère, Emmentaler and Sbrinz.

On the surface this should have made life better for the cheesemakers of L'Etivaz. Gruyère had long been the favoured cheese in the area, its production following ancient traditions of transhumance. Cows were taken high up into the Alpage every summer once the snow had melted, where wheels of cheese were made in copper cauldrons over open fires in wooden chalets.

But by the 1930s, the cheesemakers of L'Etivaz had grown disillusioned with being subsumed as part of a centralised system that they felt was weighted to larger producers in valley dairies much further down the mountains. At the same time, the quality of their own cheeses was suffering from being stored in rudimentary stone cellars beneath their mountain chalets. So in a typically forthright and practical manner, 76 producers got together and formed a co-operative, abandoning the name Gruyère in favour of L'Etivaz and building a central maturing cellar in the town, which opened in 1935.

In the conservative world of Swiss cheese, the decision to strike out on their own was a radical and risky move. But in the long run it has turned out to be an inspired one. By no longer being part of a much bigger brand, the cheesemakers can tell the story of what makes their cheese different – the seasonality, the traditional production methods and the diverse high mountain pastures that the cows graze on. Most importantly, it has helped preserve their mountain culture and economy.

L'Etivaz was the first Swiss cheese to receive protected AOP status, in 2000, which codified its unique characteristics into Swiss law. The cheese can only be made between May 10 and October 10 at altitudes between 1,000 and 2,000 metres (3,280 and 6,560 feet) above sea level, which ensures the cows have access to a colourful bouquet of herbs, flowers and wild grasses that thrive in the thin, rocky soil. And it's still made in wooden chalets dotted around the mountainsides, with raw milk poured into copper cauldrons, which are hung over log fires where the curd is scalded to over 50°C (122°F). Smoke and soot hangs in the air, permeating the wooden walls and the curd itself.

Once made into wheels weighing 15–35kg (33–77lb), they are stored in the central L'Etivaz maturing rooms typically for around 6 to 12 months, or occasionally much longer (a rare version called *Rebibe* is aged for 30 months). The Maison de l'Etivaz has been regularly enlarged over the years as demand for the cheese has grown, and there is now a shop, café and even a virtual-reality cheese experience, along with tours of the maturing rooms.

Even so, production is still tiny. There are around 70 L'Etivaz producers today, some of which have just 20 cows and make a couple of wheels a day. Around 430 tonnes (423 tons) of L'Etivaz is produced a year, which shrinks into insignificance against the 30,000 tonnes (29,500 tons) of Gruyère made in Switzerland annually.

So little has changed in the way the cheese is made that it's often said that to try L'Etivaz is to experience how Gruyère might have tasted 100 years ago. That is probably going a bit too far. There are still Alpage Gruyères made in a very similar way in the mountains during the summer. But there's definitely an epic sense of time and place about L'Etivaz, with big differences between different producers and even batches depending on where the cows have been grazing and at what point in the season. Flavours can roll between dried pineapple and smoked bacon to nutmeg and roasted hazelnuts, but there is often an underlying smoky intensity to the cheeses.

L'Etivaz is a counterpoint to the centralisation and homogenisation of food culture. It's also utterly delicious. PM

ORIGIN: Vaud, Switzerland
PROTECTED STATUS: AOP
MILK: Raw cow's milk
RENNET: Animal
AROMA: Fruity, meaty, smoky
FLAVOUR: Brown butter, smoked bacon, roasted hazelnuts
TEXTURE: Dense, crystalline
MATCH: An aged Chasselas (the name of the grape and the wine) from Switzerland has complementary nutty and honey notes. Smoked charcuterie pairs nicely with the smoky notes of the cheese.

WORLD CHEESE AWARDS: Super Gold 2024 (Coopérative Des Producteurs de Fromages D'Alpages)

Harbison

ORIGIN: Vermont, USA
PROTECTED STATUS: N/A
MILK: Pasteurised cow's milk
RENNET: Animal
AROMA: Woodsy, pungent, umami
FLAVOUR: Meaty, mushroomy, earthy
TEXTURE: Gooey, silky
MATCH: Strong amber ales and Pinot Noir. As a dip for crudités, crusty bread, or roasted new potatoes.

WORLD CHEESE AWARDS: Best USA 2023

It may seem as though cheese is a static food that hasn't changed much down the decades, but there is plenty of innovation and development if you look closely. One of the big trends at the World Cheese Awards in recent years has been the emergence of new styles of soft cheese that are bound in spruce.

Encircling a cheese in strips of bark is nothing new in the Jura in eastern France and the Swiss Alps, where cheesemakers have used the technique since the eighteenth century to make Vacherin and Mont d'Or (see page 134). But the popularity of these traditional cheeses has led to a burst of innovative thinking among cheesemakers around the world.

Anne Harbison, known as the 'Grandmother of Greensboro', where Jasper Hill Farm is based, lends her name to Harbison cheese; the farm also produces Bayley Hazen Blue (see page 104).

A small 260g (9oz) wheel aged for six weeks, the cheese has an oozy texture, with a pungent, woodsy aroma and meaty, earthy flavour. The best way to eat it is by removing the top of the cheese and spooning out the silky cream inside. Pop it in a warm oven and see it melt into molten goo.

Mature spruce trees are harvested in spring when they're producing sap. Loggers remove the bark in sheets, which are peeled away without damaging the tree, then cut into strips and cured before being dried ready for use. Producers cut the strips to size and use them to wrap young cheeses, securing them with rubber bands. The wheels of cheese grow around the bark, which imparts its flavours into the paste. The cheese is washed constantly to encourage the growth of aromatic micro-organisms that give the wheels their characteristic orange hue and smell.

There are plenty of others in the same style, including two raw milk cheeses made in the US: Winnimere, also made by Jasper Hill Farm, and Rush Creek Reserve, made in Wisconsin; Rollright from Gloucestershire in the UK; L'Adoray made in Quebec, Canada; and even one made in Santa Catarina in Brazil, called Morro Azul.

It seems a strip of bark is still the ultimate fashion accessory in the cheese world. CY

Langres

It's easy to spot Langres on a cheese counter. With its cylindrical shape and bright orange rind, it stands out like a little washed-rind beacon among the yellows and whites of other cheeses. The other tell-tale sign is a concave indentation on the top, which resembles a crater. This is known as the *fontaine* (fountain) and provides a big clue to how the cheese is matured.

While most soft cheeses are regularly flipped as they mature so the moisture inside is evenly distributed, Langres is turned twice at most, or often not at all, so the cheese starts to collapse in on itself, leaving a sunken dip at the top.

The cheese is named after the town in Haute-Marne in the Champagne region of north-east France, and there is a much-quoted tradition that involves pouring the famous sparkling wine into the *fontaine*. It's a serving suggestion that makes absolutely no sense to me. Maybe I've been doing it wrong, but the Champagne runs everywhere, while at the same time making the cheese slimy and sludgy. I prefer a glass of fizz next to my Langres, not in it.

In the nineteenth century there were dozens of farm-based cheesemakers in the Haute-Marne, but production dwindled between the wars so that today there are just a handful left. The PDO that covers the cheese allows production in the Côte d'Or, Haute-Marne, Vosges and the canton of Neufchâteau, and allows for both pasteurised and raw milk.

Two of the best-known makers are Fromagerie Schertenleib and Fromagerie Germain, which buy milk from local farms with herds of Montbéliarde, Brown Swiss and Simmental cows. There is also one last remaining *fermier* (farm-based) producer using raw milk from its own animals: Fromagerie Remillet in Genevrières.

ORIGIN: Haute-Marne, France
PROTECTED STATUS: PDO
MILK: Raw or pasteurised cow's milk
RENNET: Animal
AROMA: Yeasty, earthy, milky
FLAVOUR: Savoury, lactic, vegetal
TEXTURE: Chalky when young; soft and gooey when mature

MATCH: A vintage Champagne cuts through the richness of the cheese and picks up on the yeasty notes. A few slices of sweet, salty *jambon* emphasise the savoury cheese.

WORLD CHEESE AWARDS: Gold 2022, 2024, Super Gold 2023 (Fromagerie Germain)

The rind of Langres is a beautiful sight. Delicate and undulating with velvety wrinkles, it has a blushing terracotta hue to it that wouldn't look out of place on a fancy paint colour chart. This comes from the addition of annatto to the brine used to wash the cheese (the same vegetable colouring used in Red Leicester and Mimolette). Some makers also add Marc de Bourgogne or Marc de Champagne to the wash (grape spirits made with the must from wine production) to add a fruity, boozy aroma that can be piercingly powerful in mature cheeses.

Most Langres are matured for between two and three weeks, but some affineurs take them longer, washing the rind even more to amp up the flavour. The pale interior of Langres is mild and chalky with a tangy, yoghurty flavour when young, but more mature cheeses start to break down under the rind into a glossy goo that is savoury, fruity and vegetal with a pleasing bitterness at the finish.

If you want to know where a Langres is in its life cycle, one trick is to look at the *fontaine*. The deeper the indent, the more mature the cheese is likely to be. Just don't bother filling it with Champagne. PM

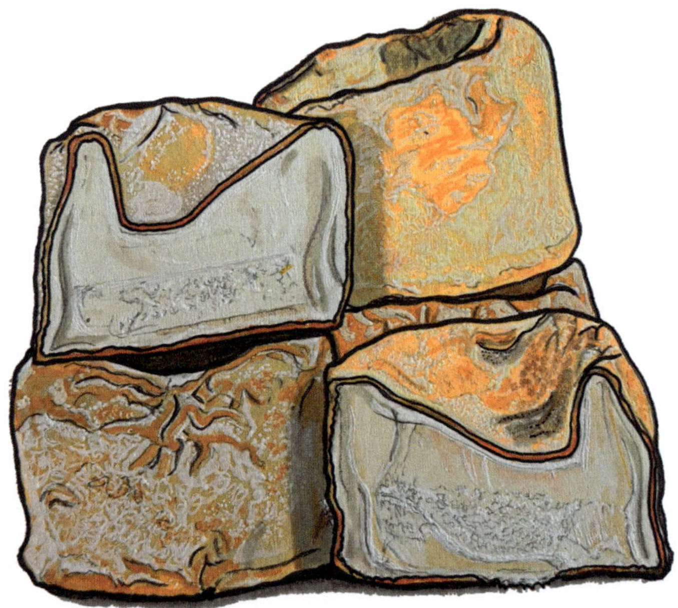

Michel

It was the Chernobyl disaster that made Backensholzer Hof farm rethink everything. Owners Ernst and Martina Metzger-Petersen, third-generation dairy farmers in the far north of Germany, were horrified by the nuclear reactor catastrophe in Ukraine in 1986, which saw radioactive fallout spread as far as Germany.

It marked a turning point for many consumers worried about the environment, but was also the catalyst for the family to switch to organic production in 1989. The guiding principle of the new approach was to 'give more to the world than you take from it'.

Making cheese was an important part of the new ethos, with a cheese dairy – Backensholz Hofkäserei – set up in 1991 at the farm close to the Danish border and the North Sea. Adding value to the milk by turning it into unpasteurised cheese meant the farm could operate in a less intensive way. The cows could be rotated between fields, so that the pasture had time to regenerate naturally, meaning synthetic pesticides and fertilisers were no longer required, while the animals were happier and healthier.

Metzger-Petersen's sons Thilo and Jasper, who took over the business in the 2010s, have taken the original concept and run with it. Jasper looks after the farm, which grows almost all of its own feed and produces enough electricity in a biogas plant and solar modules to power the farm and the cheese business as well as 2,000 local homes.

In the dairy, Thilo has remained fully committed to using raw milk to create a range of 15 different cheeses that are sold in the farm shop and the organic restaurant built in 2019. There's even a kindergarten at the

ORIGIN: Schleswig-Holstein, Germany
PROTECTED STATUS: N/A
MILK: Raw cow and goat's milk
RENNET: Animal
AROMA: Aromatic, fruity, nutty
FLAVOUR: Roasted nuts, caramel, umami
TEXTURE: Pliable when young; brittle when mature
MATCH: The malty sweetness and refreshing bubbles of Bock (a German dark lager) is a fitting partner. Also nice with a drizzle of date molasses.

WORLD CHEESE AWARDS: Super Gold 2023, 2024

farm, which teaches young kids about the importance of nature.

It's a holistic approach to farming that is not only sustainable and profitable, but just as importantly results in absolutely wonderful cheese. Michel is the pick of the bunch, winning Super Gold in 2023, where it made the final 16 and was named Best German Cheese. But we could equally have picked several of their other cheeses. Deichkäse Gold, which has won several awards over the years, is another gem. It's made with raw cow's milk and aged for well over a year until it is crumbly and crystalline and packed full of umami.

Made with a 50/50 mix of cow and goat's milk in 4.5kg (10lb) wheels, Michel is matured for four months or up to 16 months to create two same-but-different eating experiences. Young Michel has a tender texture and sweet fruity flavour, while the more mature cheese (which won the awards) is much harder and grainier with deep caramel and roasted nut notes, plus an intense savoury finish.

The depth and complexity of the cheese embodies the farm's circular approach and the dairy's dedication to raw milk, but is also a reflection of Thilo Metzger-Petersen's background. A tall, strapping chap with a cheeky grin, he learned cheesemaking in Italy and Ireland, as well as working as a chef before he re-joined the family business in 2015. He is obsessed with flavour, as you might expect from a former chef. Or as he puts it, 'a love of pleasure'.

There's certainly plenty of pleasure to be had from a slice of Michel. PM

Mt Fuji Chèvre

Few natural landmarks are as instantly recognisable as Japan's Mount Fuji, an enduring symbol in art, culture and tradition. Matsubara Masanori's cheese homage is perhaps the most delicious tribute to the mountain in central Japan. The 120g (4oz) goat's milk cheese is shaped like a volcano, its base coated in edible ash to mimic the dark rocks, while white mould blooms on top as if the cheese were covered in snow.

Masanori makes Mt Fuji Chèvre from raw milk from his own free-grazing herd. The animals feed on chestnuts, mushrooms, knotweed and bamboo grass that grow on his 9-hectare (22-acre) parcel on the outskirts of Miyoshi in the Hiroshima prefecture in southern Japan. He chose to raise his animals (around 60 goats and 20 cows) following *yamachi rakunō*, an agro-forestry practice devised in the 1960s and used to create pastures on hill and mountain sides so that cows and goats can wander freely, while also helping to maintain mountain landscapes.

Masanori's journey started in Australia working in cattle farming. After becoming disillusioned with industrial farming there, he began exploring more sustainable practices, first learning forestry techniques in his prefecture, then travelling to France to study cheesemaking.

Upon his return to Japan in 2004, he founded Mirasaka Fromage and started making cheese with milk bought from the local dairy co-operative. Masanori won a couple of local awards for his cheeses, but his dream was to make products using his own milk. In 2006 he found the plot he currently farms and spent two years saving to buy it, before clearing trees by hand (chestnut and acorn trees were left to provide food for his livestock) and planting native Japanese grasses in the clearings. Kunie, Masanori's wife, runs Mirasaka Fromage cheese café and shop, which has become a tourist destination, also known for its goat's milk soft-serve ice cream.

The cheese is made seasonally from spring to autumn, allowing the goats to dry off during the winter following their natural breeding cycles. The animals under Masanori's care live outdoors year round thanks to the temperate climate of Hiroshima prefecture. CY

ORIGIN: Hiroshima, Japan
PROTECTED STATUS: N/A
MILK: Raw goat's milk
RENNET: Animal (kid)
AROMA: Lactic, fresh, earthy
FLAVOUR: Milky, citrussy, umami
TEXTURE: Dense and chalky, but soft
MATCH: Pair with a green tea or a sake cocktail. Match with red berry jams or honey on a cheeseboard.

WORLD CHEESE AWARDS: Silver 2022, Bronze 2023, 2024

OG Kristal

Belgium is probably not where your mind goes first when thinking about the great cheese nations of Europe. It's home to just a single PDO-protected cheese (the pungent washed-rind Herve) and is better known for beer and chocolate. For most of its history, cheesemaking has largely been left to its dairy powerhouse neighbours of France and the Netherlands.

But change is in the air. Belgium has been quietly upping its cheese game over the past 40 years, and there are now more than 300 different varieties being made there, many by hand on small farms. And word is starting to spread. Belgian cheeses have regularly been picking up Gold and Super Gold medals at the World Cheese Awards over the past decade, and exports are increasing to the UK and US in particular.

One of the most successful is the red waxed Gouda OG Kristal, a psychedelically delicious cheese from West Flanders, which comes in 10kg (22lb) wheels and has a crystalline texture and rich, butterscotch flavour. It's a cheese that stops you in your tracks.

Made by 't Groendal in Roeselare and aged for 18 months, it's also known as Brokkeloud Roeselare and Old Groendal, but was re-christened OG Kristal for export to the US to make it easier for cheesemongers to pronounce. This instantly boosted the cheese's street cred – OG could also be interpreted as a nod to 'Original Gangster', a term that grew out of hip-hop culture to describe something respected or influential, while Kristal is similar to the high-end Champagne brand Cristal, long a favourite tipple of US rap stars. You read it here first: Belgian cheese is cool in the US.

An affineur called Kaasaffineurs Van Tricht was largely responsible for this clever marketing approach. The company, which has an excellent shop at a former brewery in Antwerp, buys young cheeses from 't Groendal and matures them in its state-of-the-art maturing rooms in the city's Wilrijk district, before selling them around the world.

Exports used to account for 5 per cent of the business, which was set up in 1970 and is today run by Frederic Van Tricht (the grandson of the founder), but now make up around 30 per cent of sales to destinations including the US, UK, Dubai and Singapore.

Van Tricht is a genial presence at international cheese shows and exhibitions, his jolly personality and laid-back approach belying a super-sharp business brain. As well as OG Kristal, the company takes cheeses from dozens of other small farms in Belgium and transforms them into new products in its maturing rooms by ageing them for different periods of time, flavouring them with ingredients, and washing the rinds in different Belgian ales.

Belgium's proud history as one of the greatest beer countries of the world has helped its cheese sector to grow, according to Van Tricht, who argues that they make for a perfect pairing. As the craft beer movement has spread around the world, so has the demand for cheese, because it is a delicious accompaniment to a brew. The bubbles and bitterness help refresh the palate, while also quenching your thirst from eating salty cheese, says Van Tricht, whose father Michel wrote a very fine book on the subject, sensibly titled *Beer & Cheese* (2012).

It's hard to disagree when you nibble a crunchy sliver of OG Kristal with a golden Belgian ale. The intense sweet and savoury cheese dovetails with the powerful fruity beer in a very refreshing way. It feels like they were made for each other. PM

ORIGIN: West Flanders, Belgium
PROTECTED STATUS: N/A
MILK: Pasteurised cow's milk
RENNET: Vegetarian
AROMA: Caramel, chocolate, pineapple
FLAVOUR: Butterscotch, cherries, cocoa
TEXTURE: Firm, crunchy
MATCH: Blonde Belgian ales, such as La Chouffe, create a killer combo, while mango chutney picks up on the sweet, spicy flavour of the cheese.

WORLD CHEESE AWARDS: Gold 2019, Silver 2024

Olavidia

It's hard to think of a better name for a dairy making cheeses that resemble lips, hearts and pillows than Quesos y Besos (Cheeses and Kisses). Silvia Peláez makes these deliciously romantic cheeses using the milk of the family's herd of Malaga breed goats. The pampered animals live in the Sierra del Trigo in Andalusia and feed on thyme, acorns, wild hay and, most importantly, olive leaves.

Quesos y Besos surprised everyone in 2021 at the World Cheese Awards, when its soft, wrinkly-rinded goat's cheese Olavidia was named World Champion, upstaging some of the most iconic cheeses to win the competition. The 250g (9oz) square cheese's distinctive rind is formed by *Geotrichum candidum*, a yeast that breaks down the interior from a chalky, dense paste to a runny, gooey cream. But even more unusual is the dark line of olive stone ash that runs through the heart of the cheese. It certainly caught the eye of the judges at the awards, who then fell in love with its flavour. It combines the earthy, fresh notes of white almonds with the distinct herbaceousness provided by the olive's ash. It is like tasting the air in the olive fields.

Jason Hinds, director of British cheesemonger Neal's Yard Dairy, was so impressed with the little goat's cheese with a heart of ash that he championed it in the final, where he famously (at least in cheese circles) declared that the cheese had stolen his heart. 'It's like nothing I've seen before,' he told a room full of cheese fans. 'It had an incredibly rich, unctuous, creamy texture, it was pillowy, warm and comforting, and the flavour was rich, round and long. I just wanted to go to bed with it.' If that's not a reason to try a cheese, we don't know what is.

Andalusia in southern Spain, where the cheese is made, is known for its olive groves and warm weather. When you visit the region, the aroma of olives is everywhere.
This is not surprising as the local producers

report that there are around 66 million trees in the region. Peláez and her husband decided to quit their jobs in 2016 to dedicate themselves to farm life; with a vision of highlighting the region's terroir, they make a range of lactic cheeses using no rennet. The milk is special as the goats eat olive leaves, known to increase milk production and improve rumen health by improving protein synthesis. Peláez ensures the milk is minimally handled to create a delicate cheese full of flavours from the environment in which the goats live.

In 2018, Luisa Villegas, head of the Instituto del Queso in Spain, discovered the cheese while judging the national competition and promoted it to win the top prize. Villegas would eventually advise Peláez to enter the cheese in the World Cheese Awards where it won the ultimate recognition. Their win was not pure luck, however. Peláez had understood that to create a new cheese, many conditions had to be met. She couldn't just copy a recipe and hope it would sell well.

Instead, she took stock of her environment and conditions, the competition and the gaps in the market. She quickly realised that a cheese that reflected the terroir of Andalusia would do well. From the selection of the breed of goats, to the inclusion of a by-product of the premier industry of the region (the olive stones), to making a soft cheese for a market dominated by hard cheeses, she succeeded in crafting something authentic and new. CY

ORIGIN: Andalusia, Spain
PROTECTED STATUS: N/A
MILK: Pasteurised goat's milk
RENNET: None (lactic set)
AROMA: Lactic, herbaceous, earthy
FLAVOUR: Fresh, creamy, mineral
TEXTURE: Soft, dense, creamy
MATCH: A glass of Spanish Cava or Sauvignon Blanc. Try chocolate-covered dried orange slices or fig spread.

WORLD CHEESE AWARDS: World Champion 2021

Passionata

A spot on the Super Jury of the World Cheese Awards is a coveted post for any cheese professional. Each judge on the panel chooses one cheese from among the hundred or so Super Gold medallists to showcase during the final. It's a chance for each judge to bang the drum for their favourite cheese, even though at this point they still don't know who made it or where.

If you're a cheesemaker, you definitely want Jason Hinds, director of Neal's Yard Dairy, on your side. A regular member of the Super Jury, Hinds has a way with words that is hard to resist. As we saw with Olavidia (see page 186), once the tall, charming Englishman starts waxing lyrical about cheese, it's hard not to agree with everything he says.

So when he picked an unusual cheese (later revealed to be Passionata, made in Brazil) in the final in 2024, people immediately started to pay attention. It was a hard cheese to ignore anyway because of its distinctive appearance and flavour.

Passionata comes in a 1.8kg (4lb) ball that looks more like fruit than cheese. The bottom half is covered with calendula flower petals, while the top part is encrusted with *maracuyá* (passionfruit) seeds. The cheese is washed with a passionfruit infusion after the curd is partially drained, giving it a fruity and floral smell and taste. The paste is firm yet creamy, with a flexible texture, but it's the aroma and flavour that stand out thanks to a big burst of sweet passionfruit notes that are wonderfully heady and perfumed.

The first Brazilian entry to ever make the final, Passionata was created by a team of dairy researchers at the Paraná Biopark in south-west Brazil, led by Kennidy de Bortoli. Since 2019, a programme called Projeto de

ORIGIN: Paraná, Brazil
PROTECTED STATUS: N/A
MILK: Pasteurised cow's milk
RENNET: Vegetarian
AROMA: Fruity, floral, tropical
FLAVOUR: Tangy, sweet, creamy
TEXTURE: Firm, creamy

MATCH: Caipirinha, a sweet cocktail made with cachaça. Serve on a cheeseboard with guava fruit paste.

WORLD CHEESE AWARDS:
Super Gold, Best Latin American Cheese 2024

Queijos Finos ('Project for Fine Cheeses') at the Biosciences hub has incubated 22 small artisan companies in the dairy sector. Bortoli's job has been to design new cheeses along with fellow researchers Aline Gouveia and Isabelli dos Passos.

A former chef, Bortoli wanted to create a cheese that embodied his country's food culture and was inspired when he passed a pile of passionfruit in the street, and thought, 'What's more Brazilian than passionfruit?'

This cheese is part of an increasingly large number of cheeses from Brazil, which have been entered into the awards thanks to the efforts of cheesemonger and judge Falco Bonfadini, who has been in charge of co-ordinating consignments from his home country each year.

In the end Passionata didn't take the top prize. It finished ninth out of the 14 cheeses in the final, although Jason Hinds did make a compelling speech in support of it after votes had been cast. A regular visitor to Latin America, Hinds argued that this part of the world is now making some of the most interesting, innovative and delicious cheeses. As usual, it was hard to disagree. CY

Patagonzola

Patagonia, at the southernmost tip of Latin America, is often referred to as 'the end of the world'. This vast and rugged region, shaped by the Andes, remains mostly wilderness. Indigenous communities were the first to inhabit the region, surviving through hunting, fishing and foraging. By the mid-1770s, Jesuit missionaries tried to establish settlements in the region, followed by waves of Welsh, German, Swiss and Italian settlers, who left a lasting imprint on the culture and economy.

Cheesemaking did not exist in Patagonia until the arrival of European settlers, who introduced dairy animals to the region. Cattle were brought to Argentina in the 1580s primarily for meat production. By the eighteenth century, small-scale dairy production took place in rural *estancias* (ranches), where families produced cheese and butter for local markets, particularly in the central provinces of Santa Fe, Córdoba and Buenos Aires. Patagonia, in contrast, remained focused on large-scale sheep farming, which expanded in the early twentieth century to meet European demand for wool.

Argentinian cheesemaking is dominated by large commodity producers, who focus on Italian-style cheeses like Mozzarella and Parmesan (see pages 80 and 38). However, in the last two decades smaller producers

have started to experiment with new styles of cheese. Quesería Ventimiglia is one of these new producers, with Mauricio Couly at the helm.

Couly's path to becoming one of the most recognised cheesemakers in Argentina started in the kitchen. Along with his twin brother Darío and his older brother Edgar, in 2004 they opened an Italian restaurant in Neuquén in the northern part of Patagonia using local ingredients in their food. The restaurant needed a good supply of Mozzarella, so Mauricio started making it with the milk of one cow named Lourdes. His mother also started making Dulce de Leche – a milk caramel sauce typical of Argentina. However, his dream was to make blue cheese. He had trained as a chef in Spain and England and was adamant he wanted to create something authentic to his place of origin, but which built on his European experiences.

He settled on a Gorgonzola-style cheese, with a twist. That came from adding sheep's milk to the mix, which brings its own unique flavour, developing a 3kg (7lb) wheel that was creamy and minerally, but with the distinctive piquancy of sheep's milk blue cheeses on the finish. The cheese is matured for 90 days in Couly's small dairy, along with two hard cheeses and three other blues. Following the ethos of his family restaurant, he named the cheese Patagonzola to pay homage to the region and the style of cheese.

Think of it as Gorgonzola with an Argentinian accent. CY

ORIGIN: Rio Negro, Argentina
PROTECTED STATUS: N/A
MILK: Pasteurised cow and sheep's milk
RENNET: Animal
AROMA: Minerally, tangy, earthy
FLAVOUR: Buttery, creamy, salty with umami and piquant notes of blue mould
TEXTURE: Creamy, crumbly, soft
MATCH: Pair with a full-bodied Malbec or Pinot Noir from Patagonia. Serve with pears and honey.

WORLD CHEESE AWARDS:
Super Gold 2024

St Jude

Hang out with cheesemakers long enough and at some point one of them will probably utter the phrase, 'You can't make good cheese from bad milk.' There usually follows solemn nods of agreement all round. It makes perfect sense when you consider that, bar a sprinkle of salt and tiny amounts of starter culture and rennet, cheese is essentially solidified milk.

Cheesemaker Julie Cheyney understands this better than most. She fell in love with the white stuff when she was a teenager with a weekend job milking cows at a farm in Hampshire, a formative experience that sparked a life-long fascination with all things dairy.

Cheyney developed the Camembert-style cheese Tunworth with Stacey Hedges in 2005, before she went it alone in 2010, working in the maturing rooms of Neal's Yard Dairy while she figured out what to do next. For a self-confessed 'cow nerd' (as she once described herself to me), it didn't take long to get back to milk and cheesemaking, and in 2012 she started making St Jude (named after the patron saint of lost causes) at a small dairy in Hampshire. A tiny, soft cow's milk cheese with a crumpled rind, which is similar to Saint-Marcellin, St Jude weighs just 95g (3oz) and comes in an open wooden box. Like its French cousin, it's a lactic cheese, made slowly by letting the milk acidify over 24 hours, before the delicate curd is hand-ladled into moulds.

St Jude has always been made with raw milk, initially from Hampshire, but when Cheyney heard a radio report about a farm in Suffolk that had invested in a herd of French Montbéliarde cows she was intrigued. Jonny and Dulcie Crickmore, who own Fen Farm Dairy in Bungay, had sold half their black-and-white cows and replaced them with Montbéliardes following a whirlwind tour of the Jura in eastern France, where the milk is used to make Comté and Mont d'Or (see pages 63 and 134). The couple wanted to make a Brie-de-Meaux-style cheese called Baron Bigod back home in Suffolk, and their French cheese consultant was adamant they needed French cows. If the story sounds familiar, it's probably because the Crickmores' experience was used as the inspiration for a storyline in the BBC radio drama *The Archers*.

Milk from Montbéliarde cows is loved by cheesemakers because it has just the right balance of protein and fat, plus high levels of a particular protein that helps form lovely shiny curds. It's also a hardy breed that can handle the marshy fens of Suffolk, just as well as the slopes of the Jura. The Crickmores dedication to good milk struck a chord with Cheyney, who gave them a call and discovered they were looking to rent out an ancillary dairy at the farm to another cheesemaker. One thing led to another and Cheyney ended up moving her life and business to Suffolk in 2014, setting up St Jude Cheese company in the small dairy at Fen Farm, where milk from those prize Montbéliardes was in ready supply.

It was a good move. St Jude has won plenty of accolades at the World Cheese Awards since then, but that's not to say that Cheyney's cheese is the same every time you taste it. What the cows are eating and where they are in their lactation cycle changes the composition of the milk throughout the year, which is reflected in the cheese. St Jude tends to be more buttery in the winter when the animals are housed in sheds and fed hay and silage, but in the spring and summer, when they are at pasture, there are more grassy and farmy notes. This seasonality is celebrated by Cheyney, who uses minimal amounts of starter culture so that the natural bacteria in the raw milk are allowed to express themselves through complex flavours in the cheese. 'I try to let the milk sing,' is how she puts it.

The length of time St Jude is matured also makes a big difference. At two weeks, it has a feathery texture and bright, zingy flavour, but becomes silky and soft with a stronger, earthy character at six weeks. The company also makes a washed-rind variation called St Cera, which has a funky orange exterior, plus a bouncy St Nectaire-style cheese called St Helena, created by Blake Bowden, who works with Cheyney.

Cheyney's quest for good milk doesn't end there, however. As this book went to press, she was in the process of moving her dairy once again, to a different farm in nearby Norfolk. The remarkable success of Baron Bigod Brie, which has become a smash hit on British deli counters, means that the Crickmores need more space to grow. So Cheyney is setting up her own dairy in a converted barn at a dairy farm in Beccles, owned by the Burroughs family. The farm has a herd of pedigree Friesians and has long championed raw milk by selling it in their own farm shop.

How the move will translate in terms of the flavour and texture of St Jude will be fascinating to follow in the coming years, but you can guarantee that any changes will be embraced by Cheyney, who just wants her milk to sing. PM

ORIGIN: East Anglia, England
PROTECTED STATUS: N/A
MILK: Raw cow's milk
RENNET: Animal
AROMA: Milky, buttery, yeasty
FLAVOUR: Young: buttery, citrussy; mature: earthy, farmy
TEXTURE: Fluffy when young, silky and gooey when mature
MATCH: Champagne, Cremant or English sparkling wine are effervescent matches. A few spears of roasted asparagus pick up on vegetal notes in the cheese.

WORLD CHEESE AWARDS: Multiple awards, including Super Gold 2024

St Malachi Reserve

'How did you get into cheese?' is one of the most common questions we're asked. Patrick began as a food writer, and I started as a cheesemonger. But there are many paths to the cheese life. Some people start as cooks, becoming fascinated by fermentation and dairy science, while farmers often seek to add value to their milk through cheesemaking. Even millionaires from finance, music and fashion have found their way into cheese, following their passions in unexpected ways.

In 2008, Richard Hayne, co-founder and CEO of high street fashion chain Urban Outfitters, purchased The Farm at Doe Run in Chester County, Pennsylvania, with a vision of pursuing a life of high-quality, small-scale cheesemaking. He recruited cheesemaker Kristian Holbrook, who developed several cow's milk cheeses, including St Malachi, named after a local church.

The cheese is made by adding lactic cultures typical of Alpine-style cheeses to the milk. Once the milk is set and cut, the curds are washed in a warm brine solution following a Gouda recipe. This raises the temperature, encouraging thermophilic (heat-loving) cultures to multiply. Then the curds are drained in medium-sized moulds weighing approximately 7.5kg (16lb) and aged for about 10 months in natural quarry stone caves. An extra-aged version, known as St Malachi Reserve, is matured for 16 months, developing a firmer texture and more pronounced sweet-savoury balance and the sought-after cheese crystals.

St Malachi is a delicious cheese made with Jersey cow's milk, known for its high fat content, perfect for making long-aged cheeses. The bright orange hue of the interior contrasts with its light grey natural rind, making it visually striking and distinctive.

The mix of styles employed, which combine techniques used for Alpine and Gouda cheeses, is most likely in response to consumer demands for cheeses that are sweeter and aged, with toffee and caramel notes. The sweet flavour is achieved by the use of *Lactobacillus helveticus*, a starter bacterium commonly present in Alpine cheeses. This culture contributes nutty to sweet flavours to cheeses, depending on the ageing conditions, and is also known to prevent bitterness in Swiss-style cheeses.

Today, the head cheesemaker is Miguel Vivanco, who continues to innovate recipes. Research and development is costly, not only in raw materials and production, but also in maturation times, and cheesemakers need deep pockets to support such an endeavour. Fashion clearly pays better than cheese. CY

ORIGIN: Pennsylvania, USA
PROTECTED STATUS: N/A
MILK: Pasteurised cow's milk
RENNET: Vegetarian
AROMA: Buttery, roasted, earthy
FLAVOUR: Hazelnut, caramel, sweet
TEXTURE: Creamy when young; brittle as it ages
MATCH: Try it with a Kentucky bourbon cocktail. A thyme cracker brings out a lovely woody note.

WORLD CHEESE AWARDS:
Super Gold 2022

São Jorge

ORIGIN: São Jorge, Azores, Portugal
PROTECTED STATUS: PDO
MILK: Raw cow's milk
RENNET: Animal
AROMA: Fruity, buttery, piquant
FLAVOUR: Spicy, fruity, farmy
TEXTURE: Close, crumbly when mature
MATCH: A glass of Madeira is a great all-Portuguese match, while a few slices of fresh pineapple accentuate the fruitiness.

WORLD CHEESE AWARDS: Multiple awards, including Super Gold 2022 (7 months, Continente Seleção), Gold 2023 (4 months, LactAçores)

Nearly a thousand miles off the coast of Portugal lies the volcanic island of São Jorge, which rises dramatically from the Atlantic. Part of the Azores archipelago, the island has a humid, subtropical climate and fertile soils thanks to its position in the Gulf Stream. Wild hydrangeas, azaleas and heathers grow among its rolling hills and sheer cliffs, but it's the lush green grass and the cows that graze upon it that are the origin of São Jorge's reputation as the 'land of cheese'.

When Flemish traders discovered this fertile oasis in the ocean in the fifteenth century, their eyes must have lit up. Hailing from a proud cheesemaking nation, it wasn't long before they shipped cows there and set about making cheese. It was such a good place for rearing livestock that São Jorge soon became famous for its eponymous hard cheeses as the island flourished as a stop-off point for passing ships.

São Jorge remains the jewel in the Azorean cheese crown. It accounts for around three-quarters of the island's economy and is home to over 20,000 cows (more than twice the human population), which graze the fields and meadows covering the central plateau, where 360-degree ocean views are not uncommon. Their raw milk is turned into a hard cheese that is crafted in a similar way to Cheddar.

Portugal's largest cheese, weighing in at anywhere from 8 to 12kg (18 to 26lb), it is made by fermenting the milk with home-made whey starter cultures and calf's rennet, much as it would have been by Flemish cheesemakers. Like Cheddar, the curd is cut into small pieces and cooked in the vat before the whey is drained and the dry curd salted, then pressed in wheel-shaped moulds. São Jorge is aged for anywhere from 90 days (the minimum allowed under its PDO) to 7 or 12 months, and sometimes much longer.

The Cheddar comparisons also hold partly true for the eating experience. São Jorge has a close, even texture with the odd small hole, and becomes more brittle and crumbly with age. There's a fruity, farmy and savoury quality to the cheese, which is Cheddar-like, but there is also a distinct spiciness, which is a common characteristic of Portuguese cheeses. You often get a pleasant tingly sensation on your lips when tasting a piece of mature São Jorge.

Those Flemish cheesemakers knew cheese paradise when they saw it. PM

HERO CHEESE

Serra da Estrela

On a crisp November afternoon, we arrived at the modest Queijaria Quinta da Pena, nestled in the quiet town of Carragozela in central Portugal. The air was still, save for the distant bleating of sheep, and for a moment it seemed as though only the watchful farm dogs were here to greet us. At the western edge of the Serra da Estrela mountain range, the location carried an air of solitude, as if time itself had slowed to match the quiet rhythms of rural life.

Cheesemaker Inês Pessoa, who greeted us at the dairy door, is an integral part of these rural rhythms. She is the second generation of her family to make an iconic Portuguese cheese that has a history stretching back more than 2,000 years.

Queijo Serra da Estrela honours two gifts of the region: the raw milk of Bordaleira Serra da Estrela and Churra Mondegueira sheep; and the cardoon flower, a humble plant that is used instead of animal rennet to set the milk and has defined cheesemaking in Portugal for centuries.

As Pessoa showed us around her small dairy, it was clear there is not only pride in her culture, but also hope that this cheese will endure for generations to come.

Queijo Serra da Estrela, celebrated for its sumptuously creamy texture, is perhaps the finest example of a much-loved Portuguese soft cheese style known as Amanteigado. The cheese is also classified as a *Torta*, a native Iberian tradition represented by Azeitão, also from Portugal, and Torta del Casar (see page 151) and La Serena from Extremadura province in Spain. What unites them all is the use of thistle rennet, extracted from the cardoon flower, giving them their signature silky consistency and delicate bitter undertones.

Amanteigado is thought to be Portugal's oldest cheese, with its origins in Roman times, when the Iberian peninsula was separated into two provinces. Both Extremadura and what we know as Portugal today were part of Hispania Ulterior, established in 197 BCE while Rome was still a Republic. In 1287, long after the Romans had left, King Dom Dinis established the first official cheese market in Celorico da Beira, within the Serra da Estrela region. The cheese was eventually protected under national laws and gained European PDO protection in 1996.

Serra da Estrela is a complicated cheese to make. Not only do the quantities of milk and rennet have to be exact, but the production methods are laborious and the maturation difficult. Its stringent PDO regulations, high cost of production, and labour-intensive craftsmanship pose challenges that often deter cheesemakers from attempting it.

Many producers prefer instead to make Queijo de Ovelha Amanteigado, following the same traditional techniques as Serra da Estrela, but using milk from different sheep breeds or producing outside the designated 18-municipality region recognised by the PDO.

For other producers, crafting both cheeses side by side ensures financial stability while continuing to preserve their heritage. At Quinta da Pena, Inês Pessoa and daughters Lúcia and Maria Edite Pessoa have taken things a step further by infusing their Amanteigado with piri-piri chilli, creating a vibrant, fiery twist on the traditional cheese. It is another way to keep their heritage alive after over 30 years of making cheese with the milk of their animals.

During our visit, Inês guided us through the process of preparing thistle rennet, a simple but essential technique to make Serra da Estrela cheese. A cloth pouch, filled with the dried stamens of cardoon flowers, is submerged in a small amount of water or milk, allowing the enzymes in the plant to infuse the liquid. This dark 'tea' is then poured into the vat, coaxing the milk into curds. Cardoon thistles (*Cynara cardunculus*), which bloom in the summer with spiky purple flowers, thrive wild in the surrounding fields. Lúcia gathers hundreds of fresh blossoms by hand, drying them meticulously in-house before carefully separating the tops. Other cheesemakers take different routes. Some purchase pre-dried flower crowns, while others opt for a concentrated liquid coagulant sourced from larger producers.

With a proud smile, Maria Edite led us into their maturation room as we waited for the milk to curdle, where hundreds of wheels of cheese stood patiently, awaiting their journey to their biggest customer: Casa Portuguesa do Pastel de Bacalhau, a famous 11-restaurant chain known for its cheese-filled codfish cakes. Inês recounted how the restaurateurs behind the brand arrived at a

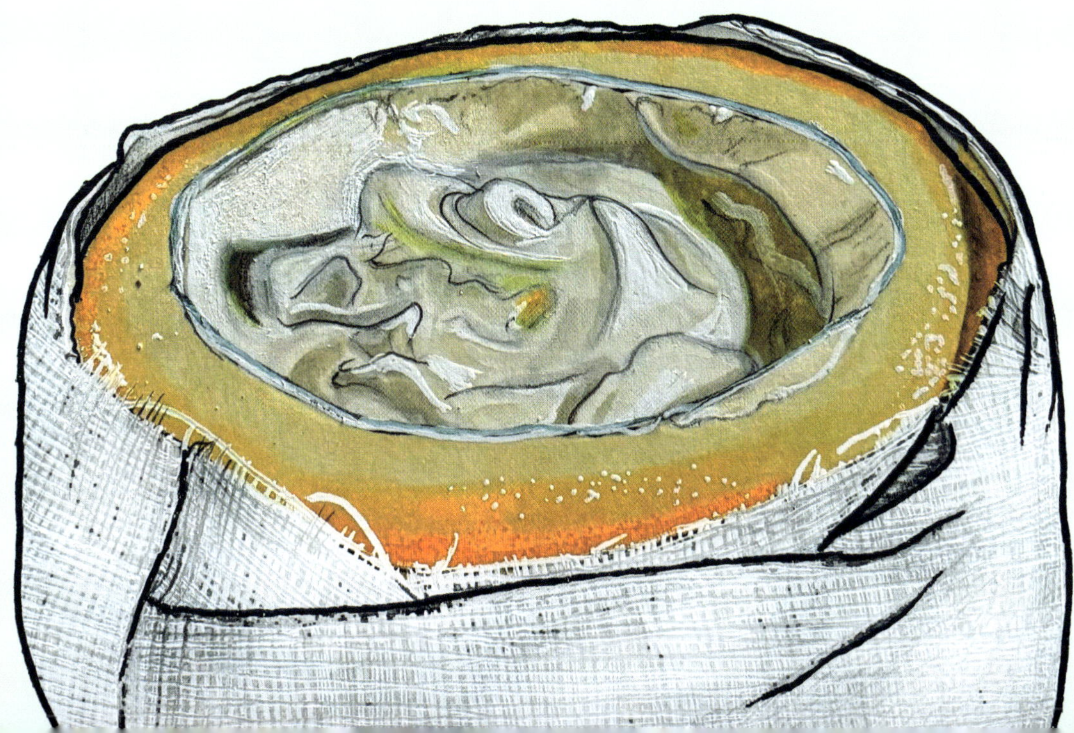

ORIGIN: Serra da Estrela region, Portugal

PROTECTED STATUS: PDO

MILK: Raw sheep's milk

RENNET: Vegetarian (thistle)

AROMA: Creamy, acidic, mineral

FLAVOUR: Buttery, tangy, slight bitterness

TEXTURE: Gooey, soft, silky

MATCH: Vinho Verde or a Gouveio white wine. Serve with crusty bread, olives and cured meats.

WORLD CHEESE AWARDS: Multiple awards, including Super Gold 2021 (Pingo Doce)

key moment, offering a lifeline just when her farm needed it most. Today, they buy nearly their entire inventory, ensuring that Queijaria Quinta da Pena can focus on making cheese rather than worrying about sales. For small producers, partnerships like these are more than business, they are a promise of survival, a hope for traditional cheesemaking. Having tried one of their famous fish cakes in Lisbon, I can tell you that the tangy creaminess of Serra da Estrela is the perfect balance to the salty richness of Portugal's beloved dried cod.

But there are still plenty of challenges facing the makers of this ancient style of cheese. Lúcia told us that the thistle is losing its strength to curdle milk as flowers are stressed from longer drought periods. Similarly, sheep are facing tougher conditions in a warming climate.

Farmers like Aurélio Pinto of Quinta da Estaca, who later in the day took us to his fields to see the region's famous Bordaleira sheep, told us about the difficulty of keeping animals in dry pastures. The reality of this type of subsistence farming is that many variables are at play, and one season of bad weather or the loss of a large client can mean total failure. In many ways, Queijo Serra da Estrela is only possible because of the dedication of these farmers and makers.

Our day had begun at the break of dawn, eager to witness the magic of cheesemaking at Quinta do Tinte – another small cheesemaker in the area. Most producers are already hard at work before sunrise, as the first task of the day is always milking. With raw milk at its most delicate, cheesemakers waste no time in preserving its character.

After a short walk down a long driveway, we were greeted with warm smiles from Aida Lopes and her team of four women. The creamery was small but efficient, a place of precision where only the essentials were allowed. The air in the room was thick with the comforting aroma of whey, a scent so familiar to me it made me feel at home.

We watched in fascination as they salted the milk before coagulation, a surprising step that sets this cheesemaking method apart. For pretty much every other cheese I know, salt is added at the end of the cheesemaking process, once the milk has been set and the curd formed. Brining, dry rubbing salt onto the rind or breaking up the curd and then sprinkling it with salt, is the usual way to go about things. Quite why it is added to the milk in Serra da Estrela is a mystery, at least to me. That's just the way it has always been done.

Just beyond the cheesery, two well-stocked maturation rooms stood, their shelves lined with cheeses at various stages of ageing. In the adjacent space, finished wheels were gently washed and carefully bound in cloth, an important detail ensuring they held their form as they slowly aged. Each wheel was between 0.8 and 1.7kg (1lb 12oz and 3lb 12oz) and aged from 30 to 60 days.

This style of cheese is commonly eaten by slicing the top off and scooping out the gooey interior. The characteristic bitterness is balanced by the creaminess of the sheep's milk. Queijo Serra da Estrela also has a long finish, developed during the maturation process, in which the wheels are maintained at a specific humidity to prevent the rind from breaking. Washed-rind cheeses vary around the world, but they are all made by cleaning the exterior with water or brine. This process removes moulds and encourages certain micro-organisms.

In 2024, the World Cheese Awards Super Jury crowned a cheese resembling Serra da Estrela. We had hoped it was from a producer we'd visited, but in a twist, the champion wasn't a Serra da Estrela PDO, it was a Queijo de Ovelha Amanteigado, made by Queijaria Quinta do Pomar, a small dairy that stunned everyone by winning the World Champion title. For the first time a Portuguese cheese earned the top honour, marking an important moment for the country's rich dairy heritage. CY

Sinodun Hill

When Fraser Norton and Rachel Yarrow took a well-earned holiday in Sicily in 2014, they weren't expecting their lives to change forever. But that's exactly what happened when they read an article about a goat's cheese maker in an old copy of *Woman & Home* magazine at their rented villa.

Norton was a project manager and Yarrow an English teacher, but both had itchy feet and were looking for something new. The article was the catalyst they needed, prompting them to give up their careers, buy a herd of goats and set up their own company called Norton & Yarrow, making cheese at Earth Trust Farm in Oxfordshire.

If that sounds like a great leap into the unknown, it makes more sense when you learn that both have farming in the family. Norton's grandparents had an 80-hectare (200-acre) farm in Nottinghamshire, and Yarrow's parents worked on a sheep farm in South Wales in the 1970s.

Their first creation was a lactic, pyramid-shaped soft cheese they named Sinodun Hill after a local landmark. Originally based on a recipe for a French cheese called Pouligny-Saint-Pierre, which has a similar shape and wrinkly rind, the cheese was quick to mature and sell, and good for cashflow. It was also the perfect vehicle for showcasing the creamy milk from their floppy-eared Anglo Nubian goats.

Think of British cheese and you probably picture a hunk of Cheddar or a marbled wedge of Stilton, but the country's more recent cheesemaking history has a distinctly Continental feel. Over the past 40 years British cheesemakers have followed in the footsteps of their European counterparts to create the kind of soft, pungent cheeses you'd expect to find in a French *fromagerie*.

There's Tunworth, which is now made in Lancashire and which French chef Raymond Blanc once described as the best Camembert in the world, while Baron Bigod from Suffolk has taken the place of French Bries on many British deli counters. Then there's the Morbier-inspired Ashcombe from Gloucestershire, complete with a line of ash, and the Roquefort-esque Beenleigh Blue, which is made with sheep's milk in Devon.

The lactic goat's cheeses of the Loire Valley in France, where Pouligny-Saint-Pierre is made, have also been a rich source of inspiration for British cheesemakers, with dozens of new cheeses in shapes ranging from logs and buttons to pyramids and bricks launched over the past few decades. They've found a receptive audience among British shoppers, who have fond memories of tasting *chèvre* (goat's cheese) on holiday in France, but want to support British farmers.

Sinodun Hill, which was first launched in 2016, has quickly risen to become a benchmark for the new style, winning Best Artisan Cheese at the World Cheese Awards in 2022 and Best British Cheese the year after, along with two Super Gold medals.

Its success is a measure of its consistency, but is also due to its unique character that is quite different to French cheeses. Sinodun Hill is distinctly British, with a clean, creamy flavour, plus a light, mousse-like texture, which is partly to do with the goat breed, but also because the method for making Sinodun has evolved away from the original French recipe.

Rather than using animal rennet, the couple

use thistle rennet from cardoon flowers to set the milk – a technique associated with Spanish and Portuguese cheeses – which helps create a more delicate, fragile curd. While most French cheeses are drained in plastic moulds and salt added by rubbing directly on the rind, the curd for Sinodun is drained overnight in muslin bags before being broken up and the salt mixed in. Only then is the curd scooped into moulds by hand, a method that helps give it a fluffy, whipped texture.

In 2018, Sinodun Hill was joined by a sister cheese – the soft, round Brightwell Ash – which led to the company quickly reaching capacity at the farm in Oxfordshire. So in 2025 Norton & Yarrow relocated its herd of goats to a larger farm in the Brecon Beacons in Carmarthenshire, Wales, where the couple are planning to implement regenerative agricultural methods and create new cheeses.

In a strange twist of fate, the farm is the same one that Yarrow's father worked at in the 1970s. Maybe it was written in the pages of a magazine all along. PM

ORIGIN: Oxfordshire, England (but now made in Carmarthenshire, Wales)

PROTECTED STATUS: N/A

MILK: Pasteurised goat's milk

RENNET: Vegetarian (thistle)

AROMA: Citrus, yoghurt, yeasty

FLAVOUR: Creamy, grassy, almondy

TEXTURE: Light, fluffy

MATCH: Sauvignon Blanc or Picpoul de Pinet are easy matches, but white port is also good, bringing nutty tones. Cherries are a refreshing, summery accompaniment.

WORLD CHEESE AWARDS: Super Gold and Best Artisan Cheese 2022, Super Gold and Best British Cheese 2023

Syrna Torbynka

It was a bittersweet moment when Syrna Torbynka won a Super Gold medal at the World Cheese Awards in 2022.

The smoked cow's milk cheese, which is similar to Scamorza, was the first ever Ukrainian cheese to win a top prize in the competition. For an up-and-coming cheese nation, this was a moment to celebrate. But the joy was tempered by the hard reality of war. Originally the competition had been scheduled to take place in Ukraine's capital, Kyiv, but judging was moved to Newport in Wales after Russia's invasion of Ukraine in February 2022.

Under such circumstances, it was a minor miracle that Syrna Torbynka, along with 38 other Ukrainian cheeses, made it to Wales to be judged at all, and testament to the determination of the country's cheesemakers to carry on in a crisis. If the awards couldn't be held in Ukraine, then they sure as hell weren't going to miss out on taking part.

This fighting spirit was embodied by Ukrainian cheese expert and judge Oksana Chernova, head of an organisation called ProCheese, which works to raise standards and the profile of Ukrainian cheese. She was key to organising the complex logistics involved in getting cheese from war-torn Ukraine to Wales, helped in her mission by the Guild of Fine Food, which waived any fees for Ukrainian entries and paid for transport in a show of solidarity.

Of the 39 cheeses that were entered, 13 of them won awards, but it was Syrna Torbynka that was named Best Ukrainian Cheese, and for good reason. Made by former music teacher turned cheesemaker Natalia Palchak at a small

ORIGIN: Ivano-Frankivsk, Ukraine
PROTECTED STATUS: N/A
MILK: Pasteurised cow's milk
RENNET: Vegetarian
AROMA: Fragrant, sweet, resinous
FLAVOUR: Fruity, milky, smoky
TEXTURE: Elastic, dense

MATCH: Dark ales lean into the smokiness, while plum or cranberry chutney bring sweetness and sharpness.

WORLD CHEESE AWARDS: Super Gold and Best Ukrainian Cheese 2022

dairy called Stanislavs'ka Syrovarnya in the western Ivano-Frankivsk region of Ukraine, the cheese is made a little like Mozzarella (see page 80) by stretching cow's milk curd in hot water until it becomes elastic. But unlike Mozzarella, the cheese is formed into small bag shapes by hand (*syrna torbynka* means 'small bag'), then hung over gently smouldering alder wood chips.

The finished cheese has a semi-hard, pliable texture and golden waxy exterior. It's a fine snack on its own or can be melted into a stringy goo, and has a harmonious mix of sweet dairy and umami flavours, plus a slightly tannic note near the rind, which is almost resinous.

It's also delicious with beer, as I discovered at an event in London to showcase the winners from the 2022 awards, where we paired the cheese with a smoked honey porter. The sweet, chocolatey ale worked very nicely with the dairy notes in the cheese, while there was a pleasing smoky harmony. Chernova explained how tough it was (and still is) for cheesemakers in Ukraine, who are battling power cuts, labour shortages and logistics disruptions.

Despite these challenges, Ukrainian cheesemakers are somehow managing to produce more cheese now than they did at the start of the war, and have continued to enter the World Cheese Awards. There is hope that one day the competition will finally take place in Kyiv.

In the grand scheme of things, Syrna Torbynka winning an award was a small victory. But a victory nevertheless. PM

THE FUTURE

Where will cheese go next and what will be considered the world's best in years to come? Here are 10 cheeses that have not yet won major honours at the World Cheese Awards, but which we think deserve more recognition. They also show how artisan cheesemakers can flourish, whether that's by working collectively and staying true to traditions, or creating cutting-edge cheeses that push boundaries.

Above: Storico Ribelle (see page 224)

Bandel

If you love Indian desserts like *rosogolla* (*rasagulla*) or *sandesh*, you should meet their salty sister: Bandel cheese. These three iconic Bengali dairy delights share a common origin, tracing back to the colonial kitchens of Portuguese-occupied India. All are crafted from *chenna*, a fresh curd, but while the desserts are soaked in sugar syrup, Bandel cheese takes a different path. It is heavily salted for preservation, and sometimes smoked, resulting in its bold, earthy flavour. Traditionally shaped into small 20g (¾oz) discs, this unique cheese embodies history, technique and taste, and is a testament to Bengal's rich culinary culture.

Bandel is traditionally soaked in water or milk overnight to soften the cheese, and eaten along with rice or left dried to grate on top of salads, omelettes or tandoori dishes. In recent years, Bandel has experienced a revival, driven by a growing interest in traditional and artisanal cheeses across the subcontinent.

The story of this cheese starts with the arrival of Portuguese traders to the Bengali coast, where they settled in the town of Bandel about 50km (31 miles) north of Kolkata in north-east India. While cows were prevalent and sacred, the curdling of milk was considered a religious taboo under orthodox Hinduism. Still, in colonial kitchens, cooks from Myanmar under the supervision of the Portuguese tried to replicate *queijo fresco*, popular in the Iberian peninsula but impossible to import in good condition because of the long sea voyage. The local religious prohibition on killing cows meant that animal rennet was not available, a fact that remains the same today in India for commercial production, and therefore these home cheesemakers had to employ a lactic set (using lactic cultures to acidify the milk until it curdles). Portuguese producers are known for making cheese without the need for animal rennet, instead using thistle flowers to coagulate milk.

Cheesemakers in India use citrus fruit juice, vinegar or other acidic agents, plus heat to curdle milk to make a simple fresh cheese. Once drained, the curd is milled by hand and salted to preserve the cheese. It is left to dry and age, but can be eaten soon after. Some cheesemakers used to smoke their small discs to give them an even longer ageing time. Nowadays, it seems only the Ghosh family of Bankura district in West Bengal continue to make this cheese.

Saurav Gupta, owner of The Whole Hog Deli in Kolkata's New Market, handles all trade, and, along with researchers in the Jadavpur University, is seeking Protected Geographical Indication status for the cheese, after it was almost lost during the COVID-19 pandemic when the producer had to discard 12,000 discs of cheese.

I tried the cheese in 2019 during a trip to India and was surprised by its salty, umami flavours. I instantly imagined this cheese would be a favourite to top many foods, and to add an extra complexity to spicy dishes. I had the pleasure of speaking with Gupta, as well as other cheese experts from India, including friends Mansi Jasani and Namrata Sundaresan, who all mentioned the importance of chefs in India incorporating cheese in their dishes as a way of supporting the entire production and supply chain and to ensure the cheese doesn't disappear.

I consider Bandel a strong contender for future medals at the World Cheese

Awards. Like many cheeses from regions outside Europe and North America, it faces the risk of disappearing, yet it remains a unique and culturally significant product. As the awards gain broader influence and more producers from diverse backgrounds enter the competition, there is a growing acknowledgement that these cheeses hold a rightful place in local cuisines. They serve as key ingredients in preserving culinary authenticity, no matter where a dish is prepared. CY

ORIGIN: West Bengal, India
PROTECTED STATUS: N/A
MILK: Pasteurised cow's milk
RENNET: Vegetarian
AROMA: Nutty, piquant, some are smoky
FLAVOUR: Earthy, salty, umami
TEXTURE: Firm, crumbly, grainy
MATCH: Serve grated on fruit salad or jaggery ice cream. Pair with sparkling fruit waters or a gin and tonic.

WORLD CHEESE AWARDS: None

Le Barriquet

If you are born into a family of Comté-makers and want a life in cheese, it's a safe bet you will make Comté, just like your parents and grandparents before you.

The history and tradition of French cheese is one of its greatest strengths and explains why it has so many PDO-protected cheeses (48 at the last time of counting). But there is an argument that tradition, and especially the rules set out in PDOs, can also act as a pair of golden handcuffs, providing security, stability and strength in numbers, while at the same time stifling innovation and change. You'd be a brave Comté-maker to go it alone and make a brand new cheese.

But there are signs that the French cheese industry is starting to embrace change. In areas such as Brittany and Provence, where there are fewer PDOs and strong demand for local foods, younger, well-travelled cheesemakers are developing their own styles. Respected affineur and *fromager* Mons is a good example. The company was set up in the 1960s by the Mons family and matures cheeses in a former railway tunnel in Saint-Haon-le-Châtel in the Loire. In 2016 owner Hervé Mons also set up a dairy, Laiterie de la Côte Roannaise, where exciting new cheeses are being forged.

Which brings us neatly to Le Barriquet: a relatively new cheese that provides a glimpse of what the future might hold for French *fromage*. Made with organic, raw goat's milk from a local farm, the barrel-shaped cheese (*barriquet* means 'barrel' in

French) is most unlike the soft PDO *chèvres* that the Loire Valley is famous for. Cheeses such as Selles-sur-Cher (see page 91) involve adding starter cultures and a tiny amount of rennet to the milk, which slowly acidifies over several days into a delicate, fluffy curd. But Mons's production space is too small to house multiple vats of curd sitting around for days on end.

Instead, Le Barriquet is made quickly, with more rennet and different starter cultures that produce less acid to create a firmer, springier curd that can be moulded into barrel shapes.

These are then washed in brine as they mature on damp straw to create a pungent, orange rind that is very different to the delicate wrinkly and ash-covered coats of most Loire goat's cheeses.

To finish, the outside is printed with two thin silhouette-style illustrations of goats and a shepherd using annatto, which encircle the cheese like the hoops of a barrel.

It's an impressive little cheese to look at, but there's much more to Le Barriquet than its dinky shape. The bouncy texture is reminiscent of a young Tomme or Reblochon, but with sweet, floral notes from the goat's milk, while the peanut-coloured rind brings smoke and meatiness, a bit like Raclette.

It's a cheese that feels familiar in some ways, but completely new in others. It's definitely not Selles-sur-Cher, or Comté come to that. PM

ORIGIN: Loire, France
PROTECTED STATUS: N/A
MILK: Raw goat's milk
RENNET: Animal
AROMA: Savoury, earthy, milky
FLAVOUR: Caramel, honeysuckle, smoky
TEXTURE: Springy, supple
MATCH: Dessert wines, such as Sauternes. Smoked saucisson dovetails nicely with the smoky, meaty rind.

WORLD CHEESE AWARDS: None

Bola de Ocosingo

This unique *queso* from southern Mexico has a special place in my heart, and not just because it's from my home country.

Made in large spheres (*bola* means 'ball' in Spanish) from raw cow's milk, it is really two cheeses in one. The outer shell is made with a hardened Mozzarella-style curd using skimmed milk, while inside is a pale yellow, crumbly paste that is aromatic with tangy umami flavours. It tastes tropical with notes of green mango, with a dense texture that coats the palate.

Queso Bola de Ocosingo, as it is officially named under a collective trademark, is made in and around the city of Ocosingo in Chiapas, which despite being one of the poorest states in Mexico, is rich in culture, with a proud independent Indigenous heritage, and strong culinary traditions.

The crumbly filling is made by fermenting cheese curds in hanging muslin bags. After the milk has coagulated, the curds drain for up to eight days, which changes the acidity of the paste, giving it a distinctive tangy taste. The process is essential as the climate in Chiapas is warm and many foods are made acidic to help preserve them.

Once the paste is ready, cheesemakers form it into balls of one of two sizes, either 250g (9oz) or 500g (1lb 2oz), and cover them with two thin layers of Mozzarella-style cheese. The process requires skill and speed. The curd skins need to be both hot enough to stretch and thin enough that they don't cook the cheese inside.

While you can appreciate Bola's unique taste unaccompanied, where it really comes alive is crumbled, like so many Mexican cheeses, atop a dish like enchiladas, over soupy black beans, or added to a raw shredded beetroot and carrot salad. A little goes a long way, and the concentrated intensity of the cheese allows it to stand up even to spicy salsas, adding complexity, when other more subtle cheeses would be lost on a chilli-numbed tongue.

There is no official, agreed-upon history of how the cheese was created. However, most credit an enterprising matriarch looking to replicate the form of a well-known Dutch cheese. Edam had become popular in the Yucatan Peninsula, north of Chiapas, as the port towns there received ships sailing to the Caribbean. Yet while Queso Bola may look like an Edam from the outside, inside it is an entirely different cheese.

It's not just the quirky shape, cheesemaking method and history of Bola de Ocosingo that appeals to me. Our family business in Mexico owes its beginnings to cheeses from Chiapas. After returning from an inspirational visit to meet cheesemakers in the region in 2010, I decided to launch a cheese blog called 'Lactography', with the tagline: 'Mongering cheese knowledge'. My sister, Georgina, was similarly inspired and took things to the next level, setting up a distribution and retail company with the same name. Back then, Bola de Ocosingo wasn't available outside Chiapas. My husband, having tasted it, encouraged us to find a way to bring it to Mexico City. We saw an opportunity to create a domestic market to support rural cheesemakers, and have stocked the cheese ever since.

I prefer the version made by cheesemaker Charito Bassoul at Quesos Laltic. Her cheese has competed in the World Cheese Awards multiple times, but is yet to win a trophy. It's a cheese that can be confusing at first contact due to its unusual shape and vibrant flavour. International judges have yet to fully appreciate the flavour profile and how to cut it open. The best way is to soften the hard exterior by placing it in a bowl of warm water for several minutes and then slice the top off. The paste inside will be firm, but can be scooped out.

Bola de Ocosingo has survived by becoming part of the gastronomic culture of the region, while also finding a new market. The export of Latin American ingredients from different regions is continuously redefining how we enjoy the cuisines of those cultures, and cheeses are a huge part of that complexity. CY

ORIGIN: Chiapas, Mexico

PROTECTED STATUS: Collective trademark

MILK: Raw cow's milk

RENNET: Animal

AROMA: Lactic, sour, mineral

FLAVOUR: Tangy, creamy, umami

TEXTURE: Paste is dense and crumbly; exterior shell is hard and chewy

MATCH: Pair with a light lager or a margarita. Sprinkle on black bean soup or on top of grilled beetroot.

WORLD CHEESE AWARDS: None

Cotija

Order enchiladas in Mexico City and you will get some salty white cheese crumbled on top. Vendors will tell you it is Cotija, but they are not giving you the whole story. Cotija has become a generic name used to describe any hard, salty white cheese made in central Mexico. It is sprinkled liberally on all manner of street food snacks, from *flautas* (rolled tacos) to *tlacoyos* (thick, oval-shaped corn tortillas). But here we are not writing about the generic cheese. I want to tell you about the 'real' cheese, which is one of just a handful to still be made in the mountains of Latin America.

The mountain range Sierra Jalmich extends across the central Mexican states of Jalisco and Michoacán. The mountains run north to south-east and give the town of Cotija a mild temperature throughout the year. The sierra plays an important role in capturing and distributing water to the adjacent valleys. The grasses that grow on the hills are wonderful forage for the cattle that travel up the mountains during the rainy season.

The milk produced from June to September is high in fats, perfect for making true mountain Cotija. This milk is kept raw and used to produce large wheels of cheese (around 20kg/44lb), which are first held by the cheesemakers in their finishing rooms and then brought to special cellars to mature. There is a minimum requirement of three months' ageing in the town of Cotija for this cheese to be certified as a Cotija de la Región de Origen (the official name in Spanish), though some wheels can be aged for up to 24 months.

Mountain Cotija is firm and easy to shave or crumble. It has creamy, soured butter notes and a distinct savoury flavour. This comes from the rock salt rubbed onto the

ORIGIN: Sierra Jalmich, Michoacán and Jalisco, Mexico

PROTECTED STATUS: Collective trademark

MILK: Raw cow's milk

RENNET: Animal

AROMA: Buttery, tangy, animal

FLAVOUR: Tropical, salty

TEXTURE: Hard, firm, crumbly

MATCH: Chocolate stouts or a fruity tequila cocktail. Perfect with Mexican corn-based snacks known as *antojitos*.

WORLD CHEESE AWARDS: None

surface during the early stages of *añejamiento* (ageing). It is this hard and salty profile that has been copied by industrial cheesemakers across Mexico. However, you will recognise a true mountain cheese by its colour. With a pale-yellow paste and a dark brown rind, the cheese looks very rustic, but the flavour is mellow and sometimes even tropical, with grilled pineapple notes.

The cheese is used for a typical lent dish called *capirotada*, made with leftover bread, raisins and sugar syrup. And like many other cheeses with a lot of umami notes, it is also used during the Christian holidays when meat consumption is restricted.

In the early 2000s, the cheese producers of the region tried to gain protected status with a Denomination of Origin. The project was led by the late Dr Esteban Barragan and his wife Professor Rogelia Villa, owners of El Mesón del Cotija, the central ageing facility for this cheese, where all cheeses are matured before being recognised as real Cotijas. However, the pro-business government of the period decided to deny the protection and instead created a collective trademark, arguing that the name of the cheese had become generic so enforcing full protection would be difficult.

This watered-down trademark didn't prevent the use of the name to describe any cheese made around Mexico, effectively unlinking origin and product. The decision paved the way for another cheese-naming fight, one that has caused very big issues with Spain and the European Union in international trade negotiations (see Manchego, page 76). Mountain Cotija has some legal protections, but lately drug cartels have threatened farmers to give up their lands or extorted them for money, causing a mass exodus of farm workers and putting the survival of this cheese in danger. Cotija was included in Slow Food's Ark of Taste to promote its permanence, but it may become extinct before long. Hopefully, greater international awareness of the cheese will stop it from disappearing completely.

There are cheeses which are made in the exact same way but are aged outside of the town of Cotija. These are commonly known as *curesmeños*, which translates to 'those of the lent period', which shows how important this style of cheese is in the gastronomy of this religious region that has its high holiday season during Easter. This cheese is mostly made in the summer rainy season, and it is perfect eight months later. Next time you order enchiladas, ask for real Cotija. CY

Grayson

'At root, all farming is just harvesting sunlight,' is the philosophy behind Meadow Creek Dairy, the makers of Grayson. This seasonal cheese is made from raw milk during the months when the cows graze freely on the lush pastures of the Appalachian Mountains in the eastern United States.

Grayson, named after the county in which it is made, comes in a square shape, weighing approximately 1.6kg (3.5lb), with a striking bright orange, sticky rind that exudes a pungent, earthy aroma. Its interior is soft and fudgy, offering deep beefy and umami notes. A bold, washed-rind cheese that commands attention, Grayson is one I often consider among my favourite cheeses in the world.

Grayson checks many boxes for me, but above all, it stands out as a highly sustainable cheese. The team at Meadow Creek practices Management Intensive Grazing (MIG), a method that involves rotating cattle between paddocks, encouraging deep-rooted grass growth and preventing soil erosion while promoting continuous, healthy re-growth without the need for chemical fertilisers.

Farmers use this approach, which is sometimes referred to as regenerative farming, to enhance pasture quality while fostering biodiversity. Additionally, Meadow Creek Dairy makes this cheese while the cows are on fresh grass from April to October. The milk dries up during the autumn and winter, allowing the cows to have a natural calving cycle and prolonging their lives. Small actions like these are all part of a holistic vision to run an environmentally sustainable business.

The herd has been developed by crossbreeding Jersey, New Zealand Friesian and Montbéliarde genes, selecting for specific traits using artificial insemination. This has been a crucial step as the farm needed smaller cows producing good-quality milk for cheesemaking that could live in the hot summers of the Virginia Highlands. These cows

ORIGIN: Virginia, USA
PROTECTED STATUS: N/A
MILK: Raw cow's milk
RENNET: Animal
AROMA: Stinky, brothy, earthy
FLAVOUR: Beefy, umami, grassy
TEXTURE: Fudgy, silky, gooey

MATCH: Gewürztraminer or a Red Ale. Serve it melted on roasted potatoes or mix it with polenta.

WORLD CHEESE AWARDS:
Silver 2022

require less water and are nimble enough to climb mountains to graze on pastureland. Seasonal grazing also means that cows are transforming grass into milk at the time of year when sunshine is most abundant, which encourages faster plant growth. The careful management of paddocks and other regenerative agricultural methods ensure Meadow Creek Dairy has perennial pastures that can be relied upon to provide nutrition year after year.

All this work in the fields has paid dividends in the cheese dairy, where owner Helen Feete and her daughter-in-law Ana can use the milk without pasteurisation to make a cheese that is aged for 90 days and expresses the bounty of the region. Feete and her husband Rick started their dairy in 1988 in the town of Galax. He and their son, Jim, take care of the farm, while daughter Kat is responsible for all business management.

There's no denying that cheese, alongside milk, is one of the most environmentally impactful foods. From the animals' emissions, including methane, to the feed and water needed to maintain ruminants, cheese can be resource-hungry.

The industry as a whole has been slow to adopt changes to reduce carbon emissions and control consumption of resources. Big dairy is mostly responsible for the highest emissions, but smaller farms also need to address the challenges. The overuse of plastic, constant refrigeration, and in some cases long transportation distances to get cheeses to markets around the world, are some of the issues the dairy industry is trying to tackle.

Some of these can be addressed by the consumer on an individual basis, such as eating seasonally and buying mostly local cheeses from independent shops or cheesemakers themselves, to reduce the use of long-haul transportation and excess packaging. However, parts of the system need a total re-think, so it's exciting that producers like Meadow Creek Dairy continue to innovate and lead the way.

Grayson may not be a cheese that you will see in Europe any time soon – high tariffs and long distances make it hard to export – but while in season it is very easy to find in independent shops in the US. Stores all over the country wait patiently for their allocations, and when the cheese is on counters, there is real excitement from those in the know. CY

Kirli Hanım

So far in our search for the best cheese in the world, we've spent a lot of time in Europe and North America with a few forays into Latin America, Australia and Asia. But perhaps we should have been looking in the place where it all began.

Exactly where, when and how cheese was first invented is a matter of archaeological debate, but most agree that it was somewhere in the Fertile Crescent – a region that spans much of what is today North Africa, the Middle East and southern Turkey. This is where Neolithic settlers began to farm for the first time around 13,000 years ago, and started to get a taste for dairy.

Cheese was probably first invented when someone tried sheep or goat's milk that had naturally curdled into yoghurt and thought it might be a good idea to drain off the whey and add salt. This type of strained yoghurt cheese is still popular across the region, where it is widely known as labneh, but there are plenty of other curd cheeses with ancient roots that reflect the gradual evolution of cheesemaking.

Turkey in particular is home to some fascinating cheeses that have histories stretching back millennia, from *süzme yoğurt* (strained yoghurt) and soft whey cheeses made like Ricotta (Lor), to goat's cheeses that are preserved in brine (Beyaz) or aged in animal skins (Tulum).

Kirli Hanım is another of these early cheeses, which was once lost to history but has since been given a new lease of life. A sheep's cheese that was common in the Balıkesir region of north-western Turkey, it used to be made as a means of storing the glut of milk that would come in the spring and summer. The soft cheese was left on racks outside to dry in the warm sun and vigorous winds in this part of Turkey, during which time a grey mould would form on the previously pristine white cheese (*kirli hanım* translates as 'dirty lady', in reference to this mottled appearance).

With the moisture level lowered, the cheese could be stored for several weeks, or would be baked to dry it even further, so that it would last for a year or even more. Production slowly died out over the centuries, but was resurrected by two intrepid Turkish cheese writers – Neşe Biber and Berrin Bal – who read about it as they researched a book charting 52 cheeses from the seven regions of Turkey.

Intrigued by the idea of this long-lost cheese, the two writers wrote a small section highlighting its history and encouraged a local cheesemaker to try making it as an experiment so they could take photos for their 2017 book, *Peynir Aşkına* (For the Love of Cheese).

The dairy created a soft, cylindrical sheep's cheese, which was dried on wooden racks in the sun for 30 days, before being baked at 200°C (390°F) to seal the rind and create a much firmer final cheese with a sweet, sheepy kick. It turned out so well that a photo of Kirli Hanım was used on the front cover of the book, which caught the eye of other cheesemakers in the region who started making it again with the support of Biber and Bal, who also stocked it in their Istanbul deli Antre Gourmet.

Interest continued to snowball, with the cheese registered as part of Slow Food's Ark of Taste, which protects and preserves rare traditional foods. They also managed to get the local council in Balıkesir to support sending the cheese to the World Cheese

Awards in 2023 – the first time a Turkish cheese had ever been entered. It duly won a Bronze medal.

There are two types of Kirli Hanım made today. One is created by heating the whey left over from another popular sheep's cheese called Sepet ('basket') cheese. This is aged for a shorter period of time and served fresher. The harder aged version, which was recognised at the World Cheese Awards, is made by coagulating full-fat sheep's milk with rennet before ageing and baking.

Kirli Hanım's revival is hopefully a sign of things to come. Turkey's strong dairy credentials are at odds with its modest showing at the awards, but that is largely because the country has not entered its cheeses in the competition down the years. According to Biber and Bal, this is due to several factors, including the absence of a national promotion strategy for cheese and bureaucratic obstacles when exporting to EU countries.

But after successfully getting Kirli Hanım to the awards, Biber and Bal are determined to put more Turkish cheeses on the international stage. They even harbour long-term hopes that the awards could be held in Turkey one day. Back where it all began. PM

ORIGIN: Balıkesir, Turkey
MILK: Raw sheep's milk
RENNET: Animal (lamb)
AROMA: Fragrant, sheepy, milky
FLAVOUR: Caramel, smoky, hazelnutty
TEXTURE: Hard, grainy
MATCH: Bal and Berrin recommend rosé wines made with Turkish grape varieties Kalecik Karası and Öküzgözü. Thin slices of mature cheese can be grilled and drizzled with olive oil and pomegranate syrup.

WORLD CHEESE AWARDS: Bronze 2023 (Özem Dairy Farm)

Paipa

Colombians often claim, '*Aquí no hay quesos fuertes*' (Here there are no strong cheeses), but this couldn't be further from the truth: Queso Paipa, a semi-hard rustic cheese from the Sogamoso Valley, proudly defies this misconception. Produced in the towns of Sotaquirá and Paipa, this 400g (14oz) cheese owes its uniqueness to the valley's cool micro-climate. The industry was first established in the region during the colonial period, with the cheese made in Paipa, and the milk mostly sourced from large dairy farms in Sotaquirá.

Paipa has a creamy, lactic and tangy finish reminiscent of soured butter. Its soft, bouncy texture melts beautifully. Colombians use it to make traditional dishes like *papas chorreadas* (dripping potatoes), to snack on, and to make pizzas. The cheese must be aged for a minimum of 21 days to comply with the protections set out by its PDO, however some producers extend ageing by up to six months, during which time the cheese develops a firmer texture and sweeter, nutty flavour, perfect for grating on top of pasta. Italian dishes are very common in parts of Colombia.

Paipa was awarded a PDO in 2012, a first for a Colombian cheese, with the mission to protect this traditional product in the face of new trade agreements with the European Union. EU negotiators insisted that European Denomination of Origin protections needed to be respected by Colombian producers. Fearing the loss of their heritage, Colombian producers applied for similar PDO protections, sparking heated debates over culture, history, production methods and origin.

Ultimately, broad protections were granted, ensuring small artisan and self-subsistence cheesemakers could continue their craft. The rules also recognised the historical use of raw milk to produce the cheese. This approach emphasised the importance of high-quality milk and ethical animal husbandry to produce award-winning cheeses.

In Colombia, Bolivia and Peru, cheesemakers focus on fresh and unaged varieties, known as *suaves* (soft cheeses). It is rare to find hard cheeses in the Andean countries. They also do not traditionally produce long-aged cheeses, bloomy-rind, washed-rind or blue cheeses, collectively referred to as *fuertes* (strong cheeses).

Paipa is a remarkable exception – made for over 130 years, it is known for its flavour, developed through extended ageing. Today, new producers in the Andes are also experimenting with different styles to appeal to evolving tastes. CY

ORIGIN: Boyacá, Colombia
PROTECTED STATUS: PDO
MILK: Raw and pasteurised cow's milk
RENNET: Animal
AROMA: Lactic, soured cream
FLAVOUR: Creamy, sweet, tangy
TEXTURE: Soft, chewable, melty
MATCH: Try with a Chilean Carménère, or pair it with tropical fruits like mango or guava jams.

WORLD CHEESE AWARDS: Bronze 2021 (Kilo Alimentos)

HERO CHEESE

Queijo do Marajó

The air is thick with the lush scent of tropical vegetation. Birdsong is all around. The environment is heavy and humid. It's another morning in paradise on the island of Marajó, a secluded spot in the estuary where the Amazon empties into the Atlantic and home to one of Brazil's most fascinating cheeses.

The exact origins of Queijo do Marajó, a supple, rectangular buffalo milk cheese, remain a mystery. Local cheesemakers credit migrants from other northern regions of Brazil for introducing cheesemaking techniques to the island, initially using cow's milk before transitioning to buffalo milk.

The introduction of water buffalo to Marajó island is also the subject of fascinating tales. One legend suggests that in the early 1920s, a ship en route to French Guiana, carrying Carabao (a breed originally from Indo-China, then under French control), encountered a mishap off the coast of Pará state in northern Brazil. Apparently, some of these resilient animals swam ashore and thrived in the island's tropical environment. Initially, they were valued for their strength as draught animals and for their meat, but eventually the richness of their milk was put to good use in cheese.

Others credit Jean Marie Raul Alphonse Botreau Roussel Bonneterre, a French immigrant who married a local resident, with importing Mediterranean buffaloes from Italy in 1895. This original stock has over the years been supplemented with Murrah buffaloes, one of the most common dairy buffalo breeds, known to thrive in hot, humid climates, and well adapted to Brazilian conditions.

Regardless of its origins, buffalo farming is a point of pride for the local population, and cheesemaking a source of income for many in the region. Farmers milk buffaloes by hand due to the unreliable electricity supply, which makes using milking machines tricky. They ensure that a portion of the milk is left for the newborns, a practice used to prevent udder infection and to promote the healthy growth of the next generation.

Once the raw buffalo milk reaches the dairy, it is skimmed. The milk is then left to ferment and curdle naturally for about 15 hours, relying solely on the milk's native flora and ambient micro-organisms; no lactic cultures or rennet are added. After the milk is coagulated, the curds are cut into large pieces and steeped in a process called 'washing', first with fresh milk and subsequently with warmed water. This step adjusts the acidity of the curd, in turn

ORIGIN: Pará, Brazil

PROTECTED STATUS: Brazilian Geographical Indication

MILK: Raw buffalo milk

RENNET: None

AROMA: Milky, buttery

FLAVOUR: Low acidity, white chocolate, toasted

TEXTURE: Soft, smooth, creamy

MATCH: Serve with fresh tropical fruits. Pair with Pilsner beers or light, crisp white wines.

WORLD CHEESE AWARDS: None

making the cheese sweeter. Large stainless-steel cauldrons are used for this process, an innovation recently mandated by local health authorities. However, some producers still use wooden bowls, though these cheeses are typically for household consumption.

Following the washing, the curd is pressed to further expel whey, then broken up and salted. Cream is then reintroduced, and the mixture is cooked for an hour at low temperatures to achieve a creamy and elastic consistency. Locally, this cheese is known as Queijo Crema. A similar cheese produced in the island's western region, near the entry to the Amazon jungle, without the added cream is known as Queijo Manteiga. Both cheeses are placed into rectangular plastic moulds, weighing between 500g and 5kg (1lb 2oz and 11lb), and left to rest. After 24 hours, the cheeses are ready to be sold.

This long production process results in a cheese with a soft, compact texture and a pleasant cacao butter aroma. The cheese has a greenish-yellow hue and a slightly acidic, salty taste, balanced by the creamy sweetness of the buffalo milk. Local residents eat it as a snack with fruit paste, as part of their regular meals, partially melted on top of buffalo steak, and with their school lunches.

Buffalo milk is abundant during the rainy season from May to June. At this time up to 15 producers make cheese, however not all of them produce year-round, and the increasing droughts affect milk production, which is prioritised for the calves. Queijo do Marajó is protected by the Brazilian government with a national Indicação de Procedência (similar to a European PGI).

In 2018, a cheese produced at Fazenda São Victor by Cecilia and Marcus Pinheiro was honoured as Best in Show at the Prêmio Queijo Brasil, a national cheese competition organised by the local association Comer Queijo. This recognition marked a turning point, instilling a profound sense of pride within the community. Since then, the producers have worked hard to promote their cheese outside the island and have sought new markets in the large Brazilian cities. This has pushed them to become logistics experts.

Shipping and transport might be the last thing on your mind when you are savouring a piece of cheese, but behind every bite is a finely tuned system of trucks, planes and boats transporting foods all around the world. The cheese industry depends on perfect logistics to move perishable, often delicate, wheels across the globe, linking the most remote rural communities to cheese-lovers everywhere.

These logistics don't just move cheese, they shape it, transforming the way it is made, shared and enjoyed.

Think, for example, how a wooden box helped in the popularisation of Camembert cheese in Paris (see page 56), or how just-in-time logistics ensures a steady supply of buffalo Mozzarella cheese made in southern Italy can be enjoyed all over. In the case of Queijo do Marajó, logistical hurdles are what makes this cheese even more special when eaten outside of the island.

The first part of the journey is a three-hour ride in a wagon pulled by male buffaloes. Each hour, the buffaloes are switched to share the burden of carrying the precious cargo. This takes the cheese from the *fazendas* (farms) to the nearest dock to start a four-hour boat journey up the Paracauari river to the town of Soure. This part of the trip is only possible when the tide is high and the boat can navigate the shallow river. Upon arrival, the cheese is transferred to a larger boat for a five-hour trip to the capital city of Belém, across Marajó's bay. From here it is distributed locally or sent to the airport and on to São Paulo or Rio de Janeiro in southern Brazil, where the cheese has a devout following.

I first tasted Queijo do Marajó during a 2017 trip to Brazil, where I had been invited to judge the third edition of the national cheese competition. Before the event, international judges were introduced to over a dozen little-known Brazilian cheeses. This was an experience that transformed my understanding of the country's rich and diverse cheesemaking culture. I had visited Brazil before to speak at a cheesemakers' conference and to meet producers, but each trip revealed new layers of terroir, technique and dairy traditions.

What continues to impress me is the collaborative spirit among Brazilian cheesemakers and mongers, united in their drive to elevate their cheese culture. The country's cheese industry is vibrant and continues to pressure the government to support artisan production. Several cheeses now enjoy Geographical Indication Protections, and domestic production is appreciated and consumed locally.

There is genuine pride in supporting national producers. Among Queijo do Marajó-makers, this pride runs even deeper. It is not uncommon to see Cecilia Pinheiro dressed in traditional *vaqueira* (cowgirl) attire, made of worker shirts with intricate embroidery and palm leaf hats, passionately talking about the virtues of her land. She has so many stories to tell about her cheese, the island and what makes Marajó so special.

Cheese connects rural communities to urban centres, it reminds us of the agricultural lands that feed us, and rewards the labour of thousands of makers in every part of the world. Queijo do Marajó has yet to win a World Cheese Awards medal, but it is only a matter of time. Like many Latin American cheeses, its nuanced flavours may confuse at first, with both savoury and sweet notes, but once tasted, they are unforgettable. As logistics improve, they will start reaching a wider audience, earning them the recognition they deserve.

As the morning mist lifts and the birdsong increases in volume, it is clear that Queijo do Marajó is more than just a cheese. It is an expression of a tropical paradise and a reason for pride in the fruits of the land. CY

Stonebeck

We met Wensleydale earlier in the book, when it was being milled up and stuffed with dried cranberries (see page 96).

That was the modern, industrial version of the cheese that most people will have seen at some point on supermarket shelves. But there's a long and venerable history to Wensleydale that we felt needed further exploration. Especially because there is an exciting new group of cheesemakers in and around Yorkshire, in northern England, who have revived traditional farmhouse production and created a template for others to follow at the same time.

It's thought that Cistercian monks first brought cheesemaking to Wensleydale nearly 1,000 years ago, and the cheese was still widely made on farms until the Second World War, which proved catastrophic for its fortunes. There were 176 farms making Wensleydale in 1939, but just nine remained in 1946 as the effects of the war and rationing took their toll. The last farm gave up in 1957, with large creameries dominating production by then.

But with growing interest in artisan and local foods, there has been a revival of small-scale Wensleydale production in recent years, with new cheeses such as Whin Yeats in Cumbria, Yoredale in Yorkshire and, perhaps the most traditional of all, Stonebeck from North Yorkshire. Made by Andrew and Sally Hattan on a remote 186-hectare (460-acre) hill farm in Upper Nidderdale, this is Wensleydale as it would have been in the 1930s, long before block versions and novelty flavours.

The Hattans had tried to raise beef cattle and sheep on their farm 275 metres (900 feet) above sea level, but the land was too marginal, so they invested instead in a small herd of Northern Dairy Shorthorn cows – a rare native Dales breed that is well suited to the rugged landscape.

There are only 30 cows in the herd, milked

ORIGIN: Yorkshire, England
PROTECTED STATUS: N/A
MILK: Raw cow's milk
RENNET: Animal
AROMA: Damp soil, cream, citrus
FLAVOUR: Grassy, savoury, farmhouse butter

TEXTURE: Fudgy, crumbly
MATCH: Best bitter is a sturdy match, while a dollop of apple chutney and crunchy toasts studded with cranberries (of course) are great on the side.

WORLD CHEESE AWARDS: None

between spring and autumn when they graze outdoors on wildflower meadows and moorland. The principle is that grass-fed animals make better milk, which is just as well because Shorthorns give less than a quarter of the milk of a high-yielding modern breed, such as Holstein-Friesian.

The small-scale nature of the operation is only financially viable because of the extra value that is added by making cheese. The Hattans pieced together how Wensleydale used to be made before the war using old photos, a recipe from 1917, and by chatting to a local cheesemaker called Mabel Peacock, who was 101 at the time.

The cheese they ended up making fits around domestic life, just as it did for farming families more than a century ago. Made with raw milk, the curds are hung up in cloth bags so the whey can drain, before they are broken up for salting using a peg mill that is turned by hand. Formed in moulds using an old cast-iron press, the cheese is bound and hand-sewn in locally made calico.

It develops a pretty stone-coloured rind, speckled with patches of grey and white mould, as it matures for around two to five months, and the flavour varies depending on when in the season it was made. There's often a grassy flavour and juicy acidity, as well as a mouth-filling richness, while the texture is much softer than you might expect from a Wensleydale: dense and fudgy near the rind with a moist crumble in the middle.

Stonebeck is not cheap, retailing for more than three times the price of block versions. But far from deterring shoppers, the cheese's complexity and ethical backstory have helped it build a loyal following, while demonstrating a model that other cheesemakers could follow.

It's a cheese that tastes of the land itself, but also the people and history behind it. It certainly doesn't taste of cranberries. PM

Storico Ribelle

Every two years the small town of Bra in Piedmont is transformed into the cheese capital of the world.

Hundreds of artisan cheesemakers set up stalls in the streets, piled high with the rarest raw milk cheeses on the planet, as part of a four-day festival organised by campaign group Slow Food. Over the weekend, hundreds of thousands of turophiles descend upon the town to taste, buy and attend a packed schedule of talks, lectures and workshops. It's an event that should be on the bucket list of any self-respecting cheese geek.

Slow Food was set up by fire-brand journalist Carlo Petrini in the 1980s in response to the rise of fast-food restaurants in Italy. The movement he created continues to rebel against industrialised food systems today, campaigning to protect and preserve traditional foods that are 'good, clean and fair' in the process.

Of all the many cheeses that have appeared at the festival, there is one that embodies the rebellious Slow Food spirit more than others. The Italian cheese Storico Ribelle ('historic rebel') was born out of opposition to the creep of modernisation that threatens to dilute many traditional cheesemaking practices.

For centuries the hard raw cow and goat's milk cheese Bitto has been made during the summer months in the Bitto Valley in the mountains of Sondrio in northern Lombardy. The cheese gained PDO protection in 1996, but amendments to the rules left traditional cheesemakers unhappy. The production area was extended from the original heartland to the whole of the Sondrio region, while herdsmen were allowed to supplement the animals' diet with fodder (rather than 100 per cent pasture) and cheesemakers were permitted to make starter cultures rather than allowing the milk to curdle naturally.

A group of 16 Bitto rebels were so disenchanted that they formed a splinter group and left the PDO to make a cheese they called Bitto Storico ('historic Bitto'). Their idealistic leader, Paolo Ciapparelli, set up the Save Bitto Heritage Consortium, as well as a commercial company that guaranteed a good price for the cheese. This caused a fair amount of enmity between Bitto Storico producers and the main Bitto consortium for many years, until eventually a deal was reached in 2014 recognising both groups. The name Bitto Storico was changed to Storico Ribelle to avoid confusion.

The machinations of Bitto politics were briefly explained to me one sunny afternoon in Bra when I stumbled across the Storico Ribelle stall and got chatting to a quietly eloquent man in a fetching wide-brimmed hat. Carlo Mazzoleni, who has since taken over from Ciapparelli as president of the producers' group, was busy cutting shards of the rock-hard cheese for people to taste. These came from 9–20kg (20–44lb) wheels, which were presented like vintage wines with the year and the specific mountain pasture where they were made written on the side. Some were more than 10 years old.

The cheese I tried – a 2014 from the Orta Varga Alpine pasture – was hard and granular, while the flavours were wild, taking in fruit, leather, animal, spice and a herbal tea note. The prices were pretty wild too: 200 euros a kilo, which is about the most I've ever paid for a cheese.

But it's a small price to pay when you learn

that only around 1,500 wheels are made each year (10 times less than Bitto) by just 10 producers. They make cheese for just a few months during the summer, moving up the mountains with their Bruna Alpina cows and Orobica goats so they can access the best Alpine pastures, staying at rudimentary structures as they go. Known as *calècc*, these have stood for centuries in the mountains and comprise four low walls, made temporarily habitable by the cheesemakers who rig up a tarpaulin-tented roof. Here they can sleep and make cheese in copper cauldrons over log fires, while the animals graze the wildflowers and herbs outside (which might explain the herbal tea flavour I picked up).

The Bitto Heritage Consortium has long had the backing of Slow Food in their efforts to preserve these traditional cheesemaking practices, which has enabled them to attract investment and command higher prices. A central maturing room, restaurant and café were built in the village of Gerola Alta in 2010, where you can buy a whole wheel of that year's production, although it will only be ready to taste years later. You can even ask for bespoke messages and pictures to be painted on the rind in blueberry ink.

Judging by the crowds around Storico Ribelle's stall at the Bra cheese festival, there's clearly plenty of people willing to pay for the privilege of tasting a slice of history, tradition and place – attributes that have come up time and again as we've explored the best cheeses in the world over the preceding pages. It also goes to show that there are alternative models allowing artisan cheesemakers to secure a profitable and sustainable future. We need more rebels with a cause. PM

ORIGIN: Lombardy, Italy

PROTECTED STATUS: N/A

MILK: Raw cow and (10–20%) goat's milk

RENNET: Animal

AROMA: Fruity, savoury, animal

FLAVOUR: Herbaceous, tropical fruit, smoky

TEXTURE: Rock hard, crystalline

MATCH: Full-bodied red wines work well. Valtellina Superiore made with Nebbiolo grapes is the local match. The sharp sweetness of aged balsamic vinegar contrasts with the salty, savoury flavour.

WORLD CHEESE AWARDS: None

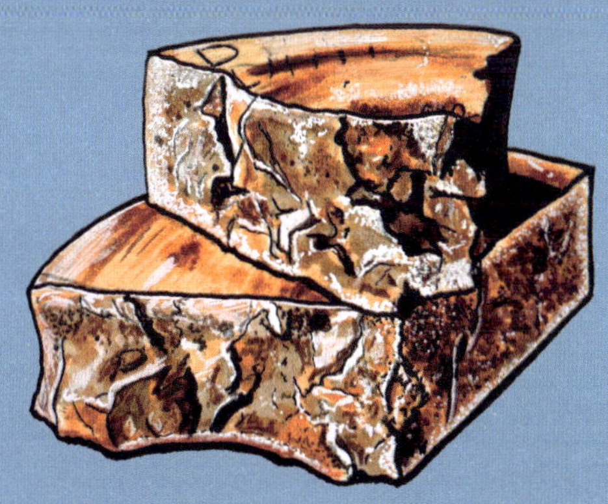

Conclusion

As you've probably already guessed from the preceding pages, we eat a lot of cheese. We also spend a huge amount of our lives thinking, writing and talking about the stuff. But even so, we've learned much more than we expected on our odyssey into the heart of the World Cheese Awards.

Over the past 100 cheeses, we've travelled from volcanoes in Japan to the outback of Australia, and from limestone caves in Cheddar Gorge to mountains in Mexico. Along the way we've met an ensemble cast worthy of a hit Netflix drama, including Italian mountain rebels, Dutch self-sufficiency idealists and US millionaires, who have helped us explore far more than just cheese. Climate, geography, identity and culture have been constant themes, but we've also ventured into history, politics, religion, economics and conflict, and plenty more besides. Cheese is not just a food; it's a way to understand people and the natural world around us.

So, taking all this into account, are we any closer to identifying the One Cheese to Rule Them All? Well, having eaten more cheese than even we are used to, and spending even more time thinking, writing and talking about it than normal, we do have a few conclusions.

What makes a cheese truly special?

After spending many eye-boggling hours poring over more than three decades of World Cheese Awards winners, there are two types of cheese that really seem to impress judges. Namely, hard, aged cheeses with a touch of sweetness, such as Gruyère and Gouda, and creamy blues, such as Gorgonzola and Stilton.

A perfect example of this is the 2024 awards in Portugal, where the 14 cheeses that made the final included five Alpine-style cheeses and four blues. This wasn't a one-off either. Le Gruyère – the ultimate expression of Alpine cheesemaking – has won the top title more than any other cheese, on five separate occasions, while Goudas have won three times. Blue cheeses have been named World Champion on 10 separate occasions.

There are a couple of reasons why these two styles are perennially popular. One is that they are both strong cheeses with a big hit of flavour. As much as judges give every entry a fair chance, the cheeses that shout loudest tend to be heard more, especially when you've already tasted dozens of others. Fresh cheeses, such as Mozzarella or Ricotta, and younger cheeses, such as Caerphilly or Tomme de Savoie, have never won the top title. They are seemingly just too quiet to rise above the noise made by more powerful cheeses.

There's also something about the flavours and textures of Alpine and blue cheeses that appeal. It's the combination of sweet and savoury in Alpine cheeses, and the creamy and spicy notes in blues that seem to make them inherent crowd-pleasers.

The Guild of Fine Food decided to do its own deep dive into finding a Champion of Champions in 2016 by collating as many historic winners as possible for a grand tasting. This was the day after the World Cheese Awards in San Sebastián, which had seen a Norwegian Blue called Kraftkar win the overall title (see page 130). The cheese took its place alongside dozens of previous winners for a special judging session. The winner? You guessed it, a blue cheese, with Kraftkar winning once again.

So does that mean a Norwegian Blue is our One Cheese to Rule Them All? Well, no. There have been other World Champion winners since 2016, and if this book has taught you anything, it's hopefully that cheese is a wonderfully varied food, due to factors ranging from what the milk-producing animals are eating through to whether the cheesemaker is having a good day in the dairy. In other words, a batch of cheese might be crowned World Champion one year and win nothing the next.

There's another big variable at the awards: the judges themselves. As Bob Farrand, who founded the awards in 1988, once told me: 'To win the World Cheese Awards, you need the right judge to taste the right cheese on the right day.' As much as there are rules and systems in place to make judging fair, transparent and consistent, there is no accounting for what appeals to a particular judge on a particular day, which could be influenced by everything from their upbringing and professional background through to how they woke up that morning. Judging cheeses is not a science. There is always a personal and subjective element to the process. That said, as the entries in this book show, there are cheeses that win year after year at the awards, and that consistency is no fluke.

A new world order?

If you'd asked us before we started the book where the best cheese in the world was made, we would have probably said France or Italy. These are countries that are home to a huge range of styles and where traditional cheesemaking is still relatively strong. But we're not so sure anymore. The EU's PDO system does protect and preserve many traditional cheeses, but by their very nature, rules and regulations can stop cheeses from evolving.

Increasingly we are finding that the most progressive farms, cheesemakers and maturers are just as likely to come from countries such as Japan, Norway, the US or the UK. These are places that either don't have long histories of cheesemaking or have had to rediscover long-lost traditions which had died out with the rise of large-scale manufacturers. Either way, they are not so constrained by tradition and are free to take inspiration from anywhere and everywhere to create new styles of cheese that blend different influences and ideas. This is being underpinned by sustainable farming practices, cutting-edge science and a strong focus on research and development.

Which brings us to another conclusion as to what makes a cheese truly special. Discussions about topics such as raw milk, terroir and animal husbandry, plus craft skills versus automated processes, have been a common feature in our cheese profiles. There are lots of things that farmers and cheesemakers can do to speed up production and reduce costs, but most of the time it doesn't make the cheese taste better. In our experience, the best cheeses tend to be made by hand with raw milk from animals that graze diverse pastures.

The reason why this might be is complex and the science is not clear. Research has shown that cheese made with milk from pasture-fed cows contains chemical compounds that make it richer, more intense and more buttery than those made with milk from animals fed with preserved feeds.

Whether raw milk also leads to more complex and interesting flavours in the final cheese is open to debate. The microbes found in raw milk are certainly more extensive and diverse compared to pasteurised milk, which many argue leads to more intense flavours in cheese. And there is research to back this viewpoint up, but there are also conflicting studies which show that people can't tell the difference or prefer pasteurised cheeses over unpasteurised in taste tests.

There are so many other factors that go into making good cheese beyond the milk that it's impossible to pin everything on one or two elements. But all things being equal, there's a richness, complexity and eyebrow-raising deliciousness to a well-made raw milk cheese that pasteurised cheeses can't quite match. Just as importantly, these kinds of cheeses also support local communities and are less damaging to the environment, while helping to maintain skills, traditions and local cultures.

The One Cheese to Rule Them All

So there we have it. The One Cheese to Rule Them All could come from one of the old European cheese powerhouses or one of the up-and-coming cheesemaking nations around the world. It could be made up a mountain in big wheels or matured in a cave with blue moulds. And it's probably made by hand with raw milk from well-tended, pasture-fed animals.

But the truth is that the best cheese is the one that tastes good to you right now. Cheese is a key to unlock the world around us, but most of all it's a food to be enjoyed.

How Cheese is Made

Coagulate, cut, drain, mould, salt and wait. The process of cheesemaking can be summarised in these six actions. Although there are variations within each step, the basic method remains remarkably similar.

It starts with milk, which can be raw, thermised or pasteurised, and is typically sourced from cows, goats, sheep or buffaloes (although there are also cheeses made from donkey, camel, yak and reindeer milk). The milk is inoculated with starter cultures (lactic acid bacteria) to begin fermentation. These cultures can be naturally present in the milk, introduced from the environment, or deliberately added. The bacteria convert lactose (sugars) into lactic acid, which helps with preservation, flavour and to curdle the liquid milk into a solid (the soluble casein proteins in the milk stick together to form a delicate curd).

But for most cheeses, a coagulant known as rennet is added, creating a firmer curd. This is a mix of enzymes that are derived from the stomachs of young animals (referred to either as animal or traditional rennet), although there are also vegetarian rennets made from microbes or plants, such as thistles.

Once the milk has set into a gel-like curd, it is cut or broken up to release moisture (whey) from the curds. Techniques such as cutting, cooking, pressing, piling or washing the curd are also used to reduce moisture content. Each method affects the cheese's texture and flavour. Spun-curd cheeses like mozzarella are heated in hot water and stretched at this stage.

To form cheese, the curd is drained and moulded to create wheels, squares or even balls. Salt is added, sometimes by rubbing it directly on the rind or by mixing it with the curd; sometimes by submerging wheels in brine. Then comes the waiting. During maturation, cheeses are cared for to develop rinds or moulds (including blue moulds), both inside and out. Each cheese follows a unique path, with maturation times ranging from a few hours to several years.

Glossary

AFFINAGE – The French word describing the process of cheese maturation (*affinage* means 'to refine'), which is widely used across the world to describe the process of ageing cheeses under controlled conditions. Techniques include controlling temperature, humidity and air flow, plus washing rinds, turning and cleaning cheeses and patting down moulds.

AFFINEUR – A person working in cheese maturation. Either trained or amateur, the job requires skill and patience.

BLOOMY-RIND CHEESES – Cheeses with fuzzy and wrinkly white rinds formed by moulds and yeasts, such as *Penicillium candidum* and *Geotrichum candidum*. The rind releases enzymes over time which break down the paste underneath, resulting in a softer texture and more intense flavours.

CASEIN – Proteins found in milk that are the basis of cheese.

CHEESE IRON/TRIER – A sharp tool used to sample cheese as it is maturing. The thin, circular blade is pushed into the cheese to extract a cross section that can be assessed.

COAGULANT – Enzymes used to curdle milk. See rennet.

ENZYME – Primarily proteins that act as catalysts, speeding up metabolic processes. Enzymes can be found in milk, rennet, starter cultures and the cultures that grow on and in cheese.

EYES (CHEESE HOLES) – Small to large holes in cheeses created by bubbles of carbon dioxide produced by bacteria in the cheese. Some cheesemakers encourage eye formation in cheeses such as Emmental, but eyes may also indicate contamination or defects in the cheese.

FERMIER – French term to describe products made with the milk produced on the same farm that the cheese is made. In the UK and Ireland these cheeses are known as 'farmhouse' and in the US as 'farmstead'.

LACTIC CHEESES – Cheeses curdled primarily through the action of lactic acid bacteria converting lactose (sugar) into lactic acid. These cheeses are typically delicate, with a tangy flavour and a soft and creamy texture.

LACTOSE – The natural sugar in milk.

PASTA FILATA – Italian term meaning 'spun paste', to describe cheeses made by heating and stretching curd to create a stretchy and elastic texture in cheeses such as mozzarella.

PASTEURISATION – Process of heat-treating milk to control microbial activity and deactivate potential pathogens. High-Temperature Short-Time (flash) pasteurisation involves heating milk to 72°C (161°F) for at least 15 seconds. Low-Temperature Long-Time (batch or vat) pasteurisation heats milk to 63°C (145°F) for at least 30 minutes.

PDO – Protected Designation of Origin. Part of a European Union quality scheme that grew out of wine appellations, designed to protect the names of traditional foods and drinks that have a strong link to the place where they are made. PDOs ensure that every part of a cheese's production, processing and preparation takes place in a designated area. For example, Roquefort PDO can only be made with locally sourced raw sheep's milk in Roquefort-sur-Soulzon in Aveyron, following a traditional recipe, and must be matured in the famous Roquefort caves. PDOs are the equivalent of national initiatives, such as Appellation d'Origine Protégée (AOP) in France and Switzerland, and Denominazione di Origine Protetta (DOP) in Italy.

PGI – Protected Geographical Indication. Part of the same quality scheme as the PDO, but the rules allow some elements of the production, processing and preparation to take place outside the designated area.

RAW MILK – Milk that has not been pasteurised, heat-treated nor cooled down beyond the body temperature of the animal.

RENNET – A mix of enzymes that turn liquid milk into a gel-like solid curd by coagulating the proteins (caseins). Animal rennet is made from enzymes found in the stomachs of young animals, typically calf, kid or lamb. Vegetarian rennet can be derived from microbes or plants.

STARTER CULTURES – Lactic acid bacteria added to milk to start the cheesemaking process. These 'good' bacteria convert lactose into lactic acid, and are important for coagulation, food safety and flavour. Cheesemakers can make their own by culturing raw milk or whey, or buy frozen starters from laboratories.

TERROIR – French concept linking the flavours found in food and drink with the weather, soil and micro-organisms in the place where they are grown and made.

THERMISED MILK – Milk that has been heat-treated at temperatures below those required for pasteurisation. Typically heating milk to between 57°C and 68°C (135°F and 154°F) for around 15 seconds. This technique is used by some cheesemakers to reduce the presence of micro-organisms that may spoil the milk while retaining more of the milk's original characteristics compared to pasteurisation.

TRANSHUMANCE – An animal husbandry practice involving the seasonal movement of herds between summer and winter pastures. Typically, animals are moved to higher elevations during the summer to graze on mountain pastures and brought down to lower valleys during the winter months.

WASHED-RIND CHEESE – Refers to cheeses that have been aged in moist environments and their rinds rubbed with water, salt brine or brine and alcohol to promote the growth of pungent micro-organisms that help in flavour and texture development.

WHEY – The liquid in curd, much of which is drained during the cheesemaking process.

Further Reading

A Cheesemonger's History of the British Isles, Ned Palmer, Profile Books, 2020

A Cheesemonger's Tour de France, Ned Palmer, Profile Books, 2023

American Farmstead Cheese, Paul Kindstedt, Chelsea Green Publishing, 2005

Camembert: A National Myth, Pierre Boisard (translation by Richard Miller), University of California Press, 2003

Cheese and Culture, Paul S Kindstedt, Chelsea Green Publishing, 2013

Cheese – Slices of Swiss Culture, Sue Style, Bergli, 2012

Cheeses of South Africa, Kobus Mulder, Sunbird Publishers, 2013

Ending the War on Artisan Cheese, Catherine Donnelly, Chelsea Green Publishing, 2019

Milk Into Cheese, David Asher, Chelsea Green Publishing, 2024

Quesos Mexicanos, Carlos Yescas, Ediciones Larousse, 2013

Reinventing the Wheel, Bronwen and Francis Percival, Bloomsbury Sigma, 2017

The Cheese Life, Mathew Carver & Patrick McGuigan, Kyle Books, 2023

The Cheese Wheel, Emma Young, Ebury Press, 2023

The Life of Cheese, Heather Paxson, University of California Press, 2013

The Oxford Companion to Cheese, Catherine Donnelly (ed.), Oxford University Press, 2016

The Philosophy of Cheese, Patrick McGuigan, The British Library, 2020

The Sheridans' Guide to Cheese, Kevin and Seamus Sheridan, and Catherine Cleary, Gill & Macmillan, 2015

The World Cheese Book, Juliet Harbutt (ed.), Dorling Kindersley, 2015

Acknowledgements

Writing a book like this one requires stamina, not only to eat so much cheese and stay focused on deadlines, but also to hold on to the purpose of the project. More than once, we asked each other: Who is our audience? If you are reading this, then thank you.

The idea for this book began during a conversation about our role as judges at the World Cheese Awards. We wanted to share insights into the process of evaluating cheese, to celebrate our friends in the industry, and, above all, to honour the cheesemakers and the cheeses that have captivated us over the years.

The project has benefited from the care and support of our families, and from the expert advice and long conversations with many cheese professionals, including: Robert Aguilera, Alex Armstrong, Berrin Bal, Neşe Biber, Falco Bonfadini, Bruno Cabral, Oksana Chernova, Rafael Domínguez González, Kristian Holbrook, Mansi Jasani, Anna Juhl, Kanako Mathys, Kelsie Parsons, Alex Porras, Claire Powell, Jilly Sitch, Namrata Sundaresan, Jon Thrupp and Luisa Villegas. Thank you for all your help.

Also love and respect to these excellent people: David Asher, Nigel Barden, Mathew Carver, Tracey Colley, Betty Coste, Simone Ficarelli, Mateo Kehler, Mike Lane, Ned Palmer, Heather Paxson, Cathy Strange, Will, Ellie and Sam Studd, Charlie Turnbull, Trevor Warmedahl and Emma Young.

We especially want to thank the Farrand family (John and Tortie; Bob and Linda) and the team at the Guild of Fine Food for their tenacity in hosting the World Cheese Awards each year, their help with this book, and for letting us be part of the greatest cheese show on Earth.

Thank you to the team at Murdoch Books, including Céline Hughes, Rachel Malig, Nikki Ellis, Sarah Fisher and our wonderful illustrator Amanda Hallam, for ushering the project along and keeping us on our toes. We also thank Holly Arnold for championing our idea.

Gracias Will, Mamá, Geo, y Stephen por su amor. Carlos.

Thank you Ruth, Archie & Bill. We'll be eating cheese on the island by the time you read this! Pat/Dad xxx

Index

Page numbers with suffix 'G' are glossary entries

About the Authors

PATRICK MCGUIGAN is a British cheese writer, presenter and teacher, who has travelled from the Swiss Alps to the pastures of Vermont in search of the world's best cheesemakers, maturers and cheesemongers. He writes extensively on the subject for newspapers and magazines, such as *The Telegraph*, *The Sunday Times* and *Delicious*, as well as appearing on TV and radio.

His first book, *The Philosophy of Cheese*, was published by The British Library in 2020. His second book, *The Cheese Life*, co-authored with Mathew Carver, was published by Kyle Books in 2023.

Patrick also hosts regular cheese talks, tastings and events, and teaches cheese courses at the Academy of Cheese and Guild of Fine Food. He has judged at the World Cheese Awards for more than a decade. He is very partial to a slice of Kirkham's Lancashire (his favourite cheese, in case you were wondering).

CARLOS YESCAS is a leading voice in traditional cheese advocacy. A specialist in food policy, resilient food systems and cross-cultural communication, his work explores the intersections of cheese, culture and public policy. His first book, *Quesos Mexicanos*, was published by Larousse in 2013. For over six years, he led a global initiative supporting raw milk and artisanal cheesemakers, developing international campaigns, multilingual research and policy responses that reshaped how traditional cheese is understood and valued.

With a background in law, political science and non-profit leadership, his career spans two decades of promoting sustainable food systems across Latin America, Europe and the United States. He has advised small producers, government agencies and charitable foundations, and has played a key role in establishing strategic direction for international food education organisations. There is always some Camembert in his fridge.

Published in 2025 by Murdoch Books, an imprint of Allen & Unwin

Murdoch Books UK
Ormond House
26–27 Boswell Street
London WC1N 3JZ
Phone: +44 (0) 20 8785 5995
murdochbooks.co.uk
info@murdochbooks.co.uk

Murdoch Books Australia
Cammeraygal Country
83 Alexander Street
Crows Nest NSW 2065
Phone: +61 (0)2 8425 0100
murdochbooks.com.au
info@murdochbooks.com.au

For corporate orders and custom publishing, contact our business development team at salesenquiries@murdochbooks.com.au

Publisher: Céline Hughes
Editor: Rachel Malig
Designers: Nikki Ellis and Sarah Fisher
Illustrator: Amanda Hallam
Production Manager, Australia: Natalie Crouch
Head of Production, UK: Lauren Fulbright

Murdoch Books Australia acknowledges the Traditional Owners of the Country on which we live and work. We pay our respects to all Aboriginal and Torres Strait Islander Elders, past and present.

EU Authorised Representative: Easy Access System Europe, Mustamäe tee 50, 10621 Tallinn, Estonia, gpsr.requests@easproject.com

ISBN 9781761501258

A catalogue record for this book is available from the British Library

A catalogue record for this book is available from the National Library of Australia

Printed by 1010 Printing International Limited, China

10 9 8 7 6 5 4 3 2 1